THE FIGHTING CORSAIRS

*The Men of Marine Fighting Squadron 215
in the Pacific during WWII*

JEFF DACUS

LYONS
PRESS

Essex, Connecticut

An imprint of Globe Pequot, the trade division of
The Rowman & Littlefield Publishing Group, Inc.
4501 Forbes Blvd., Ste. 200
Lanham, MD 20706
www.rowman.com

Distributed by NATIONAL BOOK NETWORK

Copyright © 2020 by Jeff Dacus
First Lyons Press paperback edition, 2023

All rights reserved. No part of this book may be reproduced in any form or by any electronic or
mechanical means, including information storage and retrieval systems, without written permission
from the publisher, except by a reviewer who may quote passages in a review.

British Library Cataloguing in Publication Information available

Library of Congress Cataloging-in-Publication Data available

ISBN 978-1-4930-6670-4 (paper : alk. paper)

♾™ The paper used in this publication meets the minimum requirements of American National
Standard for Information Sciences—Permanence of Paper for Printed Library Materials, ANSI/
NISO Z39.48-1992.

TIMELINE OF THE PACIFIC WAR AND VMF-215

1941
December 7—Japanese attack on Pearl Harbor brings United States into conflict.

1942
March 10—James Neefus downs Japanese flying boat off Midway Island.
August 7—Allies invade the Solomon Islands, attacking Guadalcanal, Tulagi, Tanambogo, and Gavutu Islands.
September 14—VMSB-242 becomes VMF-215 at Goleta, California.

1943
January 1—Jim Neefus brings first Corsair to Marine Corps Air Station Santa Barbara.
February 15—ComAirSols, Commander Aircraft Solomons, is established on Guadalcanal. This organization would direct Allied air activities in the Northern Solomons and against Rabaul.
February 21—Russell Islands seized by 43rd Infantry Division.
March 1—VMF-215 arrives in Hawaii.
April 13—VMF-215 arrives at Midway.
April 15—First Allied operations from Russells.
June 5—First Allied strikes on Kahili Airfield, Bougainville Island.
June 17—VMF-215 leaves Midway.
June 21—Allied landings at Segi Point on New Georgia.
June 25-26—VMF-215 stops at Wallis Island en route to combat zone.
June 30—Army and Marine units land on Rendova and Vangunu.
July 1—VMF-215 arrives at Espiritu Santo.
July 11—Segi Point Airfield operational.
July 25—VMF-215 begins operations on Guadalcanal.
August 14—Bob Owens is first to land on Munda Airfield, New Georgia.
August 15—Invasion of Vella Lavella.
September 1—ComAirNorSols created to command the final assault on Rabaul.
September 27—Vella Lavella airstrips become operational.

October 19—VMF-215 begins second tour at Barakoma on Vella Lavella.

November 1—Allied landings at Torokina on Bougainville.

November 5—Carrier strikes on Rabaul.

December 17—First fighter sweeps on Rabaul.

1944

January 6—VMF-215 begins third tour at Barakoma on Vella Lavella.

January 27—VMF-215 begins operations from Bougainville.

February 14—Three-tour pilots of VMF-215 leave for the United States.

February 20—Japanese begin withdrawal of air units from Rabaul.

Principal Aircraft Types

Japanese (italicized throughout text):

Betty—The designation for the Mitsubishi G4M twin-engine Navy medium bomber.

Emily—The designation for the Kawanishi H8K four-engine Navy seaplane.

Hamp (Hap)—The Mitsubishi A6M3, a variant of the famous *Zero*, was a Navy single-engine fighter, identified by its squared-off wing tips. VMF-215 shot down four.

Kate—The Nakajima B5N, single-engine Navy torpedo bomber. One of these was claimed by VMF-215.

Mavis—The Kawanishi H6K four-engine Navy flying boat. Jim Neefus shot down one of these before joining VMF-215.

Oscar—The Nakajima Ki. 43 was a single-engine Army fighter. VMF-215 claimed one of these.

Rufe—The Mitsubishi A6M2-N was a floatplane version of the famed *Zero*. Two of these were claimed by VMF-215.

Tojo—The Nakajima Ki. 44, single-engine Army fighter. VMF-215 pilots claimed four of these including one misidentified as a Focke Wulf 190.

Tony—The Nakajima Ki. 61, single-engine Army fighter. This aircraft was powered by a liquid-cooled engine and often referred to as a copy of the German Messerschmitt Bf-109. Seven of these were claimed by pilots of VMF-215.

Val—Aichi D3A Navy divebomber. One was claimed by VMF-215.

Zeke—The famous *Zero* series of naval single-engine fighters, A6M2 through A6M5. The Marines of VMF-215 were credited with 114½ victories over this type, including four *Hamps* and two *Rufes*.

The pilots of VMF-215 were credited with 135½ confirmed and 36 probable victories.

Allied:

Airacobra—Bell P-39 single-engine Army fighter with unusual liquid-cooled engine mounted behind the pilot and tricycle landing gear.

Avenger—Grumman/General Motors TBF/TBM, Navy/Marine single-engine torpedo bomber.

Buffalo—Brewster F2A Navy/Marine single-engine fighter.

Catalina—Consolidated PBY Navy twin-engine patrol plane, known as "Dumbo" on rescue duties.

Corsair—The star of our story, the F4U was built by Vought, Goodyear and Brewster. It was a single-engine fighter used both by the Navy and Marine Corps.

Dauntless—Douglas SBD single-engine Navy/Marine divebomber.

Duck—Grumman J2F single-engine floatplane used for rescue.

Hellcat—Grumman F6F single-engine Navy/Marine fighter.

Liberator—Consolidated B-24 Army four-engine bomber.

Lightning—Lockheed P-38, twin-engine Army fighter.

Mitchell—North American B-25 twin-engine Army bomber.

SNJ—North American single-engine trainer used by Navy and Marine Corps, known as the AT-6 Texan when used by US Army or foreign air forces.

Tomahawk/Warhawk/Kittyhawk—Curtiss P-40 series of fighter used by US Army and New Zealand.

Ventura—Lockheed PV-1 Navy twin-engine patrol bomber.

Wildcat—Grumman F4F single-engine fighter used by the Navy and Marine Corps.

Contents

Introduction

A fighter pilot must possess an inner urge to do combat. The will at all times to be offensive will develop into his own tactics.

—Col. Hubert "Hub" Zemke

BOUGAINVILLE

Monday, November 1, 1943, hundreds of Allied ships lay in the waters off Cape Torokina on the Japanese-held island of Bougainville, the largest of the Solomon Islands. Landing craft pushed through the surf to unload their cargoes before returning to their mother ships for more supplies or Marines. Landing Ship Tanks moved up on the beach to disgorge vehicles directly onto the soft dark sands. Troops and supplies pushed inland. High above the transports and their seaborne protectors was an aerial umbrella of fighter planes from the US Navy, Army, and Marines as well as New Zealand, relays of protective fighters coming and going as their fuel ran low.

In the early afternoon a division of four inverted gull-winged Marine F4U Corsairs from Marine Fighting Squadron Two Fifteen (VMF-215) took station at twelve thousand feet as medium cover over the beachhead. Circling to the northwest, they looked to the north in the direction of the sprawling Japanese base of Rabaul, where any Japanese counterattack on the ships below would originate.

Sharp-eyed Lt. Robert Hanson's body suddenly grew tense as his eyes caught the glint of sunlight on metal from the direction of Kieta Airdrome on the eastern coast of Bougainville. Peering intently, Hanson made out many shapes of what appeared to be Japanese Mitsubishi *Zero* fighters, codenamed *Zeke*. Six of the green/brown fighters were diving

ix

from about ten thousand feet in preparation for a strafing run on the crowded beaches below. His pulse quickened and he instinctively charged his guns in preparation for the attack. Glancing over at his division leader, Capt. Arthur "Thrifty" Warner, Hanson eagerly motioned toward the Japanese. Warner calmly indicated he had already seen the threat.

"Down we go," mouthed Warner, and his weathered blue Corsair fell off on one wing, curving down on the unsuspecting Japanese. The other Marines followed, swinging around and behind the six Japanese. Warner, Hanson, Lloyd Cox, and Samuel Sampler each picked out a target. The Marines knew the Japanese attack had to be thwarted or the vulnerable Marines on the beach would be slaughtered. When the first Japanese pilots realized the danger and reacted, the Corsairs were already in firing range.

Warner's target pulled up abruptly and climbed to the left as the Corsair's guns opened fire, the .50-caliber rounds from the Corsair passing closely underneath the departing enemy plane. Diving away, the dark green *Zeke* headed for the wave tops along the beach in an attempt to escape, but the faster Corsair easily closed the distance. Warner's bullets found their target, and the *Zeke* was last seen crashing into the deep, dark jungle of Bougainville, its path traced by a faint trail of sooty smoke.

Lloyd Cox sighted in on a *Zeke* and eased pressure on the trigger, but before the bullets struck home, the nimble little Japanese plane flipped over on its back, and reversed direction under the startled Marine. Banking hard left, the lean, tall Marine spotted another, square-wing *Zeke* and closed behind it. Pressing the trigger, Cox noticed to his frustration that only three or four of his six guns were working. A few seconds later, wisps of smoke indicated only one firing, but the single gun proved enough as the enemy plane belched oily black smoke, lost way, and glided toward the sea. Following from five thousand feet, Cox saw it crash just outside Torokina Bay. Cox zoomed for altitude and joined Warner who had witnessed the crash. From their lofty ringside seat, the pair saw another F4U in pursuit of a smoking *Zeke*; they assumed the lone Corsair was Sampler's.

When the action started, Sampler was separated from his section leader, Hanson, in pursuit of two *Zekes*. Firing at one target, then the other, Sampler couldn't get a good shot at either, finally concentrating on one diving away. Despite several maddening minutes of close pursuit, he was unable to get a clear shot at the wildly maneuvering Japanese. Sampler broke it off and climbed to join a passing Corsair. Moving into position on its wing, Sampler happily found himself back with Warner. Cox had been separated by clouds and continued on to their base at Vella Lavella alone.

The adventure wasn't over for Sampler; his engine was running rough and losing power. Informing Warner of the problem, the division leader responded by flying around Sampler's Corsair in an attempt to note any visible damage. As Warner checked the damage, clouds crowded around them, and the two aircraft became separated. Fortunately, both returned safely to Barakoma, the airfield on Vella Lavella, a few minutes after Lloyd Cox. The fourth member of the division, Robert Hanson, was overdue, and no one could recall seeing him after the action began. Maj. Robert Owens, the squadron executive officer, reluctantly declared Hanson "missing in action."

In the initial encounter with the other members of Warner's division, Hanson lined up one of the six *Zekes* and let fly with his battery of six .50-caliber machine guns. Too late the Japanese pilot tried evasive maneuvers as smoke, then flames, poured from the little fighter. Hanson was forced to pull up to avoid colliding with the doomed aircraft, passing just above the falling plane. But the modern-day Samurai refused to go quietly, lifting the nose of the *Zeke* and firing a defiant, wildly erratic shot that missed Hanson completely. The *Zeke* fell off to the left and burned all the way to the sea.

In a sky dotted with airplanes and punctuated with tracers and bursts of antiaircraft fire, Hanson went after another Japanese fighter and attacked from above and to the right. Lining up the enemy fighter in his reflector gun sight, Hanson fired a long burst, slightly damaging the *Zeke*. Continued firing was rewarded when the dark brown enemy plane exploded in a bright flash. Momentarily blinded, Hanson shook his head and began looking for his division.

Instead of his comrades, Hanson glimpsed ominous shapes flying in above and behind him. Turning into the oncoming aircraft, the big Marine identified the large wings of *Kate* torpedo planes. The *Zekes* engaging the Marines previously had been an advance guard to sweep away the Allied air patrols and pave the way for the *Kates* and *Val* divebombers to slip in to attack the fleet. There appeared to be no other Allied planes between the task force and the approaching Japanese bombers. Hanson decided to make a hasty attack and break up the enemy formation.

In full view of the assembled ships below, Hanson tore into the six bombers. He fired from below and to the side at one of the bombers without apparent effect, but the *Kate* broke off its attack and peeled away back toward Rabaul. Striking quickly from the other side of the formation, Hanson made a high-side run on a second bomber, getting hits and disrupting the remaining Japanese. Torpedoes tumbled away as the *Kates* jettisoned their loads and scattered in all directions, their rear gunners spraying bullets in Hanson's direction in a desperate attempt at self-preservation.

Flying through the midst of the *Kates*, Hanson pounced on another target, which had attracted his attention due to the threads of smoke trailing it as it scooted north toward safety. Hanson's guns took a toll, although they fired erratically with two or four stopping at various times. The *Kate* slowly glided into the ocean, smoothly knifing through the waves in its death throes.

Looking for more targets, Hanson ended his pursuit when he noticed his Corsair's Pratt and Whitney engine was running rough. He hadn't noticed any hits from the enemy's rear gunners, but whatever the reason, the Corsair was definitely in trouble. The action against the enemy had taken him far from the invasion beach, and he turned the aircraft toward the south, heading for home. Power continued to drop, and the Corsair became harder and harder to control. Tipping the nose down to keep airspeed up and maintain control, Hanson decided to get as close to the fleet as possible and make a water landing.

Spotting a group of six destroyers and eight transports, Hanson pointed the crippled Corsair in their direction. The wounded fighter couldn't make it any farther, and Hanson set the plane down about five miles from the destroyers. Unhooking his harness and throwing out his rubber boat, Hanson was out of the Corsair in less than thirty seconds.

He quickly inflated his life jacket, but it deflated just as fast—evidently it had a tear in it. A strong swimmer, he easily pulled himself aboard the life raft and began paddling to where he had last seen the destroyers.

At the moment Hanson set down, the invasion fleet was retiring for the evening. Some ships were moving out to sea for more room to maneuver, and the transports were heading south to pick up the next echelon of troops. Hanson was well aware of the schedule and paddled furiously to close the distance. He threw out his dye marker as a flight of TBF Avenger bombers passed overhead. Several of the planes flew back and forth near his position, but even though they passed in his proximity, they did nothing to acknowledge they had seen him. Resigning himself to his situation, he put his years of athletic training to use and slowly settled into a constant rowing pace to try to reach the beachhead.

Cruising around the invasion force was the destroyer USS *Sigourney* (DD643), a ship on its first cruise. The ship had only arrived in the Solomons on October 24 and endured the enemy attacks on this first day of the Bougainville invasion, shooting down two enemy planes during that hectic day. The crew had watched as the four Corsairs had broken up the Japanese afternoon attack, but now it was time for the ship to head south and the crew relaxed, hoping that the day's attacks were finished. At about 1805, alert lookouts spotted something in the water floating toward the turning ship. Announcing the object as a life raft, the lookouts directed the ship until the bridge spotted the raft. Sailors raced to the railings in preparation for the rescue of what was presumed to be a downed airman. Over the sound of waves lapping against the sides of the destroyer they heard a strong baritone voice booming out the popular Cole Porter tune, "You'd Be So Nice To Come Home To." After more than four and a half hours in the water, Bob Hanson was home. The *Sigourney* turned and headed south for the night.

A few days later, back in Massachusetts, Hanson's parents, the Reverend Harry A. and Alice Dorchester Hanson, would receive the dreaded telegram indicating their son was missing in action. Knowing his parents would be worried upon receiving such a notification, Hanson quickly put pen to paper as soon as he was aboard ship.

During his brief stay with the fighting Navy, Hanson was very impressed. Although he only stayed a couple of days aboard the tin can, his recollections were glowing. The food especially struck a pleasant note with an absence of any form of Spam and such niceties as ice cream, steak, and fresh eggs. He wrote home cheerfully describing his life aboard the destroyer and some of his recent adventures: "Healthy, happy, not hurt, and three more Japs under my belt. That makes five and a probable. The destroyer that picked me up was a brand new one. And, boy, what swell chow!"

The destroyer anchored off Tulagi Island, just north of Guadalcanal. Hitching a ride on a landing craft, Hanson was ferried across Ironbottom Sound to Guadalcanal. Stopping at the Supply shack to replace the gear he lost, Hanson moved on to the air group headquarters to make arrangements for getting back to Vella Lavella Island where VMF-215 was conducting operations. Instead of waiting for a later scheduled cargo aircraft, Hanson decided to ferry a new F4U up to Barakoma.

Arriving at Barakoma, he was confronted by the squadron executive officer, Maj. Robert G. Owens Jr. Hanson was not the only pilot who had been forced down in recent days, and Owens was not happy with the loss of an airplane, especially with the way Hanson had gone off on his own to confront the attacking Japanese. Despite the positive outcome of breaking up the attack of the *Kate* torpedo bombers, Hanson had lost his Corsair and nearly been killed. Planes and pilots were valuable.

"Welcome back," said the perturbed major in his smooth Carolina accent, "I expect now you'll be a little more careful!" Owens was not pleased or impressed with Hanson's solo tactics.

"Yes, sir!" replied the grinning lieutenant, "I will be more careful." Somehow the way he said it and the disarming smile that accompanied the statement did little to reassure the squadron exec. Owens knew Hanson and realized the dunking and reprimand would have little effect on the young flyer's independent style of combat.

If the world is indeed a stage, as William Shakespeare wrote, a gigantic production was being acted out all over the globe in 1943. Part of the huge cast and crew were the men of VMF-215. The action above Torokina Bay by four Marine fighter pilots was just a small part of the role played by the men of Two Fifteen in the drama of the Second World War. Later, a superior officer would write: "The destruction and damage inflicted on the enemy by Marine Fighting Squadron TWO FIFTEEN contributed substantially to the New Georgia, Bougainville, and Rabaul Campaign." Their story had begun at a small town on the coast of California the previous summer.

CHAPTER ONE

Training

The best form of welfare for the troops is first class training.
—ERWIN ROMMEL

SANTA BARBARA LIES ON THE PACIFIC COAST NORTHEAST OF LOS ANGE-les. In 1940, the city was a small town of about thirty-four thousand residents. As war engulfed much of the globe and the United States geared up for the conflict ahead, the Santa Barbara City Council contemplated the improvement of their airport. For years small planes had been landing and taking off from a small airfield with a couple of runways in the suburb of Goleta, originally built in a swampy area. The city fathers of Santa Barbara thought the threat of war might be used to their advantage. Soliciting federal funds and the business of United Airlines, the runways were lengthened, taxiways built, and two hangars with a small control tower were constructed. The Army built a few revetments for aircraft as well as ammunition storage bunkers.

As part of the nationwide buildup in anticipation of war, Army personnel arrived and did basic construction to expand the airport in January of 1942. A Japanese submarine attack on nearby Richfield oil fields in the suburb of Ellwood on February 23, 1942, added impetus to military construction at Santa Barbara. Panic gripped many civilians, and there were more calls for military improvements. Nevertheless, conditions at the base were often marginal at best and primitive at worse. The stench from a nearby slaughterhouse pervaded everything. Local water was

I

undrinkable, so fresh water was provided in trucks from town and chlorinated. The two old hangars on the field became barracks, and the large numbers of arriving troops spilled over into tents. Built in a tidal swamp, the field was frequently flooded and mosquitoes were ever present. Pilots sometimes joked about landing on "Lake Santa Barbara" and referred to their surroundings as "The Swamp."

The Army moved out, and Marines took over with the arrival of Marine Air Group 24 (MAG 24) on June 15, 1942, commanded by Lt. Col. Franklin G. Cowie. The air group was composed of three dive-bomber squadrons, VMSB-242, VMSB-243, and VMSB-244, to be equipped with Douglas SBD single-engine bombers. The executive officer of VMSB-244 was Capt. Robert Gordon Owens Jr.

OWENS

For Bob Owens, originally from Greenville, North Carolina, it started while on a trip to Pensacola, Florida, with a friend after graduating from Furman in 1938. As the two watched the airplanes flying at the nearby naval air station, the friend mentioned how fun it all looked. Owens thoughtfully agreed, and he applied for naval flight training as soon as he returned home. Before he could be accepted, he was given a rigorous battery of physical and mental examinations along with 180 other applicants. The tests had to be difficult as there were only two openings to flight training. Fortunately, Owens did well and was granted one of the positions with an assignment to the Marine Corps. Possessed of a sharp wit and dry sense of humor, Owens became a naval aviator in 1940.

After his initial assignment in California, Owens received orders to Hawaii. Once in Hawaii, he sent for his fiancée, Marjorie Frances (Fran) Hart. A young girl with little experience outside of North Carolina, Fran joined another girl engaged to Dred Parks, a member of Owens's squadron, in driving across the United States, catching a ship to Hawaii, and joining their Marines in Honolulu. The couple acted quickly; the ship docked at 9:30 in the morning on October 30, 1941, and they were married at 1:30 on that same afternoon.

Fran and the other wives enjoyed their new lives living on the beach and spending afternoons watching as the pilots "flat hatted" (showing off with various aerobatic maneuvers) above them. Nightlife was entertaining in the tropical paradise of prewar Hawaii, and the wives of the pilots enjoyed their social life while the Marines enjoyed their days full of flying. Dred Parks and Bob Owens became close friends as they waited for their new squadron, VMSB-232, to form. Officially joining the squadron on December 1, 1941, it was less than a week later that their idyllic life was interrupted by the Japanese sneak attack on Pearl Harbor.

Assigned to Ewa Air Station on Oahu, Owens was recalled from his quarters on the morning of December 7, 1941, and arrived at the airfield in time to view the devastation caused by the surprise attack. Of the forty-eight aircraft at the field, forty-seven were destroyed, and ground installations were damaged around the airstrip. The weeks after the attack were spent rebuilding and preparing for the upcoming conflict. Owens's duties were not limited to his own squadron; he also served as operations and maintenance officer for the field and other squadrons transitioning through the base. When Owens received his orders to report to Marine Air Group 24 in California during the early summer of 1942, Navy torpedo squadron VT-4 presented him with a plaque in recognition for his efforts in assisting that squadron in attaining operational status before its deployment.

With his new orders, Owens took fifty-four men by ship to San Francisco and on to Goleta to begin the expansion of the ground facilities and prepare for the arrival of the air group. Most of the troops were inexperienced. Hawaii was their first duty station before being sent back to the continental United States. An exacting and technically gifted pilot, in Hawaii Owens tried to fit in flying whenever an aircraft was available, and by the time he arrived at Santa Barbara he had accumulated over one thousand hours of flying time. Unfortunately there was little time for flying after his arrival at Goleta, as there were no planes, and the Marines spent their days in construction work. Change came at a frantic pace, and any complaints were met with a shrug of the shoulders and the flat statement: "There's a war on, you know!"

Conditions improved as more personnel arrived and new construction on hangars and living quarters started. A blessing occurred when a suspicious fire gutted the hog farm, resulting in the farm, as well as the slaughterhouse, being removed. A spur line from the main railroad directly to the base made improvements much easier, and in August a new United Airlines terminal was opened, improving civilian air travel. An Olympic-size pool, chapel, living quarters, office spaces, theater, and other buildings were slowly added to make the base livable. New hangars sprouted up around the runways. In addition to organizing his men into a divebombing squadron, Owens found himself engaged in a variety of additional duties, including handling a great deal of money in the opening of a new post exchange. Newly arriving Marines were quickly organized into squadrons and also incorporated into working parties building the infrastructure around the air station.

Although there was little time for off-base liberty, the Santa Barbara community embraced the Marines, often opening private homes to the young men far from their own families. The beach was always popular, but recreation also included roller skating, horseback riding, and other activities that allowed the locals to interact with the new arrivals. At times the interaction became more intimate, and during one month a chaplain performed fifteen weddings.

Training for both pilots and ground crews began in earnest with the arrival of the first planes, and the intensity increased in proportion to the number of planes available. Danger also increased with the arrival of more planes and pilots, as more flying meant more accidents. Over the course of the war, there were at least 101 aircraft accidents at Marine Corps Air Station, Santa Barbara, the new name for the airport. Civilian aircraft continued to use the airfield, and civilian personnel manned the control tower.

The first aircraft were a mixed lot: a J2F floatplane, SNJ trainers, and a Curtiss SBC-4 Helldiver biplane bomber. More SBCs and SNJs arrived during the summer, but it wasn't until fall that the first fighters, Grumman F4Fs, arrived. During this time the cast of characters changed as fast as the equipment, and Owens found himself serving in all the various command and administrative positions, from squadron commander on down. It was a hectic, almost frantic time, and Owens seemed to thrive under the pressure, but he was also relieved when the new squadron commander arrived at Goleta.

NEEFUS

New pilots and crews came in slowly, but less than a month after Owens arrived with the nucleus of the new squadron, their new commanding officer appeared. James L. Neefus was a quick-talking but thoughtful major who had dreamed of flying since he was six years old. By 1935, the stocky, soft-spoken New Yorker was old enough to realize his dream when he applied for the Naval Aviation program. Peacetime budgets did not always allow for a boy's dream; and, even though he was accepted for flight training, he was forced to wait almost six months before reporting for duty due to fiscal constraints. After a short time of idle frustration, federal money became available, and Neefus was ordered to Pensacola, Florida, for initial flight training. Turning his back on a possible Army commission, which was offered at the same time he was chosen for the naval program, Neefus became part of class 83-C as an aviation cadet. The academics for such a course were intense; prewar ground school covered varied skills like basic navigation, basic flying instruction, and aircraft power plants. Due to the strenuous curriculum, the dropout rate was high. Neefus proved to be more than competent as both a student and flyer, ending up as the class captain. His next assignment was the Officer's Basic School in Philadelphia to learn the fundamentals of being a Marine officer.

After Basic School, Neefus embarked on an exciting career that involved a great deal of travel and lots of flying. After carrier qualification and more stateside flying in Great Lakes BG-1s and Curtiss SBCs, both biplane bombers, he was assigned sea duty and spent time on various aircraft carriers, including aboard the USS *Wasp* on neutrality patrol in the Atlantic Ocean.

When war finally engulfed the United States with the attack on Pearl Harbor, Jim Neefus was a captain with VMF-221 aboard the USS *Saratoga* en route to reinforce the garrison of Wake Island, two thousand miles west of Hawaii. Japanese forces attacked Wake within a few hours of the Pearl Harbor attack, and the *Saratoga* task force was ordered to return to Hawaii.

When the task force turned back, VMF-221 was sent to the lonely outpost at Midway Atoll. Serving as the defensive screen for the atoll,

221's F2A Brewster Buffalo fighters were required to fly combat air patrols above the airstrips as well as help patrol bombers in looking for approaching enemy ships. Situated eleven hundred miles from Pearl Harbor, Midway was an important early warning post as well as an obstacle to any Japanese attempt to capture Hawaii. Indeed, Japanese ships had shelled the atoll at the time of the Pearl Harbor attack and were planning to destroy the American forces there and on nearby French Frigate Shoals to establish bases threatening Hawaii.

During the next few months, Japanese long-range flying boats occasionally flew reconnaissance missions over Midway's two islands, Sand and Eastern, keeping track of American progress in fortifying the atoll. On March 10, 1942, Neefus and his division of four Buffalos were part of a twelve-plane patrol that flew out to intercept one of these planes. Cruising about forty-five miles southwest of Midway, one of Neefus's Marines spotted a giant four-engine Japanese H6K flying boat, codenamed *Mavis*. Diving to the attack, Neefus made the first run himself, firing a long burst and then pulling away as one engine on the big Kawanishi spouted smoke. Lieutenants McCarthy and Somers made passes at the enemy, but their bullets seemed to have no effect. Pressing his attack too closely, the last member of the division, Marine Gunner Robert Dickey, found his plane the recipient of the tail gunner's fire and was wounded in the shoulder. The Japanese made it into a cloud and disappeared, but Neefus flew on, following the *Mavis*'s course in the hope the enemy would emerge long enough for another shot. His patience was soon rewarded as the big flying boat emerged from its fleecy hiding place just below him. Diving into his second attack, gunfire from the Buffalo's four guns set the patrol plane aflame; it broke up in midair before hitting the sea. Returning to Midway, Dickey counted seven holes in his aircraft before he was carted off to the sick bay. The other three pilots received congratulations and a bottle of bourbon from the MAG 22 commander Lt. Col. William Wallace. Jim Neefus was awarded the Navy Cross for finishing off the enemy.

The *Mavis* had been part of a Japanese attempt to investigate French Frigate Shoals as an advanced base for refueling submarines and other flying boats doing reconnaissance of Midway and Hawaii. Receiving orders to go stateside and command a fighter squadron, Jim Neefus would not be at Midway during the epic naval engagement that would be fought over a three-day period in the first week of June. Maj. Floyd Parks would lead VMF-221 in that battle. Perhaps Providence was looking out for Neefus as the men of Two Twenty One in their obsolete Buffalos and a few F4F Wildcats were slaughtered in the Battle of Midway by packs of the more swift and nimble Japanese *Zeros*. Only two of the squadron's planes survived the battle. Floyd Parks was one of the fifteen pilots killed.

Jim Neefus, VMF-215's first commanding officer, pictured at Goleta, later Santa Barbara, Marine Corps Air Station. USMC Photo

It was a mildly warm July day that greeted Jim Neefus when he arrived at Goleta to take command of the gradually growing group of pilots and ground crew that was to form the squadron. Bob Owens and the advance party had done their best to turn their field into a full-fledged air station, but planes were still scarce and most flying was done in SNJ trainers. There were still many problems, among them a most interesting identity crisis formulated by some officer or officers at Headquarters Marine Corps in Washington, DC.

At first, the unit was to be part of a divebombing group, MAG 24, flying SBD divebombers, although there were no aircraft of that type at Goleta. When Bob Owens arrived the unit was designated Marine Scout Bombing Squadron 244 under the command of Capt. R. W. Clark. Clark moved on to the Air Group Staff, and Owens commanded the fledgling outfit until Neefus arrived in late July. Scuttlebutt, as the Marines called rumors, spread that they were not to be a divebomber squadron at all but a fighter squadron. The pilots were eager to fly fighters, and they cheerfully flew whatever aircraft available to prepare for their new assignment. Unfortunately, after months of logging in as many hours as possible, hopes were dashed on September 14, 1942, when the squadron was given a new label, another divebomber designation, VMSB-242. The disappointment was fortunately short lived as the very next day they were informed they would be a fighter squadron, VMF-215. Another divebomber squadron at Goleta was designated VMF-222. Two Twenty Two would become the sister squadron to Two Fifteen and would follow it into combat.

THE SQUADRON

Doctor Ernest Neber was one of the first forty-two permanent members of the squadron that arrived with Bob Owens. From Carbondale, Illinois, Neber would prove to be the squadron's most important human asset while officially fulfilling the role of flight surgeon. With the looks and wit of the performer and comedian Danny Kaye, Neber was the perfect choice to join the boisterous pilots several years his junior. A capable family practitioner, he would have a chance to ply his medical trade among the healthy young Marines in ways he never imagined in his small hometown. In addition, they would provide him with the chance to practice other, non-medical skills, such as that of priest, analyst, confidant, brother, or father. He would grow to be a close friend to all of these boys growing rapidly into a forced manhood, and they would love him for all he did. They kidded him constantly, often accusing him of being an obstetrician before the war and totally unsuited for dealing with combat wounds, flying accidents, jungle diseases, and the male anatomy in general.

More Marines arrived in spurts and streams, some with a wealth of experience and others fresh out of flight school. Not only were there great differences in abilities and experience, but they proved to be a group of distinctly different personalities as well. One of the first was Richard Braun, an extremely capable pilot with a subtle wit, sophisticated charm, and friendly smile. He also had a wealth of flying experience.

From Training Command came one of the most gifted men ever to sit in a cockpit, Capt. Reynold G. Tomes. A stout, aggressive man, Tomes had already accumulated a substantial amount of time in the air, teaching youngsters the intricacies of flight. Men assigned to his division remarked that an airplane seemed to come alive when he took off, and his long hours relegated to a training unit left him spoiling for a fight. Tomes honed his gunnery skills instructing novices at Naval Air Station Miami. He was assigned as Two Fifteen's ordnance officer. Bob Owens, an avid card player, soon discovered that Tomes played a mean hand of bridge.

Another well-trained and experienced officer was Capt. J. B. Moore, assigned as the engineering officer. In contrast to Moore's quiet demeanor, the operations officer was a delightful, freewheeling soul, Capt. Arthur T. Warner. A former tire salesman, Warner could tell stories and make witty comments that could crack a smile on the most hardened of straight faces. He and Doc Neber would provide a seemingly endless stream of practical jokes. An excellent pilot, his days in sales earned him the sobriquet of "Thrifty."

From the Royal Canadian Air Force (RCAF) came amiable but fiercely competitive Don Aldrich. Originally from the Midwest, near Chicago, Aldrich's father had been a pilot and a mechanical engineer. The elder Aldrich owned an airplane, a sturdy Waco biplane, and by the time the boy was twelve years old he had logged nearly one hundred hours. Unfortunately, Don's father passed away while the young man was in high school, and the family was forced to sell the faithful old Waco.

Don grew up to be a tall, wiry young man and decided to follow a course similar to that of his father, enrolling in the Armour Institute of Technology in Chicago to study engineering. However, after only two years of study, the grip of flying pulled him away from school. He quit the institute and took a job at a sausage casing factory, earning enough money to continue flying a Piper Cub at Ashburn Field in his spare time. Somehow he found time to fit in romance, and he married his sweetheart, Marjorie Blievernicht. The newfound family responsibility prompted him to try for a career in the Army Air Corps, which would enable him to fly full-time and provide for his family with a regular paycheck. But the Army Air Corps in 1940 was very selective and refused to accept married men. Undaunted, Aldrich went north and enlisted in the RCAF, an air force at war with no restrictions concerning matrimony. A disarming smile on the ground, serious in the air, Aldrich won his Canadian wings in November of 1941.

The US entry into the war after Pearl Harbor provided a new opportunity as restrictions on married men were relaxed. Tired of flying novices around in Harvard (British designation for the SNJ) trainers, Aldrich returned to the States, went through naval flight training, and chose to become a Marine officer upon completion. His first assignment was with VMF-215, and though he was not loud or animated, he would prove to be a natural leader.

Aldrich was not the only RCAF product to arrive at Goleta as the squadron expanded and the first permanent barracks were built. Fast-talking Gerry Shuchter had also learned the basics flying up north. Other new pilots included eccentric young Edgar Prochnik, gravelly voiced Robert "Red" Lammerts, and a son of missionaries: sober, solid Donald Moore. A couple of pilots that had some flying experience were giant Robert Johnson and friendly, intelligent John Downs. They made up for the fresh, new faces of skinny Thomas Stockwell and baby-faced Ray Wolff. Eager young Wolff was new to Marine Corps flying, but as a young man he had worked on his father's farm for twenty-five cents an hour in order to pay the six dollars an hour for flying lessons. He joined the Navy training program after earning his private pilot's license.

Among the experienced new arrivals was also a member of a vanishing breed, that of enlisted naval aviator or NAP, in the presence of popular TSgt. Robert Keister. Harold "Hap" Langstaff and Reinhardt "Chief" Leu came straight from carrier qualifications. The two friends formed an excellent flying team after learning a few tricks from the old master Ray Tomes, their division leader. Another Owens joined the squadron in the person of J. J. Owens, nicknamed "Jig Jig." Dred Parks, who had formed a close friendship with Bob Owens and his wife in Hawaii, joined the new squadron. Neefus counted on Jig Jig and Parks, two experienced captains, to give the squadron a pair of solid leaders, but sadly they were killed when their SNJ slammed into the side of a California mountain in cloudy conditions. Unfortunately, such accidents were not uncommon, with contributing factors including the experience level of some pilots, the worn aircraft, and the rush of war. An accident rate of 25 percent hung over the new squadron.

Accidents could often prove a sobering experience, as new pilot Roger Conant found out on a morning training hop. A graduate of the University of Wisconsin, Conant had recently arrived from Aerial Photography School. He was standing on the runway when his good friend Bud Kamman died in another SNJ accident.

Most of the pilots arriving at Goleta were inexperienced. 2nd Lt. Tom Stockwell, a tall, lanky lad from Louisiana, was typical of the majority of new pilots. He later recalled his journey to join Two Fifteen:

"I enlisted in the Navy V-5 Program as a Seaman 2/C in the late summer of 1941 at New Orleans and started training at the Navy Reserve Air Base there. These bases were known as 'E' Bases. We called them 'Elimination Bases.' They were designed to take the aspiring young would-be birdmen through initial training leading to solo only. Fifty percent seemed to be about the norm for washouts there. Of the 12 of us who enlisted from Baton Rouge that summer, 6 washed out there. Four of us finally received our wings. We trained in N4N4s [*Note*: Stockwell meant the famous N3N3] which were built at the Naval Aircraft Factory in Philadelphia as I recall. They handled like a truck but were sturdy aircraft.

"My introduction to Marines occurred in New Orleans. We were drilled by members of the small Marine Detachment at the base and I greatly respected the men, especially one MSgt Harry Alms. If these men were representative of the Marine Corps, then it was the Corps for me. After soloing my orders took me to Corpus Christi for the remainder of my training and more exposure to Marines. The Marine Corps was taking 10% of each class on a volunteer basis at that time. As 40% of my class volunteered, I felt lucky and honored to be accepted. The Marine Corps may have not gotten the top 10%, but they surely didn't get the lower 30. Training at Corpus started off in basic in the ubiquitous N4N4. Later classes started in the Stearman just coming into service with the Navy—a pleasant plane to fly . . . a total of 86 hours were received in that plane in basic training. Next came 5 hours in an SNV-1 and 16 hours in an OS2U-3 for familiarization ands formation flying (Vultee and Chance Vought). Twenty hours of instrument work came next in the SNV-1. After that we went into advanced training for tactics, gunnery, navigation, aerobatics, cross country, etc., flying SNJ-3's and 4's, and F3F-2's and 3's. That consisted (for me anyway) of 91 hours in the SNJ's and 21 in the F3F's. The F3F's were pretty well worn out and the few that were then in service were pooping out and the numbers being reduced daily. My last flight in one was in an F3F-2 which was the last one in service and was the last operational flight of a biplane fighter in the Navy. . . . I really enjoyed the little Grumman. . . . Upon graduation my log showed 243 hours . . . in 5 different types of aircraft."

The people of Santa Barbara grew to enjoy the crowds of young servicemen that crowded their businesses and spent their money at local shops. Roger Conant had fond memories of being greeted by the mayor. A war was on, and the gracious folk of this sleepy community and nearby towns opened their homes to these young men who were so far from their own families. Jim Neefus was lucky enough to find a place in town owned by a wonderful couple who made him feel at home and charged him a rent that just happened to match his housing allowance. In return for the local hospitality, the Marines were often guest speakers and dignitaries at various civic functions. Some of the young Marines fell in love with more than just the beautiful California landscape and sunshine, as

Two Fifteen pilots Robert Nichols and William Deming both tied the knot with local girls.

Santa Barbara was a good place to train a fighter squadron. Most of the year the air was clear and cool, and though at times a morning fog interfered with visibility, it burned off with the arrival of the sun above the coastal town. Temperatures were mellow, rarely extreme. The ocean provided a vast training area for learning navigation skills, and the beautiful beaches were a welcome sight after a day of training or during the infrequent liberties. Combining these factors with a supportive civilian population made Santa Barbara a beautiful place to learn combat flying.

On occasion some residents were a little more than just neighborly in giving the Marines the welcoming touch. One of the newer pilots, Grafton "Sammy" Stidger, frequented a local laundry run by two lovely ladies who were quickly overcome by his wit and charm along with what one pilot described as the "puckish good looks of a young Arthur Godfrey." During his visits, one of the girls would tend to his cleaning and the other would provide him with romantic companionship. The next liberty the two laundresses would switch roles. It always seemed that the smooth-talking Stidger had the best-looking uniforms in the squadron.

With the fighting in the Pacific reaching new highs during that summer, training took on new meaning above the brown hills of California. Aircraft from various squadrons filled the air during the morning, afternoon, and evening with each outfit trying to get the most use out of the limited number of planes. Gunnery practice was flown in the few F4F Wildcats the Air Group possessed, and flying time was shared with sister squadron VMF-222. The two squadrons shared planes, living quarters, and liberty time.

Formation and night flying was done in the SNJs. Neefus kept the pilots in the air as much as possible, calmly chiding them on their mistakes and giving the pilots with low time more hours in the air to improve their skills. Owens was more direct; the pilots remembered him as a hammer in comparison to Neefus's firm but more subdued attitude. Despite his soft southern drawl and calm demeanor, woe to the pilot who faced Owens after a mistake.

On January 1, 1943, Jim Neefus brought the first Corsair
to Goleta. The new tower is in the background, and an F4F
Wildcat is in the foreground. Author's Collection

Giving new pilots a great deal of flying time and putting them in
new situations could often lead to disaster, though not always in a fatal
way. One morning several divisions were sent up for gunnery practice,
and one of the new second lieutenants, string bean Tom Stockwell, drew
the assignment of flying the SNJ that towed the target sleeve. With one
of the ground crew riding along, Stockwell dutifully flew around the
gunnery area and allowed the other pilots to practice various attacks from
above, below, and various angles. They used ammunition with different-
colored paint on the tips of the bullets to decipher the hits from the
different planes. After the exercise was completed, Stockwell returned to
Goleta and brought the SNJ in on final approach. Normally the towline
was released while on the approach to the runway, and Stockwell let it go.
However, crossing the end of the runway Stockwell felt a tug and realized
that the towed target was still attached to the plane and probably had
stuck on the boundary fence. Completing the landing, Stockwell glanced
back down the runway and noticed the field was littered with various

articles of clothing. The target line was wrapped around the tail wheel of the SNJ and somehow Stockwell had managed to snag a nearby clothesline with the tow cable. The commander of the air group quickly ensured that the correct apology and restitution were rendered, with Stockwell constructing a new clothesline to "Marine Corps specs" and returning any undamaged clothes. The owner of the garments, a middle-aged woman, proved to be another of those delightful residents of the Goleta area. She held no grudge against Tom Stockwell or with flyers in general.

The new squadrons at Santa Barbara were fortunate that pilots returning from the Pacific were routed through Goleta to reflect on the lessons they had learned in combat and pass those reflections to the new pilots. Neefus and Owens were able to glean kernels of information from discussions they had with these veterans concerning information the fledgling fighters would need to stay alive in combat above the Pacific Islands. Marine aces Marion Carl and John Smith described the twisting air battles and violent air actions that were the hallmarks of the war against the Japanese. After fighting many successful battles against the Japanese *Zero*, an aerodynamically beautiful and maneuverable aircraft, the veteran Marine flyers had a great deal of practical advice for the men of Two Fifteen.

The Marine pilots in the Solomons battles had flown the stocky F4F Wildcat, an aircraft inferior to the *Zero* in most performance categories. The *Zero* was a magnificent aerobatic airplane with good speed and maneuverability but was lightly constructed and lacked armor. Veterans like Carl and Smith told the Marines to use the Wildcat's strengths: solid construction, shattering firepower, and a heavy aircraft weight that made them superior in a dive to any Japanese planes. The veterans instructed the novices on the best tactics to use with the Japanese: using altitude to attack, diving away after attacking, and avoiding a turning combat or "dogfight." Above all, the veteran pilots, who had shot down thirty-seven planes between them, emphasized teamwork, using the basic formations of two plane sections and four plane divisions.

These lessons did not fall on deaf ears. Neefus, displaying a low-key but definite command presence, and Owens, the highly capable executive officer who readily accepted responsibility, began working the pilots harder and harder in an effort to master basic flying skills. Once those skills were mastered, they could begin combat tactics in earnest. When the basic individual skills appeared to be mastered, the pilots began to learn the elements of section (two planes) and division (four planes) tactics. Neefus lamented the lack of combat aircraft he needed to complete preparations for the tough lessons that remained.

Training tempo increased throughout the fall and into the winter, at the same time that Allied forces were fighting to turn momentum against the Axis in places like Guadalcanal, El Alamein, and Stalingrad. The year 1942 passed and another year of war loomed ahead of the hard-training Marines. This new year brought good news to the men of Two Fifteen; they were finally getting new airplanes, and with the dawn of 1943 the F4U Corsair came to Goleta.

THE U-BIRD

Operationally speaking, the Corsair was brand new, with the first squadron equipped with the powerful fighter just leaving for the Pacific. Squadrons that were already operational in combat with the F4F Wildcat would later transition to the Corsair, but Two Fifteen would begin its career with the big fighter.

Built by Vought-Sikorsky Aircraft of Hartford, Connecticut, it was easily recognized by inverted gull wings that allowed a short landing gear despite a huge thirteen-foot propeller. At six tons and with a wingspan of over forty feet, it was an imposing aircraft. Even pilots with a great deal of experience were in awe of the massive fighter; the newer men were, in some cases, terrified of the prospect of transitioning from the comparatively sedate Grumman F4F Wildcat to the still teething Vought. The bent-wing F4U weighed nearly twice as much as the little Wildcat and was pulled along by a Pratt and Whitney Double Wasp R-2800 power plant that generated over 2,000 horsepower compared to the Wildcat's 1,200 horsepower. Solidly built with armor plate and self-sealing fuel tanks, the plane was equipped with six Browning M2 .50-caliber machine guns that could tear any Japanese plane into pieces. It was faster than any Japanese plane it would encounter and, like its predecessor, could outdive the Japanese.

An early model Corsair pictured stateside in March 1943. Notice the "birdcage" canopy that restricted the pilot's view. National Archives

The "hot" Corsair had many problems that still needed to be worked out and many vices that made it a challenge to fly. Some of these, like the extreme bounce upon landing, were remedied swiftly and easily. The aircraft tended to stall rather quickly, with little notice to the pilot of such an impending action. The right wing would lose lift and almost immediately the aircraft would go into a spin, which was particularly problematic because it was difficult to recover from a spin in the Corsair. A small block of wood fitted to the leading edge of the right wing was added, which made the wings stall together, warning the pilot of the loss of lift. The Corsair was equipped with a "birdcage" canopy, a slim structure made of many glass panels that interfered with visibility. A "blown" hood, much larger and with only a couple of braces, was introduced later, solving much of this problem. Later a raised seat and longer tail wheel would also help the pilot see on the ground.

Despite improvements, some of the difficulties would never be solved. The long nose with the pilot set back behind the wings led to the sobriquet of "Old Hose Nose." The pilot's view was impaired on the ground, and the aircraft was taxied in a weaving S pattern to allow a look down the tarmac. The powerful engine and huge propeller tended to generate a great deal of torque on takeoff and landing requiring a great deal of right rudder and trim. Many a novice pilot applying full power on an aborted landing found himself nearly out of control and headed off the runway. Representatives from both Vought and Pratt and Whitney assisted Two Fifteen's maintenance sections, commanded by Lt. A. E. Ennis, in learning how to service the new planes. The factory representatives also helped each of the pilots as the young men logged their first hours in the Corsair. Jim Neefus was the first to fly one of the new planes, picking up a Corsair at North Island in San Diego on New Year's Day. He made two takeoffs and landings before departing for Goleta. In the next few days, only a few pilots managed a flight in the new plane, closely watched by the other pilots, as no one wanted to crack up in the only Corsair the squadron possessed.

A week after those first flights, more lucky pilots went to North Island, picking up a Corsair, and bringing it back to the air station until the squadron had its full complement of eighteen. It was essential that all pilots get as much time as possible on the powerful F4Us before the squadron departed for combat, for just as the first planes arrived, the orders to move out were received. Neefus tried to get each pilot at least an orientation flight, and for some of the new pilots that short hop would be the extent of their training on the six-gun fighter when the unit headed overseas.

Bob Owens had many hours of flying, but even with his experience the Corsair was something totally different than anything he had flown before. "The Corsair was a hell of a thing to fly, particularly if you'd started on a much lighter aircraft. It had so much torque that when you 'poured on the coals' to 2800 rpm, it would try to walk away from you. You had to apply full rudder in there in order to keep control. The F4U had a very large cockpit, so much so that the shorter guys could not hold their rudder all the way to counteract the torque. Some pilots used to fly with a cushion—one of my pilots, Lt. Hap Langstaff, used to have two of them in there in order to be able to push the rudder pedals further forward."

"From takeoff to landing it was like a spirited horse that required constant control," remembered Langstaff. "My problem was getting full rudder and stick movement because of my size. Being less than 5'6" I had all I could do to maintain proper control with cushions both under and behind me." The first Corsairs had no floor and the pilots looked down between long foot rails into a gaping cavern that was the inside of the fuselage. Inverted flight brought all kinds of objects down upon the pilot's head, including lost tools.

Roger Conant, another rather short, though muscular pilot, described his first flight in vivid terms: "This airplane was a big bird . . . I was just along for the ride!" Conant, a late arrival to the unit, was told to take one of the Corsairs up on his initial flight. As ground instruction, another pilot stood on the wing of the plane, showed Conant the instruments, explained takeoff and landing procedures, and that was it. Off he went! That first flight, a little over an hour, was the only Corsair hop in Conant's logbook when the squadron's planes were sent to San Diego for "pickling," weatherproofing, in preparation for the ocean voyage ahead. After less than two months with their new planes, Two Fifteen prepared to embark for overseas deployment.

CHAPTER TWO

Hawaii

*The most important thing in fighting was shooting, next the various
tactics in coming into a fight and last of all flying ability itself.*
—WORLD WAR I CANADIAN ACE "BILLY" BISHOP

VOYAGE

IN SAN DIEGO, THE AIRCRAFT WERE LOADED ABOARD THE SEAPLANE
tender USS *Pocomoke* and the transport USS *Ham*. The men and aircraft
of VMF-222 also boarded the two ships and the two squadrons sailed
west for Hawaii, *Ham* on February 12 and *Pocomoke* on February 23. It
was an uneventful trip except for pranksters who woke the others with
false alarms about Japanese submarines. For many it was their first ocean
voyage, but for veterans like Jim Neefus, the salt air had a warm familiarity.

Their arrival in Hawaii was an eye-opening experience as described
by Langstaff: "When we arrived at Ford Island, Hawaii, we were struck
by the grim realism of a shooting war. All around were the sunken hulks
of the battleships lost at Pearl Harbor, with only their smashed superstructure appearing above the surface." The *Pocomoke* began unloading in
Pearl Harbor on March 3 and the *Ham* a week later. The enlisted men
were sent to Pearl Harbor as working parties to unload the ships. The
planes were hoisted ashore on Ford Island and several pilots added to
their flight time with ferry flights from Ford to the new base at Barber's
Point. The men of the squadron were put to work at a feverish pace
to construct barracks, maintenance shops, and engineering spaces. The

Original pilots en route to Hawaii aboard USS *Pocomoke* AV-9, February 1943.
Standing, rear: Stidger, Leu, Stockwell. Standing middle row: Jordan, Haver, Braun,
Crowley, Nichols, Pickeral, B. Moore, Clark (intelligence officer), Owens, Shuchter,
Neefus, Shaw, D. Moore, Aldrich, Tomes, Deming, Wolff, Prochnik, Lammerts.
Front row: Smith, Conant, Johnson, Langstaff, Souther, Downs, Ennis (maintenance
officer). Author's Collection

thirty-one officers and 233 enlisted men were assigned to Marine Air
Group 24. Training began in earnest when the first eight aircraft off of
the *Pocomoke* reached the airstrip.

Gunnery being the first order of business, Ray Tomes and his
Marines of the Ordnance section set to bore-sighting the machine guns
of each aircraft as soon as it arrived. After a couple of days in intense
ground instruction and familiarization with the islands, the pilots rotated
on the eight available Corsairs, gaining a few more hours of flight time as
well as learning about the geography of the Hawaiian Islands.

Gradually the training took on a more warlike air, with daily gunnery
flights and a practice interception of Army B-24s on March 8. On March

10, ten more Corsairs and two SNJs were offloaded from the *Ham*, flown to Barber's Point, and prepped for operations. With the additional planes, the pilots were able to practice division and section tactics and formation flying. Some divisions had five pilots instead of four, making it necessary to rotate flyers on each mission in order to give a spare pilot a chance to fly with his division mates, necessitating numerous flights each day. When not flying, Neefus ensured ground school was in session with an emphasis on navigation as he knew most of their future flying would be over the ocean.

This Corsair of VMF-215 is caught off the Hawaiian coast during the squadron's three-week stay at Barber's Point. Author's Collection

Like any new outfit, with new men, new equipment, and a new location, little things went wrong. On several occasions the Corsairs were grounded due to little bugs that still plagued the new airplanes. Torque tubes, devices that help control ailerons and flaps, were one such problem. Hap Langstaff grumbled about running back and forth to the welding shop in an effort to repair or replace damaged manifold pipes. Disc brakes wore out at an alarming rate due possibly to abuse from novice pilots using their brakes excessively to fight the torque from the thirteen-foot, four-inch Hamilton Standard propeller. Pilot error was the most common cause of problems. Don Moore, viewed as one of the nicest guys in the squadron but an inexperienced pilot, hit a stake while making a landing, crumpling an aileron and putting an aircraft into the shop. Giant Bob Johnson nosed another Corsair over and wiped out the propeller. All of these accidents earned the ire of Neefus and Owens, as every plane in the shop reduced those available for training. Some accidents earned the anger of the other pilots.

One morning Tom Stockwell was assigned to fly an SNJ with a tow sleeve for gunnery training, flying straight and level as the other pilots dived from different angles to fire at the target that billowed along behind the trainer. Ammunition expended, the Corsairs and the SNJ headed back to Barber's Point so the scores could be evaluated. Stockwell made a good approach and made a fair landing but felt a tug on the target sleeve as he did so. Looking back, he saw that the sleeve was snagged on some concertina wire at the edge of the field, torn loose from the cable, and in shreds. Typically unfazed, Stockwell decided to let it go and headed for the barracks after shutting down. The shooters of the just completed exercise were not of the same mind and wanted to know their scores. Jim Neefus was not happy with Stockwell either, and the crestfallen pilot was forced to retrieve the shredded canvas. Unfortunately, or fortunately for the poor shooters, the sleeve was ripped and torn so badly after Stockwell pulled it from the wire that there was no way the scores could be accurately determined. Stockwell, who had also lost a sleeve back at Goleta, was followed by some very pointed stares and glares for days. Towed sleeve or not, there was no letup in gunnery training. If there were no towed targets, the pilots strafed pallets and other debris floating in the water.

Old skills were honed, and new skills were introduced. Two new areas of instruction were radar-guided interception and fuel consumption. Since the beginning of the war, the Navy had been developing fighter direction to a high level, as shore bases and aircraft carriers depended on their fighters being able to find attacking enemy aircraft before they could close on the fleet or station. Radar interceptions had been one of England's greatest weapons against the *Luftwaffe* in 1940, and lessons learned from that battle, as well as the carrier actions at Coral Sea and Midway, were incorporated into Two Fifteen's training schedule.

The Corsair was a new aircraft operationally, therefore little was known about throttle and mixture settings for the variety of missions a fighter squadron might be called upon to perform. The radar training and fuel instruction went hand in hand; it was necessary to learn how to get the Corsair into combat in the least amount of time and remain in combat for the maximum amount of time. Consumption tests and long-range interceptions were flown over and over, covering hundreds of miles of ocean. Navigation flights such as the squadron mission from Barber's Point to Hilo on the big island of Hawaii sent them out over vast expanses of water with no landmarks or over groups of unfamiliar islands.

The stay at Barber's Point was busy but short, lasting only three weeks. Training was intense, from dawn to dusk, consisting of fixed gunnery, interceptions, gas consumption, tactics, and formation flying. The mundane and routine flying around the islands could also be fun. Hawaii was an advanced base for the Allied thrust into the Pacific, and the skies were filled with all types of Army, Navy, and Marine aircraft. Army and Navy fighter pilots enjoyed bouncing planes of any service and engaging them in mock dogfights but found that the F4U was a bit more competition than they were used to. The Corsairs were as fast or faster than any Navy or Army planes, and the bent-wing Marine fighters could outmaneuver any of their opponents at high speeds, giving the Marines an advantage when it came time to initiate or break off the mock battles.

Despite the intense training and occasional mock dogfights with soldiers and sailors, the Marines were itching to get into the fight. Many chafed at the inaction and openly sought ways to get into combat right away. When a call for volunteers on a mission to the South Pacific reached Barber's Point, several leaped at the chance. Capt. D. B. Moore as well as lieutenants Red Lammerts, R. H. Haver, Edgar Prochnik, and Dave Souther parted company with Two Fifteen. When the squadron entered combat later that summer, those Marines would be patrolling above the quiet little island of Funafuti, untouched by the war.

With each mission, the pilots improved their flying skills and gained confidence. With his improved skills, Roger Conant felt that when he strapped on a Corsair it was like he became part of the plane. Despite the improving abilities of the pilots, Hawaii was becoming too crowded and provided too many distractions. Liberty was excellent for both officers and enlisted men despite the sparse opportunities, but it was time to move on. A squadron was needed to replace the defenders of Midway Atoll and the Marine Corps chose VMF-215.

MIDWAY

Lt. Gerald Pickeral took the bulk of the enlisted men along with pilots Tom Stockwell and Bill Deming; Lieutenant Ennis, the maintenance officer; and Lt. Robert Clark, the intelligence officer, aboard the USS *Henderson*. The remaining ground crew would assist the pilots in preparing the Corsairs for the long westward flight to Midway via French Frigate Shoals. All of the fuel training and the monotonous over-water navigation flights they had endured would be put to the test, as it was four hours across the Pacific to the postage stamp field at French Frigate and five hours farther to Midway.

The *Henderson* left Pearl Harbor, escorted by a destroyer, on March 30, 1943, arriving at Midway a few days later. Pickeral's advance party reported to Lt. Col. Marion Dawson's Marine Air Group 22. The men were assigned quarters, and the work began to set up the various departments: Maintenance, Communications, Ordnance, and Medical. Most of this work involved merely taking over the facilities left by the previous, departed squadron. Doc Neber and his corpsmen reported to the base dispensary.

Technically the western end of the Hawaiian Islands, Midway is no tropical island paradise, consisting of about two and a half square miles of coral land nearly devoid of vegetation and surrounded by reefs. The base actually consisted of two islands, Eastern Island being a giant airfield and Sand Island containing most of the permanent structures surrounded by barbed wire with a small airfield. Other than the military men assigned to Midway, the only inhabitants were the gooneys, large albatrosses that infested the island with their feathers, eggs, and droppings.

Gooneys are some of the worst flyers in the animal kingdom and, coupled with their sheer numbers, caused a great number of accidents and near accidents with aircraft. Personnel assigned extra duty for minor infractions often found themselves in the unenvied position of removing fried, chopped, or shredded gooneys from between the engine cylinders of the big aircraft engines. Despite the mess and noise, the birds were a constant source of entertainment as there was little else to do save watch them. When trying to land, the birds frequently forgot to put down their landing gear and spattered, end over end, to a sandy stop much to the delight of watching Marines.

Several new men joined the squadron during the time the advance party waited for their planes to arrive. Six of the new joins were pilots from sister squadron VMF-222 who would replace the flyers who went south to Funafuti: dour, serious John Breneman, gregarious Richard Newhall, little Jack Foster, pensive Lloyd Cox, and an enlisted pilot, SSgt. George Kross. The last of the new pilots was a well-built man with an infectious smile, Harold Spears.

Sometimes called Doc Spears, after a famous character in the Midwest, but usually referred to as Hal, Spears was born in Portsmouth, Ohio, and grew up in Irontown. A tough and active boy, Spears played football at Ohio University but decided he wanted to fly and left school for naval flight training. Called to active duty on October 13, 1941, Spears started initial training at Kansas City the following month. Going through the usual pilot's pipeline, he finished his training at Corpus Christi, Texas, and earned his wings on August 21, 1942. A rather boisterous and outgoing young man, he enjoyed the Marine Corps, and earned a reputation as a Marine's Marine. Originally sent to Midway to join VMF-222, Hal was transferred to VMF-215 to replace those men sent south. It was a lucky break for both Spears and his new squadron, as he would prove to be an excellent combat pilot. His entertaining, and often vulgar, mode of speaking made him a favorite of many pilots.

Back in Hawaii, Major Neefus lifted off from Ford Island on April 12, leading twelve F4Us. An R4D (the Navy designation for the DC-3 transport) led the flight as a weather and navigation plane. Two more R4Ds flew alongside as navigation aids and a PBY flying boat followed along behind to pick up any stragglers who might have to ditch in the Pacific due to mechanical or fuel problems. The fifty men of the ground echelon who had remained at Ford Island to prepare the Corsairs for the long flight now rode as passengers in the R4Ds and the PBY. It was an uneventful and boring flight with no problems, just miles and miles of ocean and the rhythmic noise from the Pratt and Whitney engines. On the way to French Frigate Shoals, Hap Langstaff provided a bit of comic relief.

Pilots in the formation noticed Hap's Corsair weaving back and forth, slightly but enough to cause the others to spread out to avoid collision. Neefus was forced to call in the errant young man, wondering if the Marine was suffering from oxygen failure or just acting up. Upon landing,

Four early-model Corsairs of Ray Tomes's division off the coast of Hawaii during the intense training period around the islands. Author's Collection

Neefus had to laugh at the explanation; Langstaff had been using the detachable relief tube on the control stick to relieve himself!

The planes remained at French Frigate overnight to refuel and rest the pilots before taking off early the next morning to journey on to Midway. Living spaces at French Frigate were provided in an old ship run aground against the coral shore. The airstrip covered all of the dry ground, consisting of piled-up coral covered by Marston matting, interconnecting steel plates, and then covered by another layer of coral. It appeared as if a wave might at any moment sweep over the entire base and render it useless.

While at French Frigate, Doc Neber ran into an old friend, also a medical man, who had been at Pearl Harbor during the December 7, 1941, attack. The friend related to the good doctor and the Marines his experiences during that event. Swamped by dozens of casualties brought before him during the infamous Japanese attack, Neber's friend was annoyed when his superior had stomped in and demanded that the good doctor clean up the messy emergency room as the admiral was scheduled for his regular weekend inspection. Gazing around the room, covered with blood and human matter, the doctor told his commander that the doctor could continue the operation or clean up the mess but not both. The embarrassed senior officer left, but the poor doctor found himself exiled to French Frigate ever since. This story of arbitrary Navy justice had a startling effect on the usually irreverent Doctor Neber. Bob Owens would later remember that both he and Jim Neefus were treated to many snappy salutes and "yessirs" for several days after.

French Frigate was desolate and forbidding and the Marines were eager to leave. They were equally disappointed upon arrival at Eastern Island at Midway as all they could see was sand, ocean, and military installations. It was a perfect training camp, with no women or liberty towns nearby to distract the pilots. Operations promptly began on April 14 with a flight of four Corsairs on alert or patrol, and the others on standby at all times. The routine was quickly set: dawn and dusk patrols each day as well as strip alert. It would remain the same for two months.

The training syllabus ranged from the usual fixed gunnery to navigation hops from Midway to Kure Island to the west. At Barber's Point the training had been more familiarization; now it became more tactical and technical. The F4Us were fitted with small bomb racks under the wings and they occasionally practiced glide bombing. Pilots with little time on the inverted gull wing Voughts were able to practice combat flying in real tactical situations, as they were on the front line of America's defensive perimeter. The squadron was split into two components, with some going to Sand Island and some to Eastern. The pilots were able to fly in formations larger than just division or section, enabling Neefus and Owens to evaluate the talent of the rapidly developing young men. Naturally some pilots impressed their leaders more than others, while some gave them headaches. As a matter of course there were accidents.

One evening, on return from the dusk patrol, Sammy Stidger did his imitation of the gooney bird and failed to remember to put down his landing gear. After the ensuing crackup, the startled pilot found himself uninjured but the poor Corsair suffered wing, engine, and propeller damage. Jim Neefus took the forgetful Stidger behind the Quonset huts for a little personal instruction. The young flyer learned his lesson and never repeated the offense.

Dick Newhall taxied into a water sprayer and "washed out" (the term actually used in the squadron diary) plane number 11. His punishment was five days restriction to quarters. One of the smaller flyers, Jack Foster, found the F4U a lot of airplane to handle, constantly fighting to show the big bird who was the boss. The Corsair ultimately triumphed in each case. Soon nicknamed "Fearless," Foster had several rather nasty near crashes with the big plane.

One morning while following Jim Neefus on takeoff, Foster's plane began to lift off the strip when the torque became too much for him, and the Corsair went up and over a sand bank that ran alongside the runway. Spectators were treated to the spectacle of the diminutive pilot jumping out of the aircraft and running around it, arms flailing in the air to warn people away for fear of fire. The Corsair never did blow up but the big fighter was severely damaged: It needed two new wings, the landing gear was nearly sliced off, and the fuselage was badly crumpled.

A few days later, "Fearless" Foster was bringing another Corsair in from a gunnery and navigation flight, ground looping right after landing.

The right wing and landing gear were wiped out, the propeller was peeled back, and the engine and cowling were banged up quite a bit. Foster was transferred to a divebomber squadron, where he was able to thrive on the smaller, less powerful Douglas SBD Dauntless. With such accidents happening with unfortunate regularity, a frustrated Jim Neefus lined up the entire flying echelon and informed them that he wished they had glass bellies so he could see if they had their head up their butt!

The pilots of VMF-215 in front of a Corsair at Midway. Unlike many Japanese pilots rushed directly into war from flight school, Two Fifteen had two months at Midway under near combat conditions to train. Author's Collection

The days became routine, typical entries in the Unit Diary records: "Dawn and Dusk patrols and standbys." Neefus and Owens ensured a full schedule of navigation, gunnery, and tactical flying to get the pilots into fighting trim and bring them all up to the same standard. Some of the problems with the new Corsair were solved at this time. Most notably the stall warning improved with the wooden block on the right wing. The pilots also learned how to trim the aircraft in dealing with the torque of the big engine and airscrew.

The strain of constant flying and training continued to take its toll. One morning Jim Neefus brought in four divisions low on the deck to buzz the ground crews and give them a good show from the airplanes they worked so hard to service. The sixteen aircraft flying wing tip to wing tip, streaking in at full speed across the atoll at low level, made an impressive sight. Ray Wolff, who earned the title "The Kid" due to his boyish looks and manner as well as a high-pitched voice, became nervous as the tower on Eastern Island loomed up in front of him, a possible hazard to himself and the aircraft next to him. His voice screeched out over the radio in a panicked tone, "Look out for the tower!" Fifteen pilots, unsure for whom the warning was intended, broke up and zoomed for altitude in all directions. One lone Corsair, Wolff's, streaked across the field, just missing the tower. Pilots spent the next few days speaking in falsetto voices mocking young Wolff.

Another morning Don Aldrich decided to buzz the small ships in the lagoon. He brought his F4U in at less than fifty feet, leaving a trail of watery spray as he came lower and lower. Aldrich showed off his excellent flying skills by pulling up just enough to clear the little vessels, scaring the wits out of the sailors below. He did come away with a small piece of an antenna from a ship's masthead. This provided all the evidence Neefus needed to confine Aldrich to quarters, a punishment often invoked but rather unusual considering there was no place to go at Midway anyway.

The strain of constant flying and the incessant sounds of the gooneys finally got to Thrifty Warner. At night the birds could be heard making moaning and groaning sounds that constantly interrupted the operations officer's sleep. After several long nights of this, and a few drinks, the birds provided the last straw. Warner had a personal radio and the birds began flying into the radio's antenna, disrupting his reception of music from Hawaii. Totally irritated, and a little intoxicated, Warner took a club to any of the poor, clumsy birds nearby. The next day he found himself on burial detail, interring the carcasses of the birds too slow to escape his previous night's onslaught. Poor Thrifty got over his aversion to the birds

The club on Midway continued the Corsair theme with the moniker of "Pirates' Den": Sitting: Shaw, Lane, D. B. Moore, Conant, Wolff, Braun, Downs, Shuchter, Warner, Ennis (maintenance officer). Center row: Newhall, Keister, Stockwell, Pickeral, Aldrich, Owens, Neefus, Tomes, Clark (intelligence officer), Neber (flight surgeon), Cox. Standing: Breneman, Kross, Johnson, Stidger, Spears, Jordan, Smith, Haver, Langstaff, Leu, Nichols, Deming. Author's Collection

and was seen one night at dusk with a drunk gooney, sharing drinks and crying like two long lost friends.

The officers were housed in bunkers, quick safety in case the Japanese returned for a rematch of their defeat the previous year, but the bunkers were humid and confining. There was an officers' club, dubbed the "Pirates' Den," that reflected the squadron's new name. No one knows who came up with the original idea, but they decided to call themselves the "Fighting Corsairs," a sobriquet that reflected a buccaneer flair that also pleased Vought aviation as an obvious reflection on their powerful new fighter plane with the piratical nickname.

VMF-215 squadron patch. Author's
Collection

Doc Neber spent a great deal of time at the club, carving his initials
and ribald ditties into the benches and tables. Often he would return
alone to his bunker late at night, giving pranksters an idea. One late
night, Neber returned from the "Pirates' Den" in darkness and pulled
open the door to his quarters, releasing dozens of screeching gooneys
that his comrades had stuffed into the cramped space of the bunker.
The birds, once all of them had been chased out, left behind a mess of
feathers, excrement, and a furious doctor. Bob Owens, Doc Neber's close
friend and the most obvious perpetrator, was seen running from the
scene, laughing hilariously, closely followed by Neber, the latter wield-
ing an ax handle. Revenge was sweet for the indomitable Neber. When
Owens returned to his rack the next evening, the executive officer literally
slipped between the sheets. The irascible doctor had spread shaving cream
between the bedding.

After several weeks stranded at Midway Atoll, the squadron began to
noticeably jell. Personalities merged together and the squadron developed
its own character, the results of nearly a year's training together. New men
fit in easily. First impressions led to some of the headstrong youngsters
chafing at the leadership of Jim Neefus, calling him "Bulldog." After
the months of training together, they learned to respect the low-key but
strict method of leadership and instruction of the man they now referred
to as "Gentleman Jim." The men easily followed Neefus's strong, quiet

method of leadership and he was able to lead without raising his voice. He allowed his subordinates the leeway to lead their own divisions and sections, leaving maintenance to the various shops, enabling the inexperienced leaders to learn the valuable lessons of command. He knew how

Robert G. Owens served as commander of VMF-215 during their last tour and shot down seven Japanese. He retired as a major general in 1972. USMC Photo

to delegate responsibility, especially to Bob Owens. The commanding officer spent a great deal of time at the group or wing headquarters and Owens was left to deal with daily problems. The pilots and ground crew respectfully began to refer to Owens as the "Big O" or just "O."

Recently promoted to major, Owens became the face of Two Fifteen. If Neefus was the commander, Owens was the boss. He was everywhere, in the shops, on the flight line, and in the air, always available and seemingly omnipresent. He knew every pilot, every man in the various echelons. The pilots he took as his personal charges; he made it his mission to get them all home. After the incident in which Dick Newhall wrecked a Corsair, Owens gave him a chewing out the young man would never forget, yet the delivery in the cool, smooth southern drawl made it difficult to miss the point and hold a grudge. Newhall knew it was done for his own good.

Days of working together high above the islands and low on the water developed a cohesiveness and teamwork among the members of each division. Flight leaders learned the importance of various signals and informing their sections or division of the next move. A nod of the head or wave of the hand indicated a bank, a turn, or a change of formation. Slipping the tail back and forth indicated the leader wanted the others to form line astern. The wingmen learned to anticipate their leader's movements and to stick with their division through all kinds of maneuvers.

The pilots were kept busy throughout May and early June. They were sent on interceptions of returning patrols that seemed to always develop into freewheeling mock dogfights around Midway. The Corsairs continued the navigation flights to nearby Kure and Hermes Islands, even once all the way back to Pearl Harbor. Though far from civilization, the men were never bored, Jim Neefus saw to that. Constant training kept all hands, both ground and air echelons, busy with little time for distractions. Maintenance people were on a twenty-four-hour schedule, and the pilots worked on night flying after a day of patrols and strip alerts. Every man would later remark that the two months on Midway were the most productive time in the squadron's history.

Flight operations slowed in early June due to poor weather, but Neefus turned it into a time for instrument flight training. Another pilot from recently arrived sister squadron Two Twenty Two, which took responsibility for Midway's defense when Two Fifteen departed, transferred to Two Fifteen during this time. Sandy-haired George Sanders would prove to be an interesting addition to the Fighting Corsairs, joining just as rumors of departure swirled around the atoll.

On June 13, 1943, orders were received to prepare the squadron to leave Midway within three days. They were at last heading southwest, although it was not a surprise as most of the Marines had been anticipating such a move over the previous two weeks. The arrival of Two Twenty Two to replace them had been a dead giveaway. A feverish pace of preparation began with packing of personal belongings, filling boxes with tools and spare parts, and all personnel files brought up to date before being packed into crates. Two days before leaving Midway, Two Fifteen received its last new pilot, energetic and outgoing David Escher, another transfer from Two Twenty Two. On June 17, the men of Two Fifteen boarded the USS *Chandeleur* and headed for the combat zone.

CHAPTER THREE

The Combat Zone

[T]here is a peculiarity about fliers, their psychology is strange, except for the rare few who stand out and go on to be leading aces. 99% of all pilots adhere to the formula they were taught in school. Train them to follow a certain pattern and, come what may, they will never consider breaking away from that pattern when they are in a battle where life and death mingle with one another.

—SABURO SAKAI

VMF-215, July 1943
Commanding Officer: Maj. James L. Neefus
Executive Officer: Maj. Robert G. Owens

Maj. Reynold G. Tomes
Capt. Donald. N. Aldrich
Capt. William N. Deming
Capt. Robert E. Johnson
Capt. Jack A. Nichols
Capt. Billie K. Shaw
Capt. Arthur T. Warner
1st Lt. John W. Breneman
1st Lt. Roger Conant
1st Lt. Harold A. Langstaff
1st Lt. Donald B. Moore
1st Lt. George P. Sanders

Capt. Richard L. Braun
Capt. John E. Downs
Capt. John R. Jordan
Capt. Gerald A. Pickeral
Capt. Gerard M. Shuchter

1st Lt. Lloyd E. Cox
1st Lt. David A. Escher
1st Lt. Reinhardt Leu
1st Lt. Richard G. Newhall
1st Lt. Lawrence M. Smith

1st Lt. Harold L. Spears   1st Lt. Grafton S. Stidger
1st Lt. Thomas D. Stockwell   1st Lt. Ray K. Wolff
2nd Lt. Robert L. Keister
TSgt. George Kross
Intelligence Officer: 1st Lt. Robert E. Clark
Flight Surgeon: Lt. Ernest N. Neber, U.S.N.
Maintenance Officer: 1st Lt. A. E. Ennis

AT THE TIME OF TWO FIFTEEN'S ARRIVAL IN THE SOUTH PACIFIC, THE Japanese were desperately fighting to hold the lower Solomon Islands. Allied strategy was based on the capture of bases in this area, using each new base to build airfields to allow land-based aircraft to cover the next landing. In doing so, the Allies often bypassed some islands in the famous "leapfrog" technique, with the ultimate purpose of capturing or isolating the fortress of Rabaul on the island of New Britain. Rabaul was the center for the Japanese campaigns in both the Solomons and in New Guinea, because any reinforcements for those two campaigns were funneled through the sprawling base. Rabaul was so formidable that Allied planners compared it to Gibraltar. Situated on the northeastern tip of New Britain Island, Rabaul Town was centrally located only 525 miles from Henderson Field on Guadalcanal, 445 miles from Port Moresby on New Guinea, and roughly 700 miles from the Japanese fleet base at Truk in the Central Pacific. No matter what plans the Allies had in the South Pacific, Rabaul had to be neutralized for any chance of success.

In order for the Allies to attack Rabaul with any strength, they first had to fight their way past several large Japanese garrisons on New Guinea and in the Solomons, capturing new bases for the short-range escort fighters that would cover the bombers involved in attacks on their next objective. As Two Fifteen entered the conflict, the Allies had just captured and were constructing bases on two islands in the Russells group, a subgroup of the Solomons only thirty miles north of Guadalcanal.

There were large numbers of Japanese bases throughout the area between Guadalcanal, secured in the fall of 1942, and Rabaul. These provided a screen of defenses between Rabaul and the advancing Allies.

Some of these bases had exotic names, such as Vella Lavella, Ondonga, and Kolombangara. Other places had a hint of their European past: Bougainville, New Georgia, and Santa Isabel. Some of the islands were covered with heavy defenses to cover a group of well-built airfields and others had only a motley garrison covering a crude dirt airstrip.

North of Guadalcanal was the large island of Bougainville. The main Japanese air bases in the Solomons were located on this massive island just north of the famous Iron Bottom Sound where the ferocious naval battles of the Guadalcanal campaign took place. On Bougainville were the fields at Bonis, Kieta, and Kahili. Farther to the north of Bougainville was the small island of Buka with a rudimentary airport on its southern tip. Just off the southern coast of Bougainville was the tiny island of Ballale, so small it seemed completely covered by its airstrip. Further south the Japanese were constructing an airfield at Munda on the island of New Georgia. There were seaplane bases spread throughout the islands, the most important being Rekata Bay on Santa Isabel.

ON THE MOVE

At sea on the way south from Midway, the men of Two Fifteen passed the time slowly and fitfully. The cruise seemed leisurely: tropical nights, pleasant sunny days, and numerous card games interrupted occasionally by a man overboard drill. Cards and cribbage boards were in abundance as the Marines searched for something to relieve the boredom. Some men read and reread the same books that soon became tattered as they passed from one reader to another. Others stood watching for hours as some played cards, the biggest participation and spectator activity of the voyage. The pilots of Two Fifteen found one particularly able opponent in the intelligence officer of an SBD squadron also embarked on the *Chandeleur*. The man was so good that even serious card players like Bob Owens and Lloyd Cox found the stranger a worthy opponent. Witty, affable, and exceptionally lucky, Lt. Joe McCarthy fleeced the Fighting Corsairs' best card players. After the war he would make a name for himself as "Tail Gunner Joe," a senator from Wisconsin who led the infamous anti-communist witchhunts of the 1950s. On the voyage there was little talk of politics, and all would part as friends upon reaching the combat zone, having no inkling as to the debacle this same man would later inflict on the nation they were sailing off to defend.

The ship crossed the equator in the third week of June. Those members of Two Fifteen that had not experienced a crossing were treated to the dubious honor of meeting King Neptune and making the age-old transition from pollywog to shellback. The costumes and color made it a memorable event, although the Marines felt the sailors went a bit too far in their hazing at times.

With little to do, some of the Marines entertained others with wild stories. Although affable and likeable, Hal Spears was a rough character and often tried to impress the rest of the squadron, especially the newer men, with his bawdy experiences. He never tired of telling graphic, crude stories of his amorous adventures. The more mature pilots knew when Spears was about to launch into one of his raunchy tales as he always started with a tired introduction: "I was standing on a street corner and this old whore came up to me and said, 'Hal, how you doin?' Now how do suppose she knew my name?" At that point the older, experienced pilots would roll their eyes and exit.

Often crass but always interesting, Harold "Hal" Spears joined the squadron at Midway Island, transferring from sister squadron VMF-222. He was credited with fifteen aerial victories. USMC Photo

On June 20 the crowded *Chandeleur* dropped anchor for a short stopover at Wallis Island. The ship spent two days at this tropical port northeast of Fiji. The time spent at Wallis started the process of acclimating to the tropical climate. This first experience in the exotic South Pacific did not impress the men of Two Fifteen. The weather was humid, the villages were dirty, the people were filthy, and elephantiasis, a disease that causes buildup of fluid in parts of the body, was widespread. Bob Owens followed Doc Neber on a courtesy call to a local hospital and came away appalled at the unsanitary conditions that included the rolling of dead bodies under the beds of the living to await burial. The deceased were interred but once a week. Returning to the ship, Owens could not get clean enough. He washed three times a day for several days but did not feel comfortable. After the long days aboard ship, the stop at the little island had been a relief, but there were no regrets as the musty shores of Wallis were left behind.

It did not take long for tedium to set in and grumbling came from various members of Two Fifteen. Most were eager to enter the new experience of combat, not just from bravado but also from continued inaction. Ray Tomes suffered from cabin fever as much as any of the others and exclaimed to anyone in earshot that as soon as they docked and unloaded the planes, he would fly over the *Chandeleur* at mast top height and roll his Corsair.

ESPIRITU SANTO

On July 1, 1943, the *Chandeleur* docked at the busy harbor at Espiritu Santo. Located in the New Hebrides, about 550 miles from Guadalcanal, Espiritu Santo was the forward staging area for the majority of Allied units in the South Pacific. It was a funnel through which units deploying into the Solomons passed and relieved units exited on their way out of the combat area. The United States poured millions of dollars into the base, building wharves, warehouses, airfields, and other installations. Damaged ships could stop for minor repairs or in preparation for moving to a major port. The living conditions were excellent, wooden Dallas and metal Quonset huts dotting the landscape. The mess halls were clean and enclosed with mosquito netting. Permanent structures housed the headquarters and service units. Most importantly, the long voyage was over and the Marines could leave the ship.

The first few days were spent unloading and moving into their quarters. The planes were immediately needed by frontline units to replace losses, forcing the pilots of Two Fifteen to work as ferry pilots, flying their Corsairs from Espiritu Santo to Guadalcanal or the Russells. Starting on one of these flights, Ray Tomes showed off his great piloting skills and, at the same time, made good on a previous boast. Swinging in low over the harbor, Tomes startled everyone by diving straight for the *Chandeleur*, slowly drifting at anchor. Screaming over the ships and boats in the harbor, the bent-wing bird bore directly at the *Chandeleur* and then slowly rolled as it passed the mast of the ship. Frightened sailors and locals went flying for cover in panic as Tomes nonchalantly pulled it up and flew off to Guadalcanal.

After a short period of inactivity, Major Neefus initiated a training program that stressed gunnery and section tactics. Part of the section tactics was the use of the weave, a tactic initiated by veteran Navy pilot Jimmy Thach early in the war when the Japanese *Zero* proved more advanced than the Navy and Marine Corps' Buffaloes and Wildcats. The weave involved a scissors action by the individual planes of a section turning into each other, always placing an attacker under the guns of an American fighter.

Training was interrupted by combat air patrols protecting a damaged cargo vessel in the Torres Islands north of Espiritu Santo on July 19 and 20. The next couple of days were spent in preparation for the final move to Guadalcanal. On the 24th the pilots climbed into eighteen new or refurbished Corsairs, most just returned from action in a damaged condition and recently overhauled. Following an R4D carrying the doctor, intelligence officer, and spare pilots, the Corsairs swung northwest and headed for the 'Canal. The ground echelon under Lieutenant Ennis stayed behind and would not rejoin the pilots for seven months.

Not long after leaving the sight of land, a giant cumulonimbus cloud formation loomed ahead of them. The thunderclouds seemed to spread out and block any path for the aircraft, but the transport pilots flying the navigation plane were undaunted and plunged into the stormy mass of

Doc Neber, considered the pilots' best friend, with George Kross, Hap Langstaff, and Chief Leu at Guadalcanal. Author's Collection

clouds, the single-engine fighters dutifully following along like ducklings after their mother. It was a near disaster as several pilots in the Corsairs became disoriented and nearly crashed. Don Moore's Corsair was smashed down as if by an invisible hand, and he pulled up a scant one hundred feet off the ocean. Weeks of training paid off as Neefus tightened the formation, pulling in the Corsairs close to each other and the R4D, and no one was lost.

GUADALCANAL

Thirty-five hundred miles southwest of Hawaii and only thirteen hundred miles north of Australia, the jungle-encrusted island of Guadalcanal had little redeeming value other than its airfields. The first morning on Guadalcanal, the men of Two Fifteen were given an orientation on the island and the surrounding areas. Several pilots had already been on the 'Canal on ferry hops, but for the majority it was a new experience. Luckily they had slowly acclimatized as their journey from Hawaii, Midway, and Espiritu Santo introduced them to the tropical climate.

After orientation, there was an intelligence briefing, and the Marines were turned loose to explore their new home. They were excited, for this was the site of the epic battle that had been declared over just the previous February. Now it was a busy jumping-off point for the offensive up the Solomons to Rabaul. Several airfields were in operation alongside famous Henderson Field with planes from several Allied nations and the US armed services launching strikes in support of operations against the next target, New Georgia.

Hap Langstaff, Chief Leu, and George Kross with a P-40 at Guadalcanal. Author's Collection

Over the next few days, the pilots played the role of tourists on the recent battlefields. They hiked into the jungle, a place only recently emptied of Japanese soldiers, in search of relics and souvenirs. Like little children at play, they clambered aboard a disabled American M3 tank and a small Japanese tankette. They smiled and horsed around as they posed for snapshots amid a jungle that was already encroaching upon the ruined machines of war. Trudging along the flight lines of the various airstrips, they checked out the different planes in use. Especially fascinating to the Marines was a Bell P-39 Airacobra they found in a run-up area. It was unlike any of the naval aircraft they were familiar with, having an inline engine situated behind the pilot and sturdy-looking tricycle landing gear. Larry Smith wandered into the brush and discovered a skinny but friendly cow. They were amazed that the cow had survived, but Smith thought it was still young and its survival was due only to the patience of the nearby mess halls that were waiting for it to mature and gain weight before slaughter.

Larry "Smitty" Smith, Hap Langstaff, and Chief Leu next to an Army P-39 at Guadalcanal. Author's Collection

Living quarters on Guadalcanal were semi-permanent with a few metal Nissen-type huts and pyramid tents with wood floors, but slit trenches and foxholes were still located nearby because of occasional Japanese air raids. The attacks were nighttime "heckler" attacks meant only to disrupt the sleep of the Marines. These aircraft, nicknamed "Washing

Machine Charlie," would drop a single bomb or just dive in fake attacks to force the Marines to seek shelter. Sometimes they would drop flares or change their engine speed or propeller pitch to make different sounds. The very first night on the 'Canal, the men of Two Fifteen were entertained by one of these attacks in which no damage was done except for a loss of sleep.

After their first night "attack," some of the Marines felt like veterans. They were pleased with the well-equipped mess facilities and semipermanent living quarters with mosquito netting, the staple of life in the tropics. The uniform of the day ranged from full stateside khakis to shorts and boondockers, Marine field shoes. Heat and humidity dictated the day's proper attire. The tropical surroundings, battlefield debris, and late-night enemy interruptions, allowed the Marines to further acclimatize in preparation for the combat that was to come.

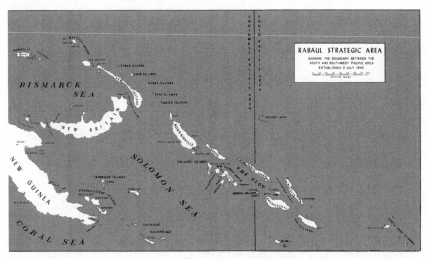

Map of Solomons Area where Two Fifteen operated. Guadalcanal lies to the lower right, and Rabaul is left of center on the eastern end of New Britain Island. From Henry I. Shaw Jr. and Douglas T. Kane, *Isolation of Rabaul: History of U.S. Marine Corps Operations in World War II*, Volume II, Washington, DC, Historical Branch, G-3 Division Headquarters, Marine Corps, 1963.

First Missions

The first official combat mission was flown on July 25. Cockpit canopies were open as the pilots took off on three flights during that hot, sultry day. Majors Jim Neefus and Ray Tomes led their divisions on the first mission patrolling Rendova, about 170 miles to the north. An Allied invasion of Rendova was in progress and the Japanese were launching violent air attacks to disrupt the landings, but the sky was empty that morning when Two Fifteen's planes arrived. Returning after the uneventful flight, Ray Tomes's engine suddenly seized up and quit, forcing him to make a water landing while his wingman Hap Langstaff circled above him. The crash took place near the Japanese-held positions on contested New Georgia Island, but Langstaff made sure there was no Japanese reaction before he headed to nearby Segi Point Airfield on the south end of New Georgia for fuel. Chafing at the slowness of fueling, Langstaff gave Air-Sea Rescue the information on Tomes's position and a search was initiated. The search was short as word came that a thoroughly soaked major had been picked up by natives and rowed to the Allied end of the island a few hours later.

The second flight of that day was an escort for a raid on New Georgia. The target was the hotly contested airstrip at Munda Point. Bob Owens and Thrifty Warner led their divisions on this uneventful flight with no enemy aircraft encountered. After taking off, Bill Deming found his well-used aircraft losing power, and he was unable to join up with the formation. He returned early to Guadalcanal, the squadron's second Corsair to fall victim to mechanical malfunctions that day. Unfortunately, these technical problems would plague not only Two Fifteen but also all of the squadrons equipped with worn and overworked airplanes.

On the third trip of the day, Don Aldrich's four Corsairs flew cover for SBDs and Grumman TBF Avengers attacking Munda. Only half of the division, Aldrich and Johnny Downs, completed the mission. Passing over New Georgia's southern tail, Bob Keister's Corsair developed a bad oil leak and his oil pressure dropped dramatically. Forced to turn back, he headed for nearby Segi Point. His wingman, Billie K. Shaw, escorted him toward safety and then tried to rejoin the formation but could not catch up and returned alone. Keister barely made it to Segi Pont, the engine quitting on landing.

The first day had been uneventful and frustrating, with no massive aerial action with dogfighting *Zeros*, but they had lost one aircraft and three others turned back for operational reasons. They had not even seen an enemy plane. The next day would be different, as they were up early the next morning for a raid on the airfield at Kahili located on the southern tip of Bougainville Island. Twenty planes led by Jim Neefus took off at 0700 and joined up with two other Corsair squadrons and some Army P-40s before heading north.

FIRST COMBAT

Unknown to the men of Two Fifteen, July 26 was to be their baptism of fire, their first encounter with the enemy. It turned out to be a disaster, not because of the Japanese but due to the condition of the airplanes they flew. George Sanders could not get off with the others and never caught up with the formation. Flying up the Slot (New Georgia Sound), Ray Tomes, Reinhardt Leu, and Sammy Stidger all suffered engine malfunctions and were forced to turn back. The formation continued on, passing Santa Isabel on their right and New Georgia on the left, the fighters weaving back and forth over and under the slower bomb-laden aircraft. Approaching the island of Choiseul, just southeast of Bougainville, a steady stream of airplanes turned back due to some type of malfunction. Bob Owens and Dick Newhall were the first, followed by Gerry Shuchter who had a bad oil leak. Five minutes later, Dave Escher and Dick Braun turned back.

About 35 miles north of Kolombangara, northwest of New Georgia, Tom Stockwell and Gerry Pickeral were weaving just behind and below the section of Thrifty Warner and Jack Jordan. The division maintained about twenty thousand feet behind the bombers. Without notice, Pickeral led Stockwell away from the other planes then criss-crossed atop the bombers twice in quick succession. Lowering down through the formation into the lower layer of escorting P-40s, Pickeral's Corsair shot up quickly past Warner's section and angled off to the side of the other planes. Stockwell was hard pressed to keep up with his formation leader's constant maneuvers, which were performed at high speed and seemed to have no purpose. Pickeral gave the signal to begin weaving again as they passed 21,500 feet. Sensing something might be wrong, Stockwell moved in closer to his wingman and tried to contact Pickeral with hand signals. Just as the two planes closed together, Pickeral's plane shot up past twenty-two thousand feet and went into a lazy wingover. In the brief moments that Stockwell had flown beside the erratic Corsair, Stockwell glimpsed the figure of Gerry Pickeral, bolt upright, with his oxygen mask hiding his leader's face as he stared straight ahead.

Pickeral's Corsair dived toward the water but pulled up, only to repeat the wingover and dive again. Gradually the F4U lost altitude, diving until speed built up and the climbing began again, white streamers peeling off the wing tips. As the speed bled off in the climb, the Corsair would wingover again into a dive. Passing eleven thousand feet, the Corsair did not pull up, gaining speed until it knifed into the waves in a giant splash. There was no visible debris as Stockwell circled at about fifteen hundred feet. Gradually an oil slick about three hundred yards in diameter fouled the ocean. Capt. Gerald M. Pickeral of Los Angeles, California, became the first member of Two Fifteen to die in combat operations.

Shaken, Stockwell returned alone to Henderson Field, leaving the others to continue on to Kahili with the bombers. Death stalked the formation as it neared its target in form of a swarm of Japanese interceptors. The run over target was made with little problem, although the Japanese tried occasionally to cut in to separate the bombers from their fighter escorts. By staying in their weaves, the Corsairs were undamaged, and their bomber charges also escaped without major loss. With one exception, the fighting Corsairs were not involved in extended combat.

Feisty Hap Langstaff lost his wingman due to engine trouble and joined up with a Corsair from VMF-214. Langstaff followed the other Marine over the target as they twisted and turned to face each approach of the Japanese. Hap was impressed with the way the unidentified Marine, with a big "66" on the side of his aircraft, handled the attacks of the enemy. The formation turned away from Kahili but as the planes neared Kolombangara headed south, the anonymous Marine turned back toward Kahili. Showing no hesitation, Hap dutifully followed his companion back toward the enemy base. Unsure of his partner's motive, Hap knew there would be action if they went back. He was not disappointed. "Enemy aircraft came from all directions," and the two Corsairs were hard pressed to keep the *Zekes* at arm's length. A *Zeke* managed to get on the tail of the Two Fourteen Corsair but Hap hefted his F4U over and let loose with a burst of .50-caliber persuasion that convinced the *Zeke* to zoom away. Several of the *Zeke's* pals fell in behind Hap and pelted him with 20mm cannon and 7.7mm machine-gun fire, but they were driven off by his anonymous wingman. Another *Zeke* made a run on Corsair number 66, and Hap again turned into the offender, firing a long string of .50-caliber bullets that drove the Mitsubishi off.

Bob Owens considered Hap Langstaff the best pilot in VMF-215. USMC Photo

The enemy attacks were pressed hard, and the Japanese seemed to be closing in on the wildly maneuvering pair. Smoke filled Hap's cockpit, and he put his Corsair into a desperate dive. He held his dive until he was at 250 feet, and he slowly pulled out and leveled off. Looking behind him, Hap saw that his heavier Corsair had left his lighter opponents far behind. His oil cooler had been hit bad, thus the black smoke, but there appeared to be no crippling damage, and he set course for home, hoping his fellow pilot was equally lucky.

Returning from Kahili, near Kolombangara, Jim Neefus retired with Jack Nichols and his wingman, sharp-featured Don Moore. The three were far from the target area and a little relaxed, weaving in a cumbersome three-plane formation. Passing through twelve thousand feet over the Slot, Neefus saw tracers flash over his wing. Startled, he looked back just in time to see a lone Japanese fighter pouring fire into Moore's airplane. The Corsair appeared to be damaged, and Neefus made a hard left turn to meet the opponent. Nichols whipped around to follow his leader, seeing the *Zeke* for the first time. Neither of the Marines was able to get a shot in as the *Zeke* went straight through them and escaped to the north. Doomed, Moore's Corsair fell off to the right with a great trail of smoke following. The F4U hit the water and burst into flames. Moore did not get out. Neefus and Nichols searched for a few minutes, but fuel was low and they were forced to return to Guadalcanal. Lt. Donald B. Moore of Wheaton, Illinois, was VMF-215's first death due to enemy action.

The fighters had done their job, and the bombers returned without a loss, but there was little celebration among the pilots of Two Fifteen. Both of the pilots that were lost had been popular, part of the original squadron that shipped out from San Diego. Pickeral had been one of the squadron's natural leaders, and Moore was remembered for his personal values. Lloyd Cox, one of the more perceptive and sensitive pilots, termed Don Moore, "one of the truly good men I've ever met." After a somber discussion with Tom Stockwell, it was decided that Pickeral's death was probably due to a malfunction in the oxygen system of his airplane. His erratic flying had been due to the gradual loss of his senses; the dives and climbs possibly occurred after he passed out. The accident reminded the men of Two Fifteen that they were not flying their own aircraft, maintained by their own ground crew. Instead they were flying planes that were shared with other squadrons, serviced by a variety of maintenance personnel, and many had been repaired quickly after suffering battle damage or mechanical failures.

Diminutive Hap Langstaff returned with the distinction of being the first and only member of the squadron to fire his guns in anger. His landing was a harrowing experience. His rudder and tail had been shot up, and control was difficult. With help from ground crewmen, Hap counted forty-two holes in the plane. It was not the hits in the wings and rudderpost that bothered him; it was the dents in the armor plate behind the pilot's seat that gave him pause. He was not the last pilot who would feel deep affection for the Corsair because of its ruggedness. Hap also learned that the pilot in Corsair number 66 returned safely.

Grimly, the pilots reviewed the day's activity. Of the twenty Corsairs that had been assigned the mission, eight did not make it to Kahili, one plane was badly shot up, and two planes, with their pilots, were lost. At the rate they were going, within ten missions the squadron would cease to exist.

FIGHTING BACK

They were given no time to dwell on their losses, as later that day Ray Tomes led eight Corsairs to escort bombers attacking an enemy transport grounded off Simbo Island, just south of New Georgia. Lloyd Cox could not get his plane to start, and Billie Shaw narrowly averted a repeat of Gerry Pickeral's death when his oxygen system failed. On the bright side, during the two missions the bombers they were escorting returned without a loss.

There was little time to grieve or ponder their losses as the men of Two Fifteen were kept busy with a constant routine of alerts, test hops, and escort missions up the Slot to Munda, Rendova, and Vila over the next few days. Mechanical problems continued to be a major problem, with six planes forced to return from the two missions on July 28, mostly due to oil leaks. As a matter of routine, ComAirSols (Commander Aircraft Solomons) would notify Neefus the day before a mission what the target was and the number of planes available. Unlike the movies, pilots had no "personal" aircraft and the operations officer would just point to an aircraft and say "Take that one!" After a few missions pilots became familiar with the characteristics of various airplanes and dreaded when they were assigned one that had a poor reputation. There were plenty of pilots and few planes, so many pilots had to wait a day or two to fly. Despite the losses and overworked airplanes, they were still eager to get into the air. Some of the divisions had more than four men, and the extra pilots flew with other divisions to make up losses.

Former RCAF pilot Donald Aldrich was an original pilot who joined VMF-215 at Goleta. Highly competitive, he was credited with twenty victories over enemy planes. USMC Photo

In six missions, Two Fifteen lost two pilots and three planes and only one man had engaged in aerial combat. Many of them had been forced to turn back from missions due to malfunctions. On July 29, eight pilots got their chance to change those grim statistics. That morning Don Aldrich and Dick Braun took their divisions on an escort for four B-25s on a barge hunt near Vila on New Georgia. It was enemy territory with fierce ground fighting taking place nearby, and the pilots anticipated action. They found a barge, larger than the usual small coastal craft seen in the islands, hung up on a reef. The B-25s made short work of the unfortunate Japanese vessel, blasting it into splinters with bombs and gunfire. Aldrich gave his Marines free rein to strafe the partially camouflaged buildings and huts that lined the shore. One after the other, the Voughts streaked in with six guns blazing. The water foamed as the bullets splashed, then sand spurted up as the bullets went up the beach into the trees. Huts simply disappeared, and boxes of supplies disintegrated in puffs of smoke and debris as the searching .50-caliber rounds found their mark. The Corsairs came in for a second pass: Aldrich then Downs, Shaw, and finally Keister. The second division followed through the smoke of secondary explosions:

Braun, then Stidger, Johnson, and Stockwell. Reforming after the second run, the Marines headed back to Guadalcanal with no losses to them or the B-25s, and no mechanical breakdowns. They had done little damage, denying the enemy a few supplies, but the action had achieved something more important. The men of VMF-215 were finally in the fight.

CHAPTER FOUR

Up the Slot

They fall into two broad categories; those who were out to shoot and those who secretly and desperately know they will be shot at, the hunters and the hunted.

—GROUP CAPTAIN JOHNNIE JOHNSON

AUGUST 1, 1943, FOUND ELEVEN GRAY-BLUE CORSAIRS TOILING SLOWLY up the Slot toward Bougainville, where they were to rendezvous with twenty-seven B-24 four-engine bombers. Gerry Shuchter did not make the flight because of a bad voltage regulator, and Johnny Downs turned back as they approached New Georgia with another of the omnipresent oil leaks. The weather was incredibly bad, and dense clouds shrouded the ocean and islands. Only nine of the promised Army bombers joined, appearing below at seven thousand feet. Jim Neefus was irritated, wanting to call off the flight, but the bombers proceeded on and the F4Us were forced to follow. Weather did not improve up the Slot, and visibility worsened as they approached Bougainville.

Closing in on Kahili, the bomber commander found the target obscured by clouds all the way up to eighteen thousand feet. He led the B-24s on a run over Ballale, a small island with a postage stamp runway across a strait from Kahili. The bombers made two runs. One straddled the southern end of the runway and the other missed the tiny island completely, splashing harmlessly into the water. Ominously, the flyers glimpsed planes taking off from Kahili into the clouds. The four-engine

57

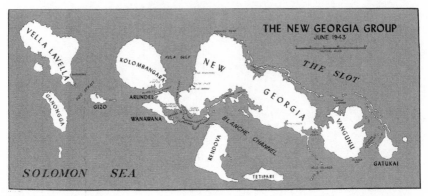

Map of the New Georgia area. Henry I. Shaw Jr. and Douglas T. Kane, *Isolation of Rabaul: History of U.S. Marine Corps Operations in World War II, Volume II,* Washington, DC, Historical Branch, G-3 Division Headquarters, US Marine Corps, 1963.

bombers turned and headed home at twenty-two thousand feet. Japanese antiaircraft fire from both airfields and nearby islands continued to track the Americans, but the explosions were consistently ahead of the formation.

Not long after the retirement began, crewmen in the bombers and some of the escorting pilots began tracking bogies, unidentified aircraft, above and behind them. The airplanes grew closer, and the big red disks on their wings revealed them to be enemy fighters. The Japanese looped and rolled, diving and then zooming up in crazy aerobatics. After a few minutes of putting on a show, the little brown fighters turned to attack, Ray Tomes's and Dick Braun's divisions turning to meet them. The *Zekes* and *Hamps* (square-winged *Zekes*) found themselves frustrated by the appearance of a radial engine snout each time they made a pass, the weaving Corsairs banking to meet each Japanese attack. Some *Zekes* managed to get in close to the bombers before being driven off, and several bombers were damaged. Flying at about fifteen thousand feet off Gizo Island, the pilots of Jim Neefus's division were startled by tracers flashing by their canopies. Neefus and Spears turned into the offending Japanese plane, but it was too late as the bullets caught Jack Nichols's fighter and it fell out of formation, on fire. Spears went into a quick roll as more fire from the Japanese plane squirted past him, but Neefus got onto the *Zeke*'s tail. The Japanese pilot pulled his little fighter into a steep climb and loop heading for the clouds with Neefus trying to stay with him. Spears found himself alone when he righted his aircraft and headed for home at high speed. Neefus lost the *Zeke* and turned for home also, briefly seeing Nichols's plane at about seven thousand feet, with Nichols in full control and the fire out. He lost sight of Nichols in the overcast. Spears returned to Guadalcanal after a stop in the Russells for fuel.

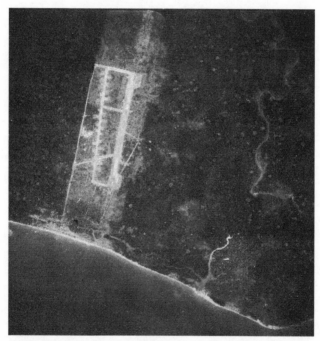

Kahili Airfield on Bougainville pictured under occupation of the Japanese. Air Corps Photo

Roger Conant was chasing a *Zeke* when he saw tracers flashing over his wings. Ray Wolff, his wingman, was too close to him and firing at the *Zeke* also, forcing Conant to break off and also making him extremely angry. Upon return to Guadalcanal, Conant stormed over to Wolff's plane as the "Kid" dropped off the big wing of his Corsair and landed on the ground. Livid, Conant's outrage spilled out, and poor Wolff staggered back. The Kid mumbled his effusive apologies but swore he hadn't been shooting. Roger was dubious until Wolff pointed to his gun ports, still covered over with the tape used to keep out dust. The bullets Roger saw must have been fired from an unseen *Zeke*!

After the short return flight, Neefus landed and went immediately to the debriefing tent to inquire about Nichols. Lt. William Crowe of VMF-124 told the commander of Two Fifteen that he had seen Nichols make a successful water landing, but Jack Nichols was never seen again.

The flight tempo intensified, training the pilots on identifying the different islands and bodies of water as well as performing the mundane duties of ground alert, submarine search, and patrols over the field. These flights allowed the pilots to get to know each other. At first with their heads covered and faces pinched by the cloth-flying helmet and oxygen mask, the pilots could not be recognized due to the glare of the plexiglass canopy and high speed of the fighters. Gradually, the pilots got to know their fellow flyers. After days together, months together, some had been a year together, they knew the shape of the man's head, his mannerisms, or the way he handled his aircraft.

August opened with the divisions of Jim Neefus, Don Aldrich, and Dick Braun sent to cover shipping off Rendova. Neefus's plane would not start, and his division arrived over the beachhead long after the others. Approaching the island, Lloyd Cox spotted an airplane flying away from the fleet to the west, and Aldrich led his division in at full throttle. It was only after they had flown out of sight of the fleet that they were able to identify the plane as a friendly Avenger bomber.

Braun heard the bogey report and spotted three *Zekes* at three o'clock below the Corsairs. Diving toward the enemy, Braun's division was confronted with two more *Zekes*. Braun attacked the pair from slightly abeam and struck one *Zeke*'s cowling, but the Corsairs were too fast and swept past the Japanese at over 300 knots. Sammy Stidger also fired some quick shots as they flashed by. Japanese fighters curved in behind the Corsairs as the second section of Marines led by barrel-chested Bob Johnson pounced on the first trio of enemy planes. Johnson and his wingman Tom Stockwell were flying too fast and were unable get in a good shot at the three *Zekes*. Flocks of Japanese joined the attack on the Americans.

Johnson failed to hit his target *Zeke* and was set upon from behind by another enemy plane. Stockwell drove the *Zeke* off as he weaved next to Johnson's Corsair. Unable to catch another *Zeke* in its climb, Johnson and Stockwell were confronted by the little fighter that turned and attacked them head on, four guns blazing. The Corsairs returned fire as the planes swept by each other. Johnson was hit, a few rounds piercing his wings. Pulling away from the fire, Johnson was enveloped by a cloud, and Stockwell joined two Corsairs, one of which he thought was Dick Braun. Two *Zekes* flashed in to hit the Corsairs, and Stockwell drove them off by firing in their direction. His day was not done; he drove off another attack merely by turning into a *Zeke*. He attempted to join a pair of Corsairs but was confronted by more enemy planes, and the dark-eyed Marine "grabbed off a cloud" until he could disengage and head for Guadalcanal.

Corsairs were equipped with a CO_2 system to fill the wing tanks as they emptied of fuel to prevent fires. Dick Braun was just purging his

Dick Braun was a born leader with a mature personality that led the younger pilots to naturally follow him. He was credited with five aerial victories. USMC Photo

wing tanks when shots passed over his head. One of the CO_2 bottles exploded and he thought, "I must have been hit!" White smoke poured into the cockpit, and he prepared to bail out. Chopping the throttle and opening his canopy, the white mist cleared and Dick realized his aircraft wasn't damaged. Diving for the deck, Braun evaded the Japanese and reached safety just above the water, covered by Sammy Stidger who scared off another *Zeke* with well-placed shots before Stidger himself had to run from other *Zekes* on his tail.

After evading the enemy fighters and setting course for home, a *Zeke* appeared from the clouds, and Stidger lined it up from dead astern. The Japanese tried to escape low on the water but Stidger held his course, firing occasionally. Finally he overtook the *Zeke* and poured in a close-range barrage of bullets. The Japanese fighter appeared to crash in the water, but the Marine was unable to confirm the defeat of his enemy as another *Zeke* was diving on him from out of the sun. The *Zeke* made a pass and then climbed away at a steeper angle than the Corsair could maintain, but Stidger followed until it reached the clouds.

Stidger rejoined Braun and went "looking for a fight." Proceeding toward a division of F4F Wildcats, Stidger took time to survey the damage to his aircraft. The left wing had lost about a foot and a half off the tip, and there was a big hole in the same wing's fuel tank with a wisp of fuel blowing back in the slipstream. There were dozens of small shrapnel holes all through the aircraft. Checking his instruments, it appeared the Corsair was fine and he waved okay toward Braun. Assuming Stidger was able to continue, Braun pulled up to join the Wildcats above them. Braun glanced back to see that Stidger was not following, so he circled around to rejoin the damaged Corsair. Sammy waved him off again, and Dick resumed his attempt to join the Wildcats. Just to be sure, Braun looked back again only to find that Stidger had completely disappeared. Braun circled for a moment and noticed Aldrich's division heading south, so he joined them.

Stidger had lost altitude and fallen behind, but when he attempted to increase his speed the Corsair began to shake and the engine coughed. He chopped the throttle, but the shudder only increased and the cockpit filled with smoke. Unstrapping his harness and pulling back on his canopy, Stidger pushed himself up and out of the stalling aircraft but did not get clear, striking the antennae post as he fell away. To add insult to painful injury, his careening body hit the vertical stabilizer with such force that several ribs were broken. Pulling the ripcord, his parachute blossomed free with a painful jolt, and he became tangled in the shrouds in an upside down position. Floating down toward the sea, he saw the engine of the Corsair vibrate completely off, and he watched, from an inverted position, as the plane fell into the sea in two separate pieces. Knifing into the water on his shoulder, he luckily suffered no further injury. A Higgins boat spotted him as he was falling and arrived just as he hit the water. The crew of the boat pulled him in so quickly that he didn't need to inflate his life jacket, which was just as well as the jacket was useless, torn and shredded in the strike against the antennae and tail.

On all missions, Doc Neber met the returning pilots with his black chest filled with various medicine bottles and medical supplies. Some pilots went straight to the post-mission interview with Bob Clark, the intelligence officer, but Doc Neber took the ones who seemed more exhausted or in shock and had them sit down in his tent. The doctor, a decade older than most of the pilots, would gaze at the array of bottles with apparent medical interest, possibly with a serious nod or quizzical look, and choose a bottle. Invariably he chose brandy, often mixed with a little fruit juice, in a container similar to those used to dispense liquor on airliners. This artificial stimulant, or depressant depending upon the condition of the pilot, and the friendly banter that went along with it, was often enough to bring a tired and stressed pilot back to a relaxed state of mind. The pilot would then go to the intelligence officer's tent to debrief. Sometimes the alcohol and soothing talk produced a deep sleep, and Neber would allow the young man to forgo an immediate debriefing.

Poor Sammy Stidger spent the next two weeks grounded on Guadalcanal, codenamed Cactus, to heal his fragile ribs. The rest of the squadron, when not on operations, stood runway alerts and wandered through the tall kunai grass that covered the island looking for loot. A distracting sidelight was the assignment to New Georgia for a day or two on base alert. On August 11, Major Neefus took Ray Tomes and Thrifty Warner's divisions with his own up to the recently captured Segi Point runway on

New Georgia for combat air patrols and strip alerts. Unable to reach Segi Point due to bad weather, the Corsairs landed at Banika in the Russells. They stayed on strip alert on Banika for two days with the exception of Larry Smith and John Breneman who returned to Cactus early.

First Victory
Two divisions of Two Fifteen under Major Owens went north on August 12 as escort for B-24s headed for Kahili. Ray Wolff missed the trip. Landing on Segi for fuel, Wolff's Corsair was crushed by another Corsair landing after being shot up earlier that day.

The flight to the target was made without incident. Once at the target, the B-24s did an excellent job of hitting the airfield squarely from twenty-four thousand feet and starting massive fires. Heading home, just past the small island of Ballale, the bombers encountered over forty Japanese fighters. The bombers turned slightly left to take advantage of a bank of clouds over Choiseul; the Corsairs and P-40s of the escort went into action to break up the incoming attack. All organization and order disintegrated as pairs or single planes became locked in deadly combat.

Owens, with Roger Conant and Dick Newhall on his wings, attacked two *Zekes* approaching the B-24s. One of the *Zekes* turned into the three Marines to take them head on. The Japanese pilot fired and Owens fired, scoring hits immediately. The *Zeke* flashed by the Marines with smoke pouring from the cockpit. Owens turned to take the other *Zeke* from behind, but only managed a wild shot before his speed pushed him past the target. Conant stayed with the major, but Newhall followed the Japanese plane as it avoided the fire from Owens's Corsair. Newhall made the mistake of trying to turn with the *Zeke*, and it turned the tables on him, gaining a six o'clock position on the Corsair. Diving for the cover of clouds at twelve thousand feet, Newhall avoided the *Zeke* and headed home at one hundred feet off the water. Owens gathered the other six planes and circled the area four times on the lookout for any stray bombers and then headed home. All landed safely without further problem, but Dick Newhall had one more burden to bear.

Alone, just passing Vella Lavella heading home, another *Zeke* appeared from a small cloud and began pelting Newhall's plane from close range with both cannon and machine-gun fire. Newhall slipped and skidded back and forth just off the wave tops enough to frustrate the *Zeke*'s aim. The Japanese pilot finally gave up, turning away in a zooming climb. Newhall briefly considered going after the enemy plane but realized he was short on fuel. After fueling up at Segi Point, he made it back to the 'Canal without further damage.

When the bombers turned and headed for home, Don Aldrich was weaving with Johnny "Loophole" Downs, so named because of his legal training. Abruptly a *Zeke* attacked from above and behind. Aldrich called break and turned sharply, but Downs did not follow. Aldrich zoomed back up to confront the *Zeke*, firing at extreme range but the *Zeke* climbed away. No sooner did that enemy disappear when another *Zeke* flew past Aldrich's gun sight. Aldrich fired and his guns quickly scored hits. The *Zeke* flashed by, flames "all over," losing speed, and falling into the water. Aldrich joined a Corsair from another squadron and headed south. Don Aldrich was credited with the first aerial victory for VMF-215.

The *Zeke* driven off by Aldrich found Downs heading for home. Downs watched the Japanese fighter, and each time it started to fire, he broke in toward it. The Corsair couldn't turn with the *Zeke*, so Downs reversed his turn and rolled into a dive, using the speed from the dive to break away from the Japanese fighter. He managed to rejoin the B-24s and broke away over the Russells. During the homeward flight he noticed his Corsair had taken some hits, with the worst damage to his flaps as he landed "hot" but safe at Cactus.

It was a busy day for the men of Two Fifteen, including those on alert at Segi Point. As the duty flight, they were sent up to patrol over Munda but encountered no Japanese. Unfortunately, Bill Deming fell victim to gunfire, but not from the Japanese. Passing over the Munda ground fighting, Deming was leading Larry Smith when suddenly his right wing exploded. Feeling a sharp pain, he realized his arm was broken. He lost control of the badly damaged plane and had to bail out. Rescued quickly by troops on the ground, Deming's time with Two Fifteen was over. Articulate and dependable, Bill Deming would recover from his injuries but would not rejoin the squadron.

DIFFERENT COMPETITION

Competition in the sky often carried over into the camp after missions in the form of card games. Not long after the first aerial victory, there was a card game right out of the old Wild West. The players were seated on cots, homemade benches, foot lockers, or whatever else that could be used as a chair. Several men sat and kibitzed around the players: southern gentleman Bob Owens, hard-playing Don Aldrich, smiling and crafty Doc Neber, good-natured Jack Jordan, and several others. Play began, with the gunfighters and the town doctor establishing rules; stakes were set, and the cards were dealt. After a few hands the game became serious, with several players dropping out due to the competition, leaving only Owens, Neber, Jordan, and Aldrich. Another hand was dealt, and shifty eyes passed over the other players as Aldrich sized up the competition as if they were a flight of *Zekes* he intended to bounce. Careless bantering stopped as bets were placed and pots were raised. Observers fell silent as "O" folded, despite a flush, and sat back to watch the outcome. Jordan went out next, a straight laid before him on the table. Only the shrewd doctor and highly competitive Aldrich remained to claim the rather large pot. Bets again were placed; Aldrich was convinced the good-natured doctor was bluffing, and he loudly yelled out, "Call!" Anxious eyes watched as the hard-charging, aggressive young fighter pilot placed a full house on the box top for all to see. He smiled smugly, as though victory was assured. With scarcely a pause, the doctor laid down four kings.

There was a moment of silence and it appeared as if Aldrich had been hit by a two-by-four between the eyes. After a short moment, Aldrich's expression slowly, ominously changed. Like a bomb going off, Aldrich burst out in mutterings and profanity. Spectators feared for the doctor's life. Neber only smiled. In a rage, Aldrich stomped out of the tent saying he "would never play again." Neber pocketed his substantial winnings, and the game began again. The betting continued, and pots were won. The noise of cheerful joking and chit-chat filled the night. There was little notice a few minutes later when Don Aldrich quietly slipped back into the tent. Within minutes he was seated with Neber and the others playing as lustily as ever.

MUNDA

On August 14, Two Fifteen became the first squadron to use the new Munda field on New Georgia Island, captured from the Japanese on August 7 and hurriedly put into action by SeaBees and engineers. On that day Owens's division was assigned as combat air patrol over New Georgia. After flying patrol for about an hour, Bob Owens brought in Corsair #76, "Spirit of 76" emblazoned on its side, for the first landing on the coral runway amid shattered trees, shell holes, and other reminders of the recent battle to capture the field. Roger Conant, Ray Wolff, and Dick Newhall followed. They were refueled and shortly after that scrambled to intercept a possible Japanese plane. The report proved false, and they spent the rest of the day on strip alert at Segi Point before returning to Cactus. Dick Braun's division landed on Munda not long after Owens departed and sat on strip alert there all day until flying back to Guadalcanal that evening.

Bob Owens making the first landing at Munda Airfield on New Georgia after its capture from the Japanese. USMC Photo

Next morning three divisions led by Jim Neefus went up to Munda and sat on the edge of the coral runway as the alert flight, on call if Japanese were expected. The muddy field had little in the way of conveniences, facilities being only what the Japanese had left, damaged in battle, or those improvised by the SeaBees or engineers. The stench of death was noticeable, and the Marines got their first look at the Japanese, unburied bodies near the airstrip. Shell holes containing dead Japanese were only hastily covered to stop the spread of disease. Sounds of nearby fighting could be heard, and the boom of artillery was unnerving. Occasionally a bullet could be heard flying across the field. Carved out of dense jungle, torn trees lined the runway, chopped off by shellfire and bombing. The debris of war could be seen everywhere. Flies covered much of the area. Except for a few Navy mechanics, there were no ground crews for the airplanes. SeaBees and Marines from nearby units were pressed into service to help with fueling from drums.

At 1145, Ray Tomes was ordered to take his division up to cover the new landings at Vella Lavella. Tomes and his wingman, George Kross, were the only ones to reach the target. Hap Langstaff could not get his Corsair started, and John Breneman's gauges went crazy about ten miles from Munda, forcing him to abort. Forty-five minutes out of Munda, the two remaining F4Us took up patrol over the beachhead at seventeen thousand feet. Only a few minutes into the patrol, they saw two *Val* dive-bombers below them at fifteen thousand feet and five *Zekes* out to the side of the bombers at the same altitude as the Corsairs. The *Vals* were a bigger threat to the shipping, and Tomes decided to ignore the escorts and go for the bombers. Tomes led the way down on the second *Val*, a little too late as its bomb fell away. They followed the *Val* as it pulled out of its dive at two thousand feet. Tomes concentrated on the *Val*, but poor Kross took enemy fire as three *Zekes* lined up behind him and poured out cannon and machine-gun fire. In a great display of flying skill, Kross continued on Tomes's wing even as he used stick and rudder to spoil the enemies' aim. Tomes first shots surprised the *Val*'s pilot, and he turned hard left at slow speed. The two Corsairs went flying past but Tomes pulled up to bleed airspeed and then rolled left into a turn in pursuit of the *Val*. Kross, noting the pursuing *Zekes* had broken off their attack due to the speed of the Corsairs, tried to turn with Tomes but couldn't follow. He fired while still out of range, flailing the air with lead. Ray Tomes, the skillful gunner who had scored 100 percent hits several times in gunnery at Miami, closed in and fired at close range. A wisp of smoke wafted back from the *Val*. Concentrating on the enemy plane, Tomes was startled by a shadow passing over his plane as Kross flew past him, firing, but Kross was too fast and his shots were wasted. The badly damaged *Val* tried to turn, but Tomes cut it off and fired a long burst. Flames appeared and black smoke poured from the doomed bomber. The *Val* straightened out for a moment and then plunged into the dense, green jungle of Vella Lavella about a mile inland. After climbing to ten thousand feet and looking for more action, the two planes returned to Munda at about 1330.

INTERLUDE

At times life on the 'Canal could be tiresome and boring, but the flyers rapidly adjusted to their surroundings. Sitting in his tent one afternoon, after all flying had been canceled due to weather, Lloyd Cox candidly

A pensive Lloyd Cox poses heroically for the official cameraman. He was credited with three victories over enemy planes. USMC Photo

described his tent mates in his diary, giving a small glimpse into their personalities: "George Kross . . . is busily studying maps of the area. A very conscientious fellow, very much concerned about the seriousness of his chosen profession. Smitty [Larry Smith] . . . is stripped to his drawers, seems to be a man concerned about improving the living conditions that surround his bunk. . . . He's bitching because of a practical joke last night . . . wrecked some of his things. He's now beginning to write letters. Conant is still sleepy-eyed from too much sack time, dearly rubbing his eyes and abusing anybody who gets on him or says something to him. Keeps calling Chief Leu "the original funny man," on account of Leu's practical jokes on everyone. . . . He keeps telling me [Cox] my diary is against all regulations. Can't quite figure Roger out . . . in any event, he's a character. Thrifty [Warner], because that's what he is, is half-heartedly composing a letter to his wife. In the last half hour he's managed one paragraph. Thrifty is much too concerned about making witty remarks about the two around him. He has the happy knack of choosing the exact descriptive word that turns a common-place incident into an extraordinarily amusing one. . . . Sam Stidger . . . seems to be memorizing the sex pictures of *Life* magazine . . . very conscious of life around him. . . . Jordan is writing, I suppose, another letter to his beautiful wife. Jordan and Warner make quite a pair . . . [Jordan] also has a keen sense of humor equaled by few men in the squadron, can be appropriately serious and understanding at times. Has a brisk manner of a typical young modern. He has no enemies, even though he can unleash the most scathing of witticisms. Like Warner, he has the happy knack of the right word at the right moment for the right occasion. Robert Clark [Intelligence officer] . . . reading a magazine, quoting various passages to the crowd in general . . . intelligent, understanding . . . boasts an inane laugh . . . delightful and fun. Harold "Cactus" Spears, stripped . . . is writing a letter. Seems to be the whoremaster of the squadron . . . boasts of his relations with women. . . . He has two aims in life: women and money. Chief Leu is rather a hard man to know, he is quiet but not dull. He speaks in . . . an often sarcastic tone."

After surveying his comrades once more, Lloyd Cox put down his pen and the pensive pilot went outside. Tomorrow would be another mission up the Slot.

CHAPTER FIVE

Leapfrog Up the Solomons

Fight as a team—you'll live longer!
—Lt. Cmdr. J. S. "Jimmy" Thach

THE MEN OF TWO FIFTEEN WOULD NOT REALIZE HOW IDYLLIC THEIR camp on Guadalcanal was, with its semi-permanent housing, mess halls with hot chow, and showers, until they moved north. The first inkling of how bad things could get was on August 17. Bob Johnson, Roger Conant, and George Kross were assigned to Munda field overnight. Sleeping in a hastily erected tent at the same time a major ground action was taking place less than a thousand yards away was a humbling experience, placing the pilots on the same level as the Marines and soldiers still fighting. The Japanese still contested ownership of the airfield, and the tents were in easy range of Japanese guns. The pilots spent much of the night in a trench next to their tent. The squadron rotated a division or two into Munda for the next week, until August 29 when thirteen of the pilots flew up to join Doc Neber and Bob Clark as permanent residents.

On August 18 Jim Neefus and Hal Spears were sent on an unusual assignment, high-altitude reconnaissance over Kahili. It was an uneventful mission without any aerial contact. Cruising above the enemy base, they reported a large transport, nine or ten smaller craft, and some barges clustering nearby bays and inlets.

Later that day, Ray Tomes and Hap Langstaff were sent on a similar flight. They flew at thirty-two thousand feet through clear sky over the jungle-covered islands, checking for any enemy activity. Counting the little ships in and around Kahili, they arrived at similar numbers as the earlier flight. Over the airfield itself, they noticed a beehive of activity: a plane taking off, one taxiing, and several approaching to land. Wanting a closer look, Tomes led Langstaff in a series of lazy S-turns. Passing twenty-nine thousand feet, in the midst of a slow turn to port, Tomes spotted six dark green airplanes with a single aircraft to the left of the others. He identified them as *Zekes*. They appeared to be at about seventeen thousand feet. Tomes led Langstaff in a stern attack on the enemy aircraft, Tomes taking the right rear *Zeke* and Langstaff the last one on the left. Tomes opened fire and his target quickly fell in pieces to the sea below, his Corsair barely avoiding the wreckage as he flew away just above the water. Langstaff also set his target on fire before joining his section leader to speed away as the other *Zekes* chased them. Upon landing, Tomes was surprised when Langstaff told him that five *Zekes* were on his tail firing at him as he destroyed his target. The swerving that Langstaff had seen from Tomes's plane was not evasive maneuvers to avoid fire, it was Tomes trying to avoid the falling wreckage and watch his victim hit the water. Tomes was only mildly interested when five bullet holes were found in the skin of his Corsair.

Munda provided all sorts of thrills for the pilots due to the proximity of the ground fighting. In addition to night raids, occasionally single artillery rounds would strike near their encampment. On strip alert one summer afternoon, Roger Conant sat in the cockpit of his Corsair waiting for the signal to scramble. Calmly he watched puffs of smoke and dirt that indicated explosions just off the far end of the runway. More shells fell, and he detected a pattern; the shells were actually traveling down the runway toward his waiting aircraft. The explosions came closer and closer, and the noise became louder and louder. Conant loosened his straps and jumped out on the wing of his plane. The better part of valor led Conant, and the rest of his division, to scramble out of their planes to seek the shelter of nearby slit trenches. Ambling awkwardly in their cumbersome flight gear, they would have been a humorous sight if not for the serious nature of their retreat. The enemy artillery passed by them, failing to hit any of the ground-bound Corsairs or any personnel.

Due to the large number of dead bodies, flies and other insects abounded. Millions of the creatures infested everything, including the food. Eating required a certain amount of skill, a quick brush of the hand on each bite before placing it in their mouths to remove the annoying flying creatures. The diet was monotonous; there were few exceptions to the C-rations and K-rations. Chief Leu remembered, "I'll never forget the crackers and sauerkraut." The men slept fitfully in their open tents on jury-rigged hammocks with a few mosquito nets to protect those attempting slumber. Giant mosquitoes, infected with various diseases, flew everywhere at night, adding to the misery of tired pilots. Hot days with no breeze made it almost impossible to sleep during the day.

Skin problems and fungal diseases were rampant. One sick pilot persisted in sleeping between dirty blankets, and his infection improved after Doc Neber insisted he sleep only between sheets. The extreme heat and humidity of the tropics affected the skin of the pilots, and Doc Neber noted that blondes were more likely to be affected than brunettes. Dick Newhall suffered an especially bad case of skin irritation, forcing him to miss several flights.

Most of the Marines lost their appetites when faced with a diet of C-rations covered in flies. Dramatic weight loss was common in Two Fifteen. Doc Neber went from 170 pounds to only 128 during his stay at Munda. The slow tropical degeneration that started at Espiritu took full hold of the men of Two Fifteen, but fortunately they were young and healthy to begin with. Occasionally, they were able to rotate back to the relative comfort of Guadalcanal for a few days. The poor soldiers, sailors, and Marines fighting on the front lines were not so fortunate.

Munda could be an immense dust bowl covered in insects, only to be turned within a few hours into a muddy, slippery pit when the frequent rains flooded the area. These first days at Munda were the worst for the men of Two Fifteen, not because the conditions would always be better in the future—because they wouldn't. Instead it was terrible because they had never faced these conditions before and they were not used to them. The diet, quarters, and climate all hit rock bottom at Munda, but the Marines slowly learned to live with such inconveniences. Some wondered why the Japanese wanted such a pesthole. It prepared them for their

Corsairs 76 and 67 just after making the first landing at Munda on August 14, 1943. Planes often used the last two digits of their Bureau Number as their aircraft number. USMC Photo

future. They were not aware that they would live in similar conditions on Vella Lavella and Bougainville during their next two tours.

Days at Munda were spent waiting for action on strip alert or combat air patrols. Occasionally the Corsairs escorted B-25s on barge patrols, strafing Japanese boats and small vessels after the Army planes dropped their bombs. Air patrols over the invasion fleet at Vella Lavella failed to produce any air-to-air engagements.

Rekata Bay, Where the Floatplane *Zeros* Play

The Japanese navy, more than any other country's armed forces in World War II, used seaplanes for every task an airplane could accomplish. They used seaplanes as fighters, converting their excellent *Zero* fighter into the *Rufe* seaplane by adding a single float beneath the fuselage and two smaller floats under each wing. Other single-engine planes performed rescue, reconnaissance, bomber, fighter, and resupply missions. Massive four-engine seaplanes like the H6K *Mavis* and H8K *Emily* served these functions and as transports or cargo aircraft. Every major capital ship in

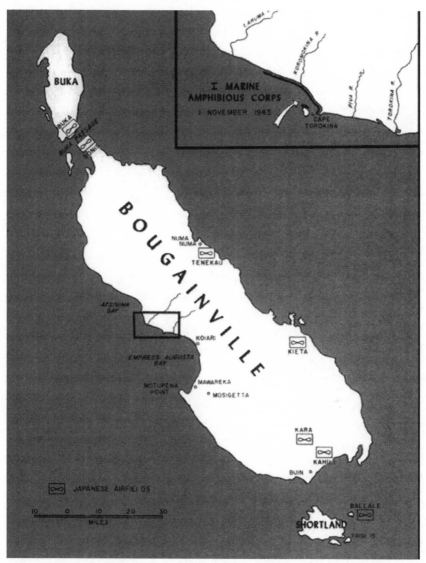

Map of Bougainville. From Wesley Frank Craven and James Lee Cate, *U.S. Army Air Forces in World War Two, Volume IV: The Pacific: Guadalcanal to Saipan, August 1942 to July 1944*, Office of Air Force History, Air Historical Group, USAF Historical Division, Chicago, University of Chicago Press, 1948–1958, 247.

the navy had a seaplane aboard. A special type of seaplane operated off submarines, and one of these bombed Oregon on September 9, 1942, in the only aerial bombing of the US mainland. Wherever the Japanese navy went, they constructed seaplane bases, and in the spring of 1942 they constructed a base on Rekata Bay on Santa Isabel's north coast.

On August 19, Jim Neefus was ordered to take four planes up to check out Rekata Bay to see if the Japanese had any aircraft moored there. Billie Shaw asked Neefus if he could take the flight, and the squadron commander agreed. Shaw took Gerry Shuchter, Hal Spears, and George Sanders, who had taken Tom Stockwell's spot on the strip alert. Weather was poor and a large squall covered the area they were to search. The four Corsairs were down at three thousand feet when they split up, Shaw and Shuchter sweeping in over the ocean while Spears took Sanders inland to avoid the weather and look for other targets. Unable to see the enemy base, Shaw circled off the coast waiting for Spears to reappear, but after several minutes of waiting, Shaw and Shuchter headed for home.

Spears wanted to take another look at Rekata Bay and flew around the northern tip of the island. When the two Marines arrived off the cloud-shrouded coast, it appeared there was nothing going on at the Japanese base. Just as the Corsairs turned to head for home, Japanese antiaircraft guns opened fire on them. Turning in to take on the gunners, the surprised Marines spotted at least five floatplanes in various stages of taking off. Diving into the attack, Spears lined up a *Rufe* fighter, and, using the wake of the taxiing aircraft as a marker, he opened fire. The bullets hit the *Rufe* just as it lifted off, and it burst into flames and settled back into the water. Spears, now at one hundred feet, sailed past his target with Sanders on his wing spraying ground positions.

The two Marines pulled up and banked sharply to attack again. Japanese guns greeted them again as two *Rufes* sailed down the bay, one behind the other, on take-off runs. Despite the enemy fire, Spears tore after the second *Rufe* just as it became airborne, and his bullets sent it down in flames. Meanwhile, the first *Rufe* was airborne, clawing for altitude, but it suffered the same fate as its comrade. Flying alongside Spears, Sanders was hit by ground fire as they ended their run but stayed with his leader. Turning back, Spears destroyed another *Rufe* and pulled up, noticing that his wingman had lost power and was circling low over the water.

Black smoke poured from Sanders's Corsair, and he decided to make a water landing. Spears flew across his front and waved for him to follow, turning him toward the open sea away from Rekata Bay. Setting up for his water landing, Sanders tried to jettison the canopy, but it was stuck and he left it in the open position as he slid onto the water. Sanders inflated his life raft, pulled himself aboard, and began paddling. He waved at Spears who waggled his wings in return. The section leader made one more pass along the shore to ensure no Japanese were attempting to get to the downed pilot and headed for Munda.

Alone

Sanders drifted in his raft until dark and then paddled for one of the nearby islands. Reaching shore at about 0330, he quickly checked the area for signs of the Japanese. Finding no evidence of the enemy, he rested until daybreak just off the beach. Sanders thought he was on Santa Isabel and spent the next day looking for natives who might help with his rescue. He saw a single enemy plane and eight Corsairs at different times during the day but they were too far off to see him. Settling in for another night, a canoe appeared with a single man in it. As the canoe turned toward him, Sanders yelled to get the man's attention but was relieved when the stranger failed to notice him. The man in the canoe had the distinctive peaked cap of a Japanese soldier!

Fading back into the darkness of the thick jungle, Sanders looked for a place close to the beach that was protected from unwanted observation. He found the perfect spot, sandy and secluded, but had to chase off an unpleasant-looking crocodile to secure his lodgings for the night. Darkness brought his second day ashore to an end and he had no problem falling off to sleep. His slumber did not last too long: "I had been lying there for quite awhile and was sound asleep. I woke up and thought I heard a noise close to me. I kept very quiet, thinking it might be a Jap coastal patrol. Then I heard a kind of crunching sound. I turned my head and there was the biggest mouth I'd ever seen—wide open. It was the same crocodile and had come back to reclaim its bed. Boy! Was I scared! I ran for the nearest tree. I heard something beside me and looked down. There was the croc. We were running side by side, me for the tree and him for the water. We were both scared as hell!" Scared also by the remains of a nearby Japanese gun emplacement, Sanders left the little island and headed for what he realized was Santa Isabel. He spent his third night there, in a native hut.

MORE ACTION

Back at Munda, Owens's division took off that third morning for a combat air patrol over Vella Lavella. It was only a short flight to their assigned position over the invasion beaches, and it was not long before the Corsairs were weaving back and forth in an aerial ballet above the invasion shipping. They had been flying such patrols for days, and it was difficult to stay alert as it appeared to be just another boring flight. Suddenly, Fighter Command vectored all fights to the southwest over Ganongga Island. Reports drifting through their headphones indicated at least ninety Japanese airplanes were inbound on the invasion fleet. It took only a few minutes for Owens, Ray Wolff, Dick Newhall, and Roger Conant to reach the island at about twenty-one thousand feet, but the sky seemed clear. Where were the enemy planes?

After scanning the skies for a few minutes, Owens spotted six low-winged fighters about three thousand feet below, traveling in the same direction. The "Big O" closed from astern on the last enemy fighter. Firing a burst from close range, the *Zeke* seemed to fly through the bullets with no effect. Overtaking the enemy planes, "O" pulled up and around to find another target.

Seeing the bullets sailing through their formation, the remaining *Zekes* broke in all directions, and the Marines noticed more Japanese all around them. Newhall continued after Owens's original target but could not get a good shot at the twisting and turning *Zeke*. Conant also got in a quick burst, but the Japanese pilot skillfully avoided his attack. Wolff got in a few rounds before Newhall finally followed the *Zeke* in a split-S down to the deck and finished it off just above the waves.

Climbing, Wolff picked out another *Zeke* and closed for the kill. Before he could open fire, the Japanese pilot pulled up in a steep loop that

Wolff was unable to follow. Another *Zeke* came at the Marine from his right just as the looping *Zeke* swerved in from the left. Sandwiched, Wolff put the heavy Corsair into a dive. With the two Japanese chasing him, Wolff dived to the deck at 450 knots, the F4U shaking and shuddering. Leveling off, Wolff found he had left the *Zekes* far behind.

Looking up, Wolff estimated fifty Japanese milling about. Feeling very lonely, Wolff latched onto a group of six Corsairs. A few minutes later, another straggler, Roger Conant, joined the group and they all turned for Munda.

Owens was still on the trail of his second target, a talented enemy pilot who seemed to frustrate each attack. Finally, "O" got in a solid stream of bullets and the *Zeke* burst into flames. With Dick Newhall still on his wing, Owens searched for more targets. Far below, the fighter director on the destroyer in control of the combat air patrols reported the Japanese were too far away to be caught by the fuel-starved American fighters. The two Marines returned to the field without further action.

On August 25, the divisions of Bob Owens, Don Aldrich, and Dick Braun took off as part of a large escort for six B-24s on a run to Kahili, with six New Zealand P-40 Kittyhawks flying along as low cover. Three of the Corsairs turned back due to mechanical trouble, and several other Marine squadrons did not take off on time and missed the flight. ComAirSols frantically called the bombers to hold up the attack, but the B-24s flew on. The Kittyhawks and Corsairs dutifully followed. The bombers flew into foul weather at twenty-five thousand feet and released their bombs somewhere over Bougainville. The low cover reported all of the bombs missed the airfield completely. The bombers turned for home and let down through the overcast.

Emerging below the clouds at eighteen thousand feet, the formation was greeted by the sight of over fifty Japanese navy *Zekes* and army *Tonys*. The Japanese attacked immediately, and the sky was filled with Allied fighters turning to defend the bombers and the B-24s clawing their way through the battle in a struggle to get home. According to Owens: "Targets were by now so numerous that it was impossible to turn without encountering *Zeros*." Owens and Roger Conant, weaving back and forth near the giant bombers, were quickly involved in intense combat. Owens chased a *Zeke* off the B-24s with a quick shot, and Conant faced another Japanese plane head on, driving it away without a single shot. A single *Zeke* was forced to break off its attack by the combined fire of the two Corsairs. One *Zeke* fell away smoking after Owens gave it a .50-caliber squirt. Flying through the maelstrom of fighters and bombers firing at each other, Owens latched on to one target and the two Corsairs followed it through the massive battle, "O" firing short bursts until it finally exploded in flames. Attacked from behind and above, "O" wisely led Conant into a cloud to escape.

Leaving the cloud, they were greeted with the sight of three *Zekes* right in front of them. Two of the enemy planes pulled up and turned into the Corsairs as a fourth *Zeke* joined them with a high side run on Owens. Firing and maneuvering, the pair of Marines evaded the attacks only to be faced by another onslaught of *Zekes*. Conant managed a solid burst into one of the attackers, and the Japanese plane burned all the way to the water. Owens breathed a sigh of relief as a P-40 approached them but the relief turned to horror as the aircraft opened fire on him and he realized that it was a Japanese *Tony*, a plane that resembled the P-40. Chasing after the enemy plane, Owens failed to notice another *Tony* on his tail. The Japanese pilot latched on to Owens's Corsair but Conant quickly slipped in behind the *Tony* and opened fire: "It seemed to stop still." In response to the continued fire, the *Tony* sprouted flame and spiraled into the sea.

Owens continued after his target, and Conant joined in the attack. The *Zeke* dropped its tank and fled in a tight turn right through the B-24s. Owens lined up another *Tony* and scored enough hits to start it smoking, but he had to make for cloud cover with several enemy planes firing at him from behind. Conant went after one of the offending *Zekes* but found only one gun working. Forced to dive away, he leveled off at one thousand feet with three *Zekes* still on his tail. He pushed the throttle forward and dived for the sea. Two of the enemy aircraft promptly gave up the chase but one hung on until the south end of Vella Lavella before turning away. Back at Munda, Conant understated, "I was very fortunate in not being hit."

"O" returned after several more short, sharp engagements, including shots from enemy antiaircraft guns on Ganongga. His Corsair was

Roger Conant demonstrates the mischievous smile indicative of his reputation as a teller of sea-stories and jolly prankster. USMC Photo

undamaged. Don Aldrich bagged a *Zeke* and probably another, but nearly did not return when he joined a formation of four airplanes that on closer inspection turned out to be *Zekes*. A few blasts from his six machine guns scattered the enemy planes, and the speed of the Corsair saved him from further trouble. Doc Neber and his traveling medicine chest were in great demand that day.

Meanwhile . . .

George Sanders finally met a native on August 24. The man took Sanders to a small village less than six miles from Rekata Bay. Such was the system of native security that there was no fear of Japanese interference. A meal of potatoes, nuts, pineapple, and, later, pig, did much to rejuvenate the tired airman. He had been subsisting on whatever he could find: coconuts, green crabs, and raw oysters. On the 25th he was taken to Boalo, a village fifteen miles from Rekata Bay. There he was treated to another healthy meal and a night of uninterrupted rest.

During the hot afternoon of August 26, George Sanders was introduced to the British District officer for Santa Isabel, Capt. Michael Forster, at the village of Nanikeo. Feeling he was just one step from returning to the squadron, Sanders was disappointed when the attempt to contact Guadalcanal failed. Forster's Japanese-made transmitter was not powerful enough to reach Cactus. So Forster's cook prepared another delightful meal, and Sanders relaxed for another evening. Taken to Forster's home at Totamba, Sanders waited in pleasant surroundings for the message that would send him home.

CHAPTER SIX

Munda and More

The more you learn before the fight, the more you'll learn during the fight and the more chance you'll have to keep on learning.
—LT. COL. CHARLES MACDONALD

WHILE GEORGE SANDERS ENJOYED NATIVE HOSPITALITY, THERE WAS little time for relaxation for the rest of the squadron. A morning flight on August 26 found Don Aldrich and Dick Braun's divisions covering B-24s bombing Kahili. Occasionally Japanese planes made quick firing runs on the Americans, but the Corsairs turned into them and scared the Japanese off. Bob Keister had a few shots at one of the enemy but couldn't tell if he scored any hits. Dick Braun and his wingman, Tom Stockwell, were separated by clouds and did not see any of the enemy. The low cover fighters observing the bombing reported excellent results and the Liberators turned for home amid tentative attacks by about twenty Japanese.

Aldrich latched onto a *Zeke* and sent it down in flames. Turning to attack another, he was jumped by several *Zekes*. A 20mm cannon shell hit his tail and rudder, damaging his controls. Fragments injured his right arm and nicked his right eye. Diving away, he succeeded in returning without further damage. The ensuing landing at Munda was exciting and required a little skill, but Aldrich brought the plane in successfully. His engagement was the only real fight of the mission.

Later that day, Ray Tomes took his division, with five New Zealanders in their tough little Kittyhawks, and a division from VMF-214

83

that included lieutenants Alvin Jensen and Robert Hanson, up the Slot to meet twenty-one Army Liberators on another raid to Kahili. Jensen and Hanson's careers would intersect with Two Fifteen on a large scale later on. Six Liberators were forced to drop out due to mechanical failure. Fierce antiaircraft fire met them as they went into their bomb run but did not affect their accuracy as they planted their bombs right on the target. In a wide, sweeping curve, the B-24s turned for their trip back to their base only to be met by swarms of Japanese fighters.

Zekes seemed to be everywhere. Some flew above the formation dropping bombs on the B-24s, others attacked from all points of the compass. Fighting in pairs, Ray Tomes and Hap Langstaff crisscrossed through the sky alongside George Kross and Reinhardt Leu. Tomes and Langstaff attacked a *Zeke*, but it escaped into a cloud. Another attack was more successful, Tomes sending a Japanese fighter flaming into the sea. Another *Zeke* passed just to the right, and Tomes set it on fire also. Tomes later noted that "everywhere we looked, we saw Zeros." One of the enemy planes latched onto Langstaff's tail, and Tomes turned into his wingman and fired at the trailing *Zeke*. The Japanese pilot zoomed up in a climb and disappeared. Tomes found himself chased by an enemy fighter, but Langstaff returned the earlier favor by turning into Tomes's pursuer. The *Zeke* pilot tried to pull up but it was too late; Langstaff's guns set him on fire, the *Zeke* bursting into a bright yellow fireball as it went down. Closing with the bombers, the pair beat off several more attacks before passing the southern tip of Choiseul where the enemy finally broke off their attack.

George Kross and Chief Leu erupted from a cloud in the midst of the aerial battle. Kross spotted a couple of *Zekes* trying to line up Leu and called to warn his wingman but found his radio was inoperative. Hand signals and wagging of wings failed to get Leu's attention. He increased speed to get in front of Leu and pulled up and over to turn into the enemy. Leu finally understood the danger and turned hard to get a shot at his pursuers. Chasing one of the *Zekes*, Kross found the other on his tail but this put the *Zeke* right in Leu's sights. A quick burst from Leu's guns and the *Zeke* fell in flames. Kross opened fire at the other *Zeke*, shattering its cockpit, and it fell off on one wing in a plunge to the sea. Weaving beside the bombers, the pair continued fending off attacks until the Japanese gradually began to run out of fuel and ammunition, forcing them to return to their fields.

Two pilots from VMF-214, the "Swashbucklers," also scored on this mission. Robert Hanson and Alvin Jensen each shot down a *Zeke* who had attacked the B-24s. The paths of these two Marines would intersect with VMF-215 again in a big way.

INTERLUDE AT SANTA ISABEL

Guided by natives, George Sanders continued with Captain Forster on his trek from Boalo to the captain's house. The sandy-haired Marine was beginning to feel at home with the natives. He perceived they enjoyed his presence as much as he enjoyed their hospitality. In each village the little party of travelers was met with throngs of little children, swarming around them with friendly wide grins and trying to shake hands with a white man. The local people showered him with gifts at each stop: shells, beads, and bracelets. On August 27, a great songfest was held at the request of Captain Forster. The entire village gathered around the visitors' hut and sang a wide variety of songs. There was laughing and dancing as they went through English, Native, and American songs. The war intruded into their songs with various tunes making fun of the Japanese and praising the United States and Great Britain. Sanders was introduced to the crowd and they clamored for him to sing something from his home. Sanders began with "The Eyes of Texas Are Upon You," and followed with several songs from the American South. The natives responded by singing a song especially created for and about the ebullient Marine from Oklahoma. Too soon, it became late, the people sang "God Save the King," and dispersed very slowly as if savoring the evening's festivities.

MUNDA

The pilots of Two Fifteen, many tired and sick with bouts of dysentery, tried to make the best of their situation. Engineers and SeaBees continued to clean up the area around the runway. Back on August 5 the airfield was declared secure, and living conditions had gradually improved. When not flying, several pilots hitched rides on P.T. boats on barge hunting expeditions around Vella Lavella and Kolombangara. Some visited the positions where the Japanese had struggled for so long, finding flags, helmets, or other relics of the defeated Japanese dreams of a Greater East Asia Co-Prosperity Sphere. Frontline infantrymen, and those who presented themselves as such, were not always trustworthy. Pilots found it was better to collect their own souvenirs than buy those offered by others. Fake flags and other spurious pieces of Japanese equipment were abundant.

A particularly easy item to find were unexploded Japanese artillery shells. The rings on the cap that fell off in flight made nice bracelets and jewelry. After removing the detonator, with a little skill and a hammer, the ring could be removed from one of these shells without exploding the fuse. Marines would gather to watch one of these local entrepreneurs make items that could be sold for a good profit. Gerry Shuchter was one of those adept at making such items.

Between missions, the men of Bob Owens's division were involved watching a Marine separating one of the rings from the cap. Owens became nervous watching the man pounding carefully at the cap of the shell, revolving it around to hit the ring at different angles. Owens moved toward the feverishly working Marine to tell him to stop just when the fuse went off. Shards of hot metal flew through the air, slicing clothes, shredding tent fabric, and tearing flesh. Several members of Two Fifteen, including Owens, were slightly nicked. Fortunately, the shell itself did not explode. Later they would joke about the "Purple Heart" award for the injury due to an "enemy shell." The careless Marine was severely injured, and Owens made sure the practice was discontinued around their living quarters.

Owens experienced another nasty surprise on August 27, during an otherwise routine patrol north of Vella Lavella. His division was bounced by a single *Tony* fighter, which sailed through the formation before anyone could fire a shot. The four Corsairs turned and gave chase. But the F4Us, supposedly the fastest fighters in the area, could not catch the *Tony*, a fighter that resembled the German Messerschmitt Bf-109. Frustrated and a little startled, the four Marines were forced to end their fruitless pursuit just short of Ballale.

Returning from another patrol that day, Dave Escher found himself low on fuel. Entering the landing pattern at Munda, his engine coughed and sputtered, out of gas. Escher's Corsair slid into the water just short of the island and the runway. His only injury, besides the embarrassment of running out of fuel, was a cut on the forehead he received when he was flung forward into the cockpit frame on landing. Sailors on Munda quickly sent out the crash boat and pulled out the bedraggled and soaked Escher after only a few short minutes.

George Kross ferried a plane up from Guadalcanal and arrived at Munda in the afternoon. He had good news; earlier that day Captain Forster had contacted Guadalcanal and a rescue was organized for George Sanders.

WATCHING A ONE-MAN SHOW

As the Allied forces moved through the Solomons, bombers had pounded the airfields on Bougainville, especially Kahili on the southern coast. Aircraft hidden under camouflage netting or in the jungle were hard to see from the altitudes that bombers operated from, so ComAirSols occasionally ordered fighters to come in low to strafe the enemy planes. Strafing by the fighters was difficult, as they were unable to maneuver coming in to shoot up the runway, which made the attacking aircraft an easy target.

The morning of August 28 was dark and gloomy, and clouds at different altitudes made visibility difficult. Flying to Kahili that day, Bob Owens and Roger Conant took part in what historian Robert Sherrod described as "one of the great single-handed feats of the Pacific War...." Originally two divisions of VMF-214 covered by Owens's division were to carry out the mission, but mechanical problems and another mission for one of Two Fourteen's divisions reduced the available aircraft to five. The two pilots from Two Fifteen were to cover a strafing attack on the airfield by three Corsairs of Two Fourteen.

The five planes met early that morning above the Slot. Flying up through the mass of islands low to avoid radar, they found a vast rain-squall barring them from their objective. Proceeding into the overcast, the planes were tossed about as though weightless, up and down until the little group was split up. Lt. Hartwell Scarborough of Two Fourteen, a veteran pilot who had downed three Japanese planes just two days before, was separated from the others and returned to Munda. Another pilot from Two Fourteen, Lt. Charles Lanphier, also was separated from the others but did not return. His brother was an Army P-38 pilot that was part of the mission that had killed Adm. Isoroku Yamamoto the previous April. Lanphier was presumed forced down and drowned, but the men of Two Fifteen would not learn of his fate until years later. It would have been better if Lanphier had died that ugly day off Kahili.

Owens flew on through the storm, Conant exhibiting great flying skill by staying on his wing throughout the vicious, dark turbulence. Owens had twinges of regret, keeping Conant in the swirling maelstrom, but he felt that the pilots of Two Fourteen would need cover. The pair of Corsairs circled at nine thousand feet above Bougainville as a single plane appeared, far below, in and out of the clouds near Kahili. It was Lt. Alvin Jensen of Two Fourteen.

Flying with Bob Owens, Alvin Jensen of VMF-214 earned a Navy Cross with his destruction of twenty-four enemy planes on the ground on August 28, 1943. He was credited with seven aerial kills during his time with 214. USMC Photo

From high above, through breaks in the clouds, "O" watched the drama unfold. Originally from South Carolina, Jensen had been flying since high school and joined the Marine Corps after earning his private pilot's license. A former enlisted pilot, he was an experienced flyer who had already claimed six enemy planes shot down.

Separated from the rest of the flight by the turbulence, Jensen found himself a few miles east of Kahili. He heard Owens say, "Let's go!" and turned to come in over the jungle-covered hills as low as possible in the first light of dawn. In actuality, Owens never gave the command to attack but it mattered little as the solitary Corsair whipped through the sky toward the slumbering Japanese airfield. The Marine ace banked hard at a point about two thousand yards off the north end of the strip, and headed south, leveling off as he turned.

The Japanese were totally surprised, and there was no antiaircraft fire to greet the Marine. He swooped into position off the north end of the airstrip. Leveling off at seventy-five feet, he roared in on the unsuspecting enemy. There were several groups of planes: a dozen twin-engine *Betty* bombers at the north end, four or five *Val* divebombers sat on their fixed gear just east of the field, and at least ten *Zekes* on the southern end. Single aircraft were haphazardly parked in between the groups, and a lone *Zeke* was warming up just off the runway. The closest *Betty*, an aircraft type nicknamed the "Flying Lighter" by its crews, filled his gun sight ring at six hundred yards. Jensen fired a long burst into the midst of the big, green bombers, using slight rudder movements to spray the entire area. Bullets passed through metal, ricocheting off engines and the ground, flying into the air in dramatic trajectories. A great explosion sent shock waves across the ground and through the murky air, buffeting the lone Corsair. At the same moment Jensen noted a bright flash reflected on his aircraft in the early morning half darkness.

New targets were already ahead of the fast-moving fighter, and Jensen slipped slightly to fire at a group of four or five *Val* divebombers sitting like fat ducks on their fixed landing gear opposite the control tower. Another long burst and fiery streams of bullets hit the planes or spattered around them on the hard-packed ground.

A large cluster of *Zeke* fighter planes loomed into sight, one pilot climbing into an aircraft as Jensen fired a final long parting burst. The *Zeke* warming up blew up in a great ball of flames, the pilot's fate unknown. A second, rewarding explosion occurred as he passed but Jensen did not wait to see the results of his efforts, pouring on the coals and banking away from nearby Ballale to avoid its antiaircraft guns.

Jensen wasted no time in checking the results of his attack. Japanese bullets were filling the sky behind him, and he flew quickly back into the squall that had allowed his undetected approach. His Corsair was untouched in the entire episode. Owens and Conant circled a few more minutes, anticipating an attack by Scarborough or Lanphier but finally turned toward Munda. Passing Shortland Island, Owens saw three distinct fires burning at Kahili. The fires could still be seen twenty miles south of the island. Scarborough, Owens, Conant, and Jensen returned home safely.

The next morning, a photo plane took photos of Kahili. Intelligence quickly checked the film, and Jensen was credited with the destruction of twenty-four enemy aircraft: twelve *Betty*s, four *Vals*, and eight *Zekes*. The dark-eyed Marine was awarded the Navy Cross.

ONE ON ONE

On Guadalcanal, Sammy Stidger, the squadron "character," was still recovering from his badly injured ribs. Sammy was a gifted flyer with a disarming personality who hoped these attributes would lead to some interesting flying opportunities after the war. He enjoyed strapping on a plane and just flying, so he let ComAirSols know he was available while he convalesced, and they were happy to have a volunteer. Stidger was assigned hack jobs for the various squadrons or test hops for the different shops. With a good ear for a faulty engine, quite often he checked out planes shunned by other pilots because "they didn't feel right." He went up one morning on such a flight, taking the Corsair up to thirty thousand feet and bouncing around the sky to test it out. Mostly he just enjoyed himself. It was a beautiful day to fly, a bit of overcast above but unlimited visibility below his bent wings. It was an exhilarating flight, alone with a powerful airplane and able to do anything he wanted.

Grafton "Sammy" Stidger, madcap and carefree, was the favorite of all who met him, especially women. USMC Photo

His fun was interrupted just as he passed Cape Esperance at twenty-eight thousand feet. Fighter Command reported a bogey on radar that was closing on Stidger from the north. The bogey failed to show the proper IFF signal. (IFF, Identification friend or foe, allowed radar operators to tell if an unidentified aircraft was friendly.) Fighter Command asked Stidger to check it out. He saw nothing as he banked around at a leisurely 140 knots. Reversing his turn, the sky was still clear. Fighter Command announced the target was coming in from the west. Scanning carefully to the west, he spotted a small dot.

The Japanese airplane was at least four miles away, at about thirty thousand feet, a small speck on the windscreen. The bogey suddenly made an abrupt course change, as though its pilot had spotted the Corsair, turning north toward Santa Isabel. Stidger headed north also, moving west to put the afternoon sun behind him. Increasing his speed to 190 knots, Stidger flew parallel to the enemy plane, watching for changes in course. As the two planes passed over the southwestern tip of Santa Isabel, down below them George Sanders and Michael Forster were rifle shooting off the back porch of the captain's residence. High above the shooters, Sammy was ecstatic, as the unidentified plane turned to the west, presenting him with a 30-degree deflection shot (a shot from behind but off to the side about 30 degrees). He was unsure of what type of enemy plane he was engaged with, but there was no mistaking the big red balls on the wings.

Stidger opened fire as he pulled around for a shot from directly astern. Firing steadily as he closed to point blank range, the target suddenly exploded. Down below, Sanders and Forster believed it was a bomb going off. Sammy knew it was not a bomb as he flew through the debris of the enemy plane. Sanders and Forster saw the flaming debris falling down, at last understanding there had been aerial combat high above them. Stidger, never seen by his squadron mate far below, returned to Guadalcanal after a very successful test flight.

Stidger's description of the plane, including a detailed drawing, matched nothing seen by the intelligence people of Fighter Command. He described it to them: "The engine was radial with a large spinner. The fuselage was bulky, with a fused canopy tapering into the tail which was also similar. The wings were tapered with round tips." Shown various three-view drawings, he picked out the aircraft he had encountered. His choice raised some eyebrows, as the picture was that of a German FW-190. How such an airplane would be flying reconnaissance in the South Pacific was a mystery. He was given credit for downing a "Fred," the nickname for an unidentified enemy plane. Sammy didn't really care as he basked in all the attention from his strange encounter. Later Marines would encounter more aircraft similar to the one he downed on that flight. It was probably a Nakajima Ki. 44 *Tojo*, a radial-engine Japanese army fighter rarely encountered in the Solomons.

Later that same afternoon, while B. K. Shaw, Johnny Downs, Gerry Shuchter, and a pilot from Two Fourteen were strafing and blowing up a barge near Gizo Island, Bob Owens led a three-plane search for a

Capt. Billie K. Shaw served as a division commander on one tour with VMF-215, winning the Distinguished Flying Cross. He later served in Korea. USMC Photo

downed flyer near Vella Lavella. The search was unsuccessful and they turned toward Munda. As they reversed course, they encountered the day's strike from Kahili on its way home. The B-24s were at twelve thousand feet, fighting off at least twenty *Zekes*. Owens spotted a lone B-24, obviously damaged, flying only a few feet above the waves. Several Japanese went in low to nail the coffin shut on the lone B-24.

Owens decided to go to the rescue of the lone bomber. He fired at one *Zeke* but overshot and failed to score any hits. Twice more he fired at fleeting shapes but the twisting, climbing targets escaped. Finally he fell in behind a *Zeke* that was concentrating on the crippled bomber and unaware of Owens's Corsair closing in. The green, red-disk covered wings filled his sight and Owens gave it a solid burst. The Japanese pilot's reaction killed him, as he pulled up right in front of the stream of bullets. The *Zeke* started to burn, flames wrapped the doomed pilot, and he went into the sea with his plane.

Roger Conant and "The Kid" Wolff remained with their division leader, covering Owens's tail. One *Zeke* slid in behind Owens, but Conant swung over and fired at the enemy aircraft. The *Zeke* began to smoke. Conant was startled as a large object fell off the Japanese plane and flew close by his cockpit. In a split second, Conant realized the object was the enemy flyer. The smoking *Zeke* went into the drink, minus a pilot. The Marines didn't see a parachute open.

A *Zeke* latched onto Conant's tail but neither Wolff nor Owens were close enough to help. Without assistance, Conant put his plane into a steep dive that the enemy plane was unable to follow. Leveling off near the water, he saw a Japanese pilot in a parachute drifting toward the water just as a *Zeke* slipped beneath the waves.

Owens was busy with a Japanese fighter that attacked him head on. Like two Wild West gunfighters, they fired at each other as the range closed but the *Zeke* pulled away at the last moment, a big mistake. By breaking off the action, the *Zeke* flew right into the guns of Ray Wolff, who was still on Owens's wing. The Japanese plane spouted flames and fell apart in midair. Wolff continued on through the falling debris of his victim but was unhurt. Now alone, at two thousand feet, "The Kid" found himself under attack again by a *Zeke* from dead astern. Wolff lowered the Corsair's long nose and pushed the throttle forward. The Japanese pilot soon fell behind and gave up the chase, enabling Wolff to return undamaged.

Owens joined on the damaged B-24, and the two protected each other, the B-24's gunners firing at approaching Japanese and the Corsair turning into possible attacks. Six *Zekes* attacked at once, and Owens was forced to dive away, zooming back up to five thousand feet after outrunning the Japanese. Free of pursuers, Owens returned to the side of the B-24 and drove off a couple more attackers. Suddenly a green apparition appeared through his propeller blades and a *Zeke* fired at him from straight ahead. Owens returned fire but suffered hits from a 20mm cannon that hit his left wing and knocked out his three portside machine guns. Another dive to the deck lost the attacker, but as soon as he pulled up several more *Zekes* attacked him. Diving away once again, the sturdy Corsair easily outran the enemy planes.

Conant heard a desperate P-39 pilot calling plaintively for help as he was in trouble and going down. Roger could also hear Owens calling for help but when he arrived at Owens's last position, the sky was empty. Conant looked around for the embattled P-39 and spotted a man in a parachute floating down near Ganongga. Assuming it was the Army pilot, Conant circled the floating man and radioed the position to Air-Sea Rescue.

After a few minutes of protective cover, Conant saw a native canoe paddle out from shore and strong hands brought in the downed flyer. Another Corsair appeared, and Bob Owens joined Conant in covering the departing canoe. A few moments later, a third Corsair arrived at the scene. Owens, Conant, and Wolff set course for Munda.

MEANWHILE ...

Friendly natives gave George Sanders a pistol taken from the body of the Japanese pilot from Stidger's downed "FW-190." The man had been cut in two by the explosion of his aircraft and had no need of the weapon. Sanders continued to live the life of a South Seas adventurer: hot tub bathing, sunbathing on the beach, and lots of good food. Sanders described the eating succinctly: "Meals were wonderful!"

CHAPTER SEVEN

Tough Missions . . . and a Break

Initiative, Aggression, Air Discipline and Teamwork are words that mean something in Air Fighting!

—ADOLPH "SAILOR" MALAN

LIFE AT MUNDA HAD IMPROVED ONLY MARGINALLY DURING THE month of August. Jim Neefus did not have many opportunities to fly as he had become the unofficial commander of operations at Munda. Food and living quarters remained spartan, and aircraft maintenance was primitive. Pilots were rotated back to Guadalcanal by flying airplanes that needed an overhaul or were facing maintenance due to flying hours. Replacement pilots flew the repaired aircraft up and stayed on at Munda. When they were assigned a mission, the pilots took whatever aircraft was available. Sometimes the assignment was met with despair, the aircraft in question having a poor reputation for reliability. Some planes were faster than others while some felt more maneuverable. Owens recalled the process years later:

"When we went into Munda it was the first time (since Guadalcanal) that there was a group of squadrons flying similar machines. Operations would assign each squadron a given number of aircraft. 'You take "No 672" and you take "No 345."' Every time it was different, and my logbook shows that I rarely flew the same airplane twice. . . . We'd take whatever planes were available and put our pilots in them. We pooled aircraft because we always had more pilots than we had Corsairs. There

97

was a time when our aircraft were painted with personalized markings. Various pilots made suggestions and the aircraft were duly painted up. I authorized the painting of an aircraft with the legend *Spirit of '76* . . . I only flew the aircraft once. Like the other pilots, I took whatever machine was assigned for any given mission."

Roger Conant remembered using the aircraft to impress the women back home. Called "Hero Pictures," the pilots used chalk to write a girl's name on the aircraft and then took a photo to send her. Once the photo was taken, the chalk was wiped off and another girl's name emblazoned on the aircraft. A new photo was taken, and the process repeated by the same pilot or another pilot as many times as necessary. Conant believed it helped morale back home. Often a number of Japanese flags were stenciled on the aircraft to show the number of "kills" the pilot was credited with. Navy and Marine Corps photographers often had each pilot sit in the same aircraft, one after the other, for these heroic publicity pictures. Unfortunately, historians mistakenly believed that the aircraft was that pilot's personal aircraft or belonged to his squadron.

A MEDAL OF HONOR FLIGHT

The pilots of Two Fifteen had strip alert on the morning of August 30. Neefus was standing among four F4Us talking to the alert pilots when a Corsair came in low over the battered trees and landed. The pilot brought it to a halt very quickly, shut it down, and hopped out, looking for someone in charge. The pilots noted the young flyer had the look of a hunter, with steely blue eyes on a wiry body. Neefus recognized him immediately as an old friend, Ken Walsh of VMF-124.

The steely-eyed Marine and Neefus were old friends, and Walsh quickly explained his situation: The Corsair he had been flying had supercharger problems and he wished to borrow one of the alert fighters to rejoin his squadron mates en route to Kahili. Neefus, waving his arms in the direction of the four alert fighters, each loaded with ammunition and fuel, simply said: "Take your pick!"

Walsh had lied about his age to join the Marine Corps in 1933. He started his career as an aircraft mechanic and eventually went through flight school in 1936. He became a naval aviator with the rank of private

Keen-eyed hunter Ken Walsh is pictured in the cockpit of a so-called birdcage Corsair. He borrowed a VMF-215 Corsair and earned a Medal of Honor. USMC Photo

first class. Walsh went through landing signal officer training as a warrant officer before he was finally assigned to a fighter squadron. He served aboard carriers and various other commands before the war began. After Pearl Harbor, Walsh joined VMF-124 and went overseas with the squadron, the first squadron to fly the Corsair in combat. Walsh had become the first Corsair "ace," downing his fifth Japanese plane on May 13, 1943. Now, thanks to Neefus, he was on his way to Kahili. Hopping into the closest blue/gray Corsair, Bureau Number 02486, he strapped in, started up, and headed down the runway.

Delayed because of the change of planes, Walsh didn't catch up to the Allied formation until they reached Shortland Island. Approaching the B-24s from astern, he joined a group of fighters behind and above the bombers. Sliding in on the wing of one of the fighters, he was startled to discover the planes were *Zekes*. There were at least fifty of them diving to attack the bombers. Frantically Walsh called out a warning to the Corsairs of VMF-123 and 124 that were escorting the bombers, and at the same time he opened fire on the last of the *Zekes*. Flames sprouted from the target, and it disintegrated. Continuing to call out warnings, he lined up an unsuspecting *Zeke* to the left and the *Zeke* fell away to the sea, pouring smoke in its death dive. Several other Japanese pilots realized the threat and broke off their attack on the bombers to strike at the lone Corsair in their midst. Others frantically scattered to avoid Walsh, unwittingly intermingling with Corsairs of the escort.

A wild melee developed, and the Japanese pilots were unable to coordinate their efforts to prevent the bombing of Kahili. Walsh was busy dodging Japanese who attacked him from all points of the compass as well as above and below. Walsh used every maneuver he could and then flew in and out of the B-24s. He thought he had a good shot at one *Zeke* but was forced to break off by several others attacking him. Joining up with several other Corsairs, he glimpsed Kahili Field far below and noted it was a buzz of activity with planes taking off and landing. Answering a call for help, the small flight of Corsairs found several B-24s in trouble over Gizo Island. Eight or nine of the bombers, and several F4Us, P-40s, and P-39s, were fighting off at least a dozen *Zekes*.

Walsh broke up an attack by six of the enemy planes approaching the B-24s, downing one. Turning to help a P-39 under attack, he fired at a single target and sent it down in flames. Low on the water, Walsh found himself under attack from four more Japanese. Pushing himself to the top of the waves, Walsh felt strikes on his plane. White smoke poured from the cowling and his speed decreased. The four enemy pilots closed in for the kill.

Suddenly a P-40 and several Corsairs appeared as if by magic and fired at the pursuing Japanese. The disappointed *Zeke* pilots turned and fled toward Kahili. Exhausted after his long flight and extended fight, Walsh nursed the battered Corsair along but it became more and more difficult to control. He coaxed the tough fighter on until he was in sight of Vella Lavella. Unable to land, he ditched into the sea off the coast near the new airstrip at Barakoma. SeaBees involved in the construction of the field saw the landing and sent a boat out to fetch the tired flyer, bringing him back wet but not injured. A long day for Kenneth Walsh and his borrowed fighter was finally over. Six months later he would be awarded the Medal of Honor for breaking up the Japanese attacks on the B-24s.

Get Kahili!

If Bougainville was to be invaded, Kahili and other small airstrips had to be taken out. Located near the small village of Buin, Kahili was surrounded by lush green jungles and spiny green ridges. Bougainville was a giant ridge sticking out of the Solomon Sea, covered by brush and dense vegetation. Kahili, located at Bougainville's southern tip, was the center for Japanese aviation on the island. It was originally believed that the first step in constructing the north-south runway involved stretching cables and netting in the trees above the construction site. Next, the trunks of the trees and all of the underbrush were cut away, leaving the tops of the trees and higher vegetation in place. The Japanese workers labored under this camouflage to construct the runway in complete secrecy. A good legend, but Allied Intelligence not only had followed the actual construction of the base but Allied planes had bombed the field several times before it was completed. Another story concerned the Japanese antiaircraft guns installed at permanent, fixed angles, forming an impenetrable screen of fire for Allied planes to fly through. Alvin Jensen and other Corsair pilots who had flown the length of the dirty airstrip knew the guns were definitely mobile and flexible. The fire over the field combined with the barrage from the nearby strip on Ballale was so heavy that new pilots entering operations were often greeted by veteran members of their squadron with "Don't let them talk you into strafing Kahili!" Whatever the truth, Kahili became the focal point of operations until the invasion of Bougainville.

Rotation of pilots out of Munda back to Guadalcanal enabled some of them to obtain a night's rest and better food. Japanese hecklers continued to bomb Munda at night making sleep difficult. There was little food available, and the best chow at the mess continued to be the less than palatable K-rations. Everyone lost weight, and many suffered from dysentery. Long hours in the cockpit and tense moments took a toll. Doc Neber recorded his medical observations: "Chronic ailments; The majority are dermatological with much fungus eczema and made worse by most not using sheets altho instructed to do so. We sent one pilot back due to severe eczema that may have been partially due to psychosomatic causes as well as heat and poor hygiene. We also had malaria, which we should not have had as it could be prevented by taking the atabrine. Dengue fever was always around and when infected, the pilots thought they would die—although the mortality rate was low and it was a self-limiting disease. Filoriosis should not have been present as the food should have been cooked thoroughly and mosquito control adequate. It was more present in the natives but some of the men, notably New Zealanders and SeaBees developed it. . . .When suspected, I sent them back to the larger general hospitals as I had nothing with which to treat them. Then there were periodic cases of other diseases, many carried by natives, and they always seemed to throw us a barbecue (pig) which I was reluctant to attend. Some, however, knowing full well the consequences. . . . I sent many to the hospital with acute appendicitis." The filth and poor hygiene could not be avoided. The lack of mosquito nets or clean clothes and sheets contributed to the pilots' discomfort. Pilots were tired and hungry, making illness more likely and prolonging their recovery time.

Dental care was also rudimentary, as Roger Conant found out in a visit to the dentist on Guadalcanal for a toothache. Diagnosed for a cavity, the dentist advised a filling. There was no electricity available, and Conant peddled to power a drill as the doctor took care of the tooth.

Artillery attacks and sporadic bombing ruined sleep for many pilots. Running back and forth to the slit trenches shattered an evening's repose, but there were additional dangers. Bob Owens did not like jumping into the trench closest to his tent due to scorpions, natural inhabitants of the island. Through the flashes of antiaircraft guns or bomb explosions, Owens would see one or two of the creatures creeping around his dirt-lined sanctuary, forcing him to choose a section of trench uninhabited by the arachnids.

On September 2, Don Aldrich and his division flew up to Choiseul to look for targets of opportunity. As they approached the west coast, they spotted two rust-red barges, one hung up on a reef and the other heading for the protection of the jungle along the shoreline. Aldrich motioned "Attack," and they gulled down in line astern. One after the other, Aldrich, Hal Spears, Billie Shaw, and Bob Keister, let fly with their six .50-calibers and left both vessels splintered wrecks.

Heading for home, Aldrich led the Corsairs around the northern tip of Choiseul and then proceeded down the east coast of the island. Near the village of Lute, Aldrich spotted an odd shape in the bushes. Closer inspection revealed a small warship or patrol boat. The division repeated the procedure they had used on the two barges with the same results, and the small vessel ended up a total wreck in a foamy patch of water.

At the same time Aldrich was hammering the Japanese watercraft, Bob Owens led three divisions of Two Fifteen and a division from VMF-123 on a strafing run against Kahili. Confusion reigned as they ran into foul weather. Owens and Ray Wolff were forced to abort due to engine trouble. Only Thrifty Warner's division remained intact. Ray Tomes's division was scattered all over the sky; Tomes joined up with lieutenants Robert Rathburn and William Cantrell of One Twenty Three, and Hap Langstaff joined with Dick Braun and Roger Conant of Owens's division. Chief Leu and George Kross missed the rendezvous completely.

It was not until the formation reached the Bougainville coast that Japanese antiaircraft fire began in earnest. Guns from nearby Ballale joined in and the sky was filled with tracers and airbursts. Thrifty Warner led his division in from the west, using the ridges near the airfield to hide his approach. Warner opened fire on a group of planes parked on the southwest corner of the runway. Lloyd Cox followed, spraying bullets into a large revetment just off the airstrip. In the revetment were several *Vals* and at least a half dozen *Zekes*.

Sammy Stidger hit a group of fighters at the southeast end, leaving several of the enemy planes destroyed. Always one to see the humorous side of things, he particularly enjoyed seeing Japanese ground personnel scrambling about in fright as his bullets splattered the ground around them. Jack Jordan spotted a twin-engine bomber and a *Val* divebomber hidden on the south end of the runway. He left them in flames. Later pilots reported six fighters and a bomber on fire from the attacks.

Japanese gunners fell victim to Roger Conant. His Corsair sped across the field at treetop level, spitting .50-caliber bullets into gun emplacements, trenches, and buildings. The startled Japanese left their guns and ran helter-skelter for bunkers and air raid shelters. After his pass, they fled from their guns whenever a Corsair began its run.

After their first passes, the airfield was shrouded in smoke, and the pilots looked for other targets. Lloyd Cox made a run on a twenty-foot boat in the harbor just off Kahili. He left it in splinters. Sammy Stidger did the same to a fifty-foot motorboat. Stidger spotted a seventy-foot-long boat loaded with Japanese soldiers, sending bullets back and forth through its hull. A giant explosion sent pieces of wood, metal, and flesh flying above the waves. He gleefully noted the surviving Japanese swimming desperately away from the burning, sinking wreckage.

Ray Tomes led the two VMF-123 pilots against nearby Ballale. Repeatedly they attacked a small barge moored near the coast, Japanese antiaircraft fire crisscrossing their path. One particular 20mm gun irritated Tomes as he made his second pass, and the stocky Marine turned on it. Down at fifty feet, shells hit the Corsair. Bob Rathburn of One Twenty Three later recalled that it "exploded and crashed in flames on the island." Tough, professional Ray Tomes, who had trained the pilots of Two Fifteen in the finer points of gunnery and was considered by many to be the finest fighter pilot in the squadron, was killed by a group of nameless antiaircraft gunners on a small island in the Pacific. Four Japanese planes had fallen to his guns in air-to-air combat. Many of his fellow pilots felt he would have been one of the greatest aces if he would have lived. But the Marine fighter pilots had to deal with the enemy on the ground as well as in the air, and this round went to the guys on the ground.

Not long after Ray Tomes went down, Don Aldrich led his second flight of the day, seven Corsairs escorting a bombing strike to Kahili. The Corsairs arrived over the target at twenty-eight thousand feet, the bombers at twenty-four thousand, and found the target obscured by large fires and smoke caused by the morning's strafing attacks. Zekes made tentative passes at the bombers but broke off over the target to avoid their own antiaircraft fire.

From his position above the bombers, Aldrich spotted a group of darkly painted, square-tipped fighters moving in behind the bombers after their bomb run. Taking Spears with him, Aldrich dived on the target and closed to firing range, only to pull up abruptly. Aldrich was embarrassed to see that the targets were not square-winged Japanese *Hamp*s but US Navy F6F Hellcats! This misidentification was unusual, as Aldrich was considered to have the sharpest set of eyes in the squadron.

Turning toward Kahili, Aldrich attacked a group of five *Zekes*, firing at the last one but helplessly watching as it pulled up and away before he could score hits. Another of the *Zekes* looped up and over to face Aldrich head on, inverted, but failed to hit the Corsair as he passed just below the Marine. Aldrich fired as the *Zeke* exposed its belly, and his guns ripped the Zeke from nose to tail. It fell into the sea, wrapped in flames. Hal Spears confirmed the kill but was separated from his wingman by the attack of four *Zekes* from behind. He put his Corsair into a steep dive and then pulled up in a zoom to eighteen thousand feet. The *Zekes* were unable to follow and he was safe, and alone.

Aldrich was also alone, for a moment. Three times he turned into a *Zeke* making an attack, trading shots head on. Each of the *Zekes* pulled up and away to avoid his fire at the last moment. One *Zeke* attacked and pulled away too late, diving after confronting the nose of the Corsair. A Corsair in a dive could catch a *Zeke* easily, and Aldrich's guns chipped away at the Japanese plane until they reached ten thousand feet where the *Zeke* burst into massive flames. It was Don Aldrich's fifth aerial victory, making him VMF-215's first ace.

Spears spotted a lone *Zeke* far below; at 2,000 feet he pushed his Corsair unto a dive to come out astern of the enemy. The faster Corsair closed the range quickly, and he fired a long burst into the brown-green *Zeke*. Smoke poured from the target, but Spears was unable to watch his victim's final descent as four more *Zekes* latched onto his tail. Again, Spears put the Corsair into a dive and pushed the throttle for all it was worth to outrun his pursuers. Briefly a *Zeke* passed before him, and he managed a quick shot that left it smoking before he was again running from the four *Zekes*.

Both Aldrich and Spears used the Corsair's greater speed to get away from the Japanese and returned to Munda over the same course, past Vella Lavella. Exhausted after their fights, they looked over their weathered blue Corsairs: Aldrich had shrapnel holes and bullet strikes in his wings, and Spears had six holes in his fuselage and one in his propeller. They met with Doc Neber for a quick pick-me-up and then sat with Bob Clark for their debriefing. Aldrich gave his usual technical, serious account of the fight, and Spears lightened up the mood with a few jokes. Their Corsairs were the only ones damaged in the afternoon action. Tomes was their only loss.

It was not uncommon for a division to fly two missions a day, sometimes three. The squadron rarely flew in any great strength, divided up piecemeal to meet the requirements of ComAirSols. The number of planes available did not always meet the number called for by Operations. Squadrons shared planes, and the ground crews worked hard to get the maximum number of aircraft ready each day. The weary but robust Corsairs were pushed to their mechanical limits without many of the usual periodic checks. Like tired but faithful warhorses, they were mounted again and again and flown into action. Planes were cannibalized when spare parts were not at hand. Divisions and sections were unable to operate together in their two- or four-plane units when planes turned back due to technical problems or pilots became sick with diarrhea or nasal infections. Division and section leaders were given a great deal of responsibility when the planes operated in groups of only four or five.

Neefus and Owens were not able to exercise squadron command in the air with the pilots split up in small groups for the different assigned missions. In addition to those harrowing flights against Kahili and enemy shipping, Two Fifteen's pilots flew dawn and dusk patrols. Especially frightening were the "Moonbeam Patrols" that required excellent night-flying and navigation skills. The Corsairs covered P.T. boat raids, spotted for artillery fire, and searched for downed airmen as well as standing the usual monotonous daily strip alerts and local security patrols.

The last mission on Two Fifteen's first tour was a strafing mission against Kahili by Bob Owens, Roger Conant, Ray Wolff, and the irrepressible Sammy Stidger. Twelve fighters from Two Fifteen and VMF-123 flew top cover for Owens's division. The escorts circled above Choiseul while Owens's four Corsairs flew up to Bougainville and turned east to attack from the northwest. Owens ordered them into a line abreast formation at one hundred feet; twenty-four .50-caliber machine guns mowed down everything in their path. Sammy Stidger was fortunate. His flight path led him directly at a revetment full of Japanese planes. Stidger's guns wreaked havoc among the parked aircraft, and the other pilots reported four planes burning after his attack. The low-altitude attack, from out of the clouds and over the ridges, was a complete surprise to the Japanese, and the antiaircraft fire was belated and inaccurate. Not one of the Corsairs was damaged.

INTERMISSION

On September 5 the fighting came to an abrupt end for the tired pilots of Two Fifteen. Marine fighter squadrons followed a policy of rotation that allowed the flying personnel of a squadron six weeks in combat, followed by several weeks of liberty and training. Each pilot was required to complete three of these six-week tours, referred to as "flights." Part of the time was spent out of action in a liberty port such as Sydney or Melbourne, and Two Fifteen would spend both of its breaks in Sydney. Training and assimilation took place at Espiritu Santo and Efate before returning to action. On this day, the pilots boarded SCAT (South Pacific Combat Air Transport Command) transports for the short flight back to Cactus, escorted by Jim Neefus, Thrifty Warner, Dick Braun, and Don Aldrich in F4Us.

As they left Munda, the tired men of Two Fifteen encountered members of their sister squadron from Santa Barbara and Midway days, VMF-222, which had just arrived for its first tour. Many of Two Fifteen's pilots had transferred from Two Twenty Two and they knew each other well. One of Two Twenty Two's pilots, John Foster, recorded his surprise upon meeting his friends whom he had not seen since Midway back in June:

"A rough growth of whiskers made them look like sourdoughs of Alaska. Their eyes were red-rimmed and bloodshot, with a black, haunted look. Creases lined their drawn faces. Their expressions were those of men who had seen death too often, who worked too hard and too long without enough food and sleep. They greeted us with the joy of men who were to be granted a few more days of life." Dramatically, Foster referred to them as "the walking ghosts of VMF-215."

The pilots of VMF-215 awaiting transport at Guadalcanal for liberty in Australia.
They have just finished their first six-week tour. Author's Collection

There was little time for the two squadrons to exchange niceties, as the men of Two Fifteen loaded their gear aboard the transport that had brought in Two Twenty Two so they could "get the hell out of this godforsaken place!" Foster enviously noted the number of souvenirs but hardly paid attention to the admonition, "Don't let 'em talk you into strafing Kahili!" Foster and his fellow pilots would learn of the hell of Munda and Kahili over the next six weeks. The R4D transport took off, and Two Fifteen left the war behind.

THE REST OF VMF-215

Ground crews, who lived in the same deplorable conditions, ate the same tasteless food, and dodged the same artillery and bombing attacks, did not get this time off and they did not get to see Sydney. While the flyers enjoyed the hospitality of the Australians, the ground echelon of Two Fifteen remained in action on New Georgia. The separation of ground and air echelons was a sore point with the pilots. During their first tour, dozens of pilots had to abort missions due to inadequate maintenance. The pilots of Two Fifteen felt that many of their mechanical problems would have been eliminated if their own "excellent" ground crews had serviced their Corsairs.

The ground crews arrived on New Georgia as the flying echelon was leaving Guadalcanal for Australia. During the next four weeks, as the pilots engaged at play on liberty Down Under, thirty-five members of the ground crew were evacuated from the island due to health problems. The maintenance people did not have time to worry which squadron they were with as they serviced the aircraft of many different squadrons, both Navy and Marine, as well as many different types of aircraft. Lieutenant Ennis and his men worked on any and all aircraft on their flight lines: P-39s, P-40s, Hellcats, Avengers, Dauntlesses, and, of course, Corsairs. Occasionally they were even pressed into service working on multi-engine aircraft like B-25s and B-24s.

They originally started in the Russells but quickly moved up to Munda, just missing the flying echelon. It was here that they suffered their casualties due to sickness. On September 26, they were sent to Ondonga Island, just off the coast of New Georgia. Part of their job was to help the SeaBees construct the runways and facilities on the island. The 37th and 82nd Naval Construction Battalions were already on the island, but they had made little progress due to the harsh conditions and lack of equipment, often stolen en route by other units.

The ground crews of VMF-215 arrived off the coast of Ondonga at dusk on the 26th and found there was nothing in the way of port facilities to help them unload their gear. They spent the next four hours slogging through the surf in an attempt to get their equipment ashore. The Japanese helped spur things along, subjecting the ordnance and maintenance people to a couple of heavy air attacks and intermittent artillery fire from nearby Kolombangara. When it was finally time to take a break and sleep, Ennis and his Marines took cover wherever they could and slept on the ground.

The aviation ground crews spent the next month constructing living quarters, shops, and preparing the field for the arrival of their airplanes. New Zealanders, Marines, and the Navy would all use the field, and the headquarters buildings for MAG-14 were constructed. Rain constantly interfered with all these projects. After a few days the air raids ceased and only the occasional night heckler, "Washing Machine Charlie" or "Louie the Louse," disturbed the nightly sojourn of the tired Marines. Their camp was constructed almost entirely by the two officers and 120 enlisted men of Two Fifteen, with important help from the SeaBees. Materials were gathered or "borrowed" from whatever source was available. The Marines felled trees and dragged the logs through camp by hand to assist in construction. They used crushed coral to build the floors of the tents and shops. Coral was also used to construct walkways and taxiways adjacent to the runway.

Sickness struck hard and early, made worse by the fact the men had not had a rest since leaving the hell of Munda where so many of their number had been evacuated. Malaria and dysentery took their toll; Ennis estimated that 85 percent of his men were sick at one time. Bill Kingsley of the Ordnance Section remembered the uniform of the day was "a helmet and toilet paper." The health care facilities were primitive or nonexistent, making it more difficult to keep the exhausted and sick men in action. Marines who were unable to work had to be flown back to Guadalcanal for hospital treatment. The men of Two Fifteen never slackened, and their persistence paid off when they were assigned to the Navy's "Skull and Crossbones" Fighter Squadron 17, which arrived on October 24 under the command of Lt. Cmdr. Tommy Blackburn.

Blackburn's squadron had been the first squadron to take the F4U on board a carrier, but the Corsair had many teething problems and they were relegated to land fields. The thirty-six Corsairs they brought to Ondonga were of the raised canopy version, the so-called F4U-1A. Most of the squadrons operating in the Solomons were flying mixes of the older models and some of the newer planes. Ennis put his men to work on a twenty-four-hour work schedule to keep up with the big Navy squadron's operations. The sailors had twice as many planes as a Marine squadron and flew the same type of daily patrols and offensive operations that VMF-215 flew. This gave the ground crews plenty to do. The Marines benefited by their association with the well-equipped Navy squadron that supplied them with large amounts of food and drink, including copious amounts of beer. The beer was flown up from Guadalcanal in the ammunition bays of the Corsairs. Most of the time the beer, usually Lucky Lager brewed in San Francisco, was hot by the time it was distributed to the ground crews. Often the taste of the beer left something to be desired, and the enlisted men put together a letter to a distributor in San Francisco, inquiring "if they had their horses tested for diabetes."

The fine training the men of Two Fifteen's ground crews had enjoyed previously at Santa Barbara, Hawaii, and Midway paid off handsomely for VF-17. During the six-week period that Two Fifteen maintained VF-17's airplanes, 98 percent of the aircraft were available. This allowed the sailors in Blackburn's squadron a chance to record a score of forty-five kills, including eighteen and one half on November 11 during the coverage of a carrier raid on Rabaul. After Two Fifteen's crews went on to Bougainville without VF-17, Blackburn wrote a complimentary letter of recommendation for the ground crews. He was impressed and later told Bob Owens of their great service: "If I got assigned an airplane . . . with no wheel or strut on it . . . I would think, I gotta go back, someone screwed up! They would say, 'Commander, just get in the airplane, we'll have it fixed by the time you get strapped in!'" Lt. Cmdr. Tommy Blackburn never missed a flight.

Chapter Eight

Rest and Relaxation

. . . and his ghost may be heard as you ride beside the billabong, You'll come a waltzin' Matilda, with me!

First to greet the returning flyers of VMF-215 at Cactus was the recently rescued prodigal son, George Sanders. He quickly became the center of attention, the pilots forgetting the past six weeks of combat and poor living conditions as he wowed them with wild tales and vast amounts of souvenirs. Bob Owens noted "he had more souvenirs than an entire Marine division out in the boondocks!" Everyone enjoyed his collection of Japanese gear and native trinkets, including a rather lurid, anatomically correct rendering of a human female.

The war slowed down once the Marines returned to Guadalcanal, but even in the rear areas there seemed to be excitement. The first day back at Cactus there was an incident of small interest but out of the ordinary. The squadron occupied the same canvas huts they had when they had passed through the 'Canal on their way to Munda. The intelligence officer, Bob Clark, decided to pull a practical joke on the flyers. They were sitting around on makeshift furniture, swapping lies and reading old mail, when Clark entered the hut. He nonchalantly tossed a hand grenade onto the floor, the spoon (safety lever) flying free as it rolled across the floor. It took only a few seconds for the room to clear, cards, letters, and books flying in the air as the room's occupants dashed for the exits. Outside, the

Marines found cover in slit trenches or behind tree trunks. After listening for a few moments, they heard no boom. Instead they heard Clark's barely disguised giggles from inside the hut. Realizing they had been had, the pilots rushed the hut and it was Clark's turn to run for cover. Clark had removed the fuse from the grenade. It was a dud, an apt description of Clark's standing among the squadron for a few weeks. His dressing down by Owens, witnesses believed, would ensure such pranks would never be repeated.

That first day back there was another, more exciting and potentially dangerous incident than Clark's thoughtless shenanigan. Fortunately, it proved to be equally harmless. Just after noon, an ammunition dump storing Japanese and American artillery shells as well as aircraft bombs caught fire. The rest of the day was spent in shelters and bunkers watching the "awesome and almost beautiful" fireworks display. It lasted until the early morning of the following day. During the afternoon at least one un-fused five-inch shell flew through the Two Fifteen area, leaving a gaping hole in one of their huts. Shell fragments and shrapnel kept the Marines' heads down, and the next morning there were numerous small tears in the huts. The Unit Diary noted sarcastically, "We all agreed . . . that it would be much safer at Munda!"

Boys will be boys and the time at Guadalcanal awaiting transport south allowed the spirit of youth to infect the pilots. Horseplay increased as the distance from combat widened. Slowly they began to unwind as they realized there would be no briefings for strikes against Kahili or Ballale. Mail arrived and was read in relative comfort. The flyers frolicked in the surf and spent hours laying in the sun on the beach. Exciting games of cards went into the late hours with no fear of a mission the following morning. The boyish pilots climbed aboard Japanese 105mm guns and had pictures taken while they played and romped through the jungle. Despite the revelry, the war could not be completely forgotten with the hulks of sunken Japanese ships along the coast and an incessant stream of aircraft flying back and forth on the various airfields near their quarters. Successive showers removed the layers of dirt and crud that had accumulated in the weeks at Munda. Despite all the cleaning and new uniforms, the smell of death from New Georgia lingered long afterward.

After a couple of days, they boarded R4Ds and flew back to Espiritu Santo on the first leg of their journey to Sydney for liberty. Jim Neefus was not with them; he had been given a job at Group level and ended his association with VMF-215. Twelve of the pilots experienced some harrowing moments on their flight south to Espiritu Santo. According to Dick Newhall: "About an hour after takeoff we ran into a severe weather 'front,' which was very dark and turbulent with rain, at about 10,000 feet. We encountered a gust of extreme violence which forced the nose up in spite of the efforts of both pilots. The plane was inverted. The twelve of us in the cabin found ourselves hurled to the roof where we remained for several seconds. The pilot recovered by pulling through the rest of the loop until very nearly vertical and then rolling out. He told us, afterward, that his speed was about 250 mph. Recovery was fully completed at 4 to 5,000 feet. We then let down to the water and completed the flight in an area of low ceiling, bad visibility, and considerable turbulence. We arrived at Espiritu Santo considerably shaken by our experience and one hour late."

Among the shaken flyers was stumpy Hap Langstaff. He reported that the twelve passengers had made a quick check for parachutes in the midst of their trial and found only eight! Sammy Stidger smiled his impish grin and suggested someone could share with him. Hap also thought the recovery from the loop had occurred at 250 feet! Whatever the height, all the single-engine fighter pilots agreed it was an experience they did not want to repeat. The big twin-engine Douglas transport was checked after it landed, and it was found that most of the rivets in the wing sections had popped and the fuselage was wrinkled. The plane was written off. Men who had survived six weeks of combat and poor living conditions nearly failed to return from a transit flight.

Espiritu Santo

After arriving at Espiritu, the squadron experienced a period of two weeks inactivity while they waited for transportation to Sydney. Conditions were obviously much better at the rear area base compared to Guadalcanal and worlds away from Munda. Living quarters were Quonset huts, and the mess facilities, as well as the food, improved markedly.

Nearby natives plied a lively trinket trade and invited the pilots to many barbecues that Doc Neber pointedly avoided. Appetites returned, and some beer was found. Several of the pilots were kicked out of nearby officers' clubs while searching for something with a little more kick.

Laughter, loud evenings, and singing were indicators that the men of Two Fifteen were becoming the boys of Two Fifteen. When they gathered together, whether in their huts or at the mess hall, singing broke out spontaneously. Some of the songs were popular favorites, or old standbys, while some were of a more ribald nature. Songs like "Ring Dang Do," "O'Reilly's Daughter," and "Big Black Bull" were lusty tunes sung far from female company. Many times it was a local favorite whose author was unknown, and the words were changed to fit the combat zone.

On a Rowboat to Rabaul
If your engine conks out now, you'll come down from forty thou'
And you'll end up in a rowboat to Rabaul

In a rowboat off Rabaul
We are throwing in the towel
'Cause they'll never send the Dumbo over here

We'll be prisoners of war, and we'll stay till forty-four
Getting drunk on Saki and New Britain Beer

There was also a rather disturbing tune referencing the dead man's G.I. life insurance:

(Sung very slowly and solemnly)
Ten thousand dollars going home to the folks,
Ten thousand dollars, going home to the folks
(Very fast refrain)
Oh! Won't they be delighted,
Oh! Won't they be excited!
(Again very slowly)
With ten thousand dollars, going home to the folks

Most of the songs were outlets for the young men who could delight in outrageous antisocial and sexual comments, much the same as any group of college-age men of any time or place.

(Sung to the tune "The White Cliffs of Dover")
There'll be Zeros over, the hills of Rendova,
For tomorrow is another day
There'll be love and laughter, and children ever after
We return to the U.S.A.
The Jappies have lost their sleep, the Marines are now on their way
We'll keep them on their feet, and on their corns we'll stay!

Another local favorite gave a quick geography lesson:

On the Road to Gizo Bay
Take me somewhere east of Ewa
Where the best ain't like the worst
Where there ain't no Doug MacArthur
And a man can drown his thirst

Where the Army takes the medals
And the Navy takes the queens
But the boys who do the fightin'
Are the United States Marines
(Chorus:)
Hit the road to Gizo Bay
Where the Jap fleet spends the day
You can hear the duds a-clunkin'
From Rabaul to Lunga Quay

Pack a load to Rekata Bay
Where the float plane Zeros play
And the bombs come down like thunder
On the natives 'cross the way
In the air to Tanolei
Losing Corsairs all the way

You can hear the pilots cussin'
You can hear the gunners pray

On the road to Munda Bay
Where the Haps and Tonys play
And the flak comes up like thunder
From Vila 'cross the bay

The local food proved an avenue to vent frustrations about combat in the Solomons in the sometimes sarcastic, critical, and always biting music:

C-ration Stew
I'm sick of their Spam and Viennas
I'm sick of dehydrated chow
I want a blonde and some liquor
And steak the size of a cow
I don't like spinach and bacon
And that horrible jungle brew
My teeth can't stand their damn hard tack
And my Gawd! That C-ration stew!

I'm done with elephantiasis
The jungle rot and spik-itch
If my kid starts out with his left foot, I'll shoot the little son of a bitch
I'm sick of the sound of motors
I'm done with the F4Us
They can jam their lousy spaghetti
And Gawd-damn C-ration stew

We ate it from Ewa to Midway
To Santos and up the Slot
Munda to Vella Lavella
And Empress Augusta was hot
We didn't mind their bombing and shelling
We sniped at the sniper too
There's only one thing we're afraid of
That Gawd-damn C-ration stew

I'm going back to God's country
I'm going to make me a change
I'm sick of the beautiful tropics
And sick of the mud and the rain
I'm sick of those stinking mosquitoes
Sick of the scuttlebutt, too
To hell with the whole South Pacific
And that Gawd-damn C-ration stew

The songs changed as they went from island to island, and squadrons often changed the words to reflect their own experiences. Verses were added or dropped with the changing situations as new pilots arrived and the old faces disappeared. These songs, like all songs throughout the history of warfare, were representative of the men themselves.

Spaghetti or Spinach?

Just before they were scheduled to fly out to Australia, an incident occurred at the chow hall that went down in VMF-215 history—as important as any aerial combat. In attendance were most of the squadron including the always-jocular Doc Neber, prankster Thrifty Warner, and wise guy Hal Spears. What happened at the meal would reach legendary proportions, especially when the good name of Ernest Neber was mentioned. It was as confusing an action as any of the squadron's fast-moving, twisting air combats.

It was the night before they were to depart for Sydney. The menu included spinach, spaghetti, and liberal amounts of real butter in little squares for the bread and spinach. Everyone was excited in anticipation of finally getting to Australia. Doc Neber and Thrifty Warner were calmly eating, enjoying the good food and engaged in quiet conversation. Spears entered the chow hall, loudly, having recently partaken of a generous supply of beer, in the company of a rowdy group of pilots. Spears proceeded to plant himself squarely opposite the mild-mannered Neber and leered. Spears playfully baited Neber with comments about members of the medical profession, but Neber only replied with a subdued "Cut that out." The inebriated pilot tried different silly ploys or comments to rile the doctor, but Neber refused to be aroused. Spears continued, despite the advice of those around him, and finally managed to irritate Neber. In a soft voice, with just a trace of displeasure, the wiry doctor informed the burly flyer that if he did not back off he would be the recipient of a bowl of spinach on his head.

This was like waving a red flag at a bull, and Spears laughed as he playfully kicked the doctor in the shin. True to his word, Neber hit Spears with a well-aimed spoonful of spinach between the eyes. On this point there is a difference of opinion; some believed it was a spoonful of spaghetti, and Owens later thought it was a pallet of butter. Whatever the missile, Spears jumped after the doctor and playfully pulled him to the floor to wrestle. Neber, seriously worried about his safety, did his best to get the heavier, stronger, and younger Spears off of him, with the rest of the room cheering them on. The noise and thrashing about attracted the officer of the day, unfortunately a new lieutenant of the rear echelon type that took the event a little too seriously. He put everyone there under arrest.

Most of the Marines were immediately released from custody, having given false names in any case. Doc Neber, never a friend of authority, protested his innocence too loudly and became belligerent with the arresting officer. Neber and Thrifty Warner, who interceded physically on the doctor's behalf, were kept in confinement the next day when the rest of the squadron flew on to Sydney. Warner took his punishment without protest and was repentant. He was allowed to fly out a few days later. Neber maintained his lack of responsibility for the incident and was not so lucky. The incident blossomed into a threatened court-martial for the good doctor, but he eventually was released. Some gave credit to the "Legal Eagle," Johnny Downs, for his escape. The future lawyer's part is a little vague; he may have tried to help Neber until his own trip to Australia was threatened. Boyish pranks hurt the poor doctor dearly. He missed the trip to Sydney.

AUSTRALIA

Khakis were donned, and the men boarded transports the day after the mess hall incident. Six weeks of combat produced eager and anxious young men, ready to leave behind all thoughts of Ballale, Rekata Bay, and Kieta. The short flight to Sydney seemed to last forever, and they were disappointed upon arrival in Sydney as their immediate entry into the city was held up by administrative niceties at the airfield. The men were assigned quarters. Some billeted with willing families while others stayed in hotels and apartments. Tailors were made available for those needing new uniforms and alterations. Ration books were issued, and a brief was given on how to treat the natives, what to buy, and where entertainment could be found. Among the items issued to the flyers was a bag containing, as Hap Langstaff called them, "disease prevention devices." Then the Marines were set loose on the city.

Sydney was a town that had been at war since 1939 and had seen young Americans at their best, and worst, since 1942. Sydney was a blend of the old world and the new, yet it had a flavor of its own. It was the closest to England most of these young men would ever get, yet it was only superficially English. The people were definitely not English, and the delightful Australian accents made an immediate and positive impression on the Americans. After years of war, the Australians were used to the strange ways of the Yanks, and the two got along famously. Bob Owens described Sydney as being "to World War Two pilots what World War One pilots wished Paris had been."

To young American boys, Sydney had a romantic and exotic feel. Bondi Beach, with its gently sloping white sands, became a favorite spot for the men of Two Fifteen. The Tarango Zoo and many museums provided cultural entertainment for those with a bent to seeing the sights. But Fort Denison and the historical sights of Sydney were unimportant to the men of Two Fifteen who were interested in companionship, the type of companionship unavailable in the Solomon Islands. Taxi drivers proved to be important guides to the city.

Stationed at the Royal Australian Golf Course were several anti-aircraft batteries manned by women. A great bond of friendship grew between these women and the men of Two Fifteen. Sympathetic taxi drivers would pick up the women at their barracks each evening and deliver them to the waiting Marines at a previously appointed place. After a night of dancing and fun among the milk bars and hotels, the drivers were equally adept at returning the young ladies to their beds before muster and discovery. It was claimed that not one of these ladies was ever late for morning formation.

Lanky Tom Stockwell and clever Sammy Stidger were standing on a street corner with several other Marines when a car pulled up to the intersection and stopped to wait for the signal to change. In the vehicle were a "handsome," older woman and a pretty young lady. The good-looking and seemingly shameless Stidger stepped into the street and, to the surprise of his companions, began speaking to the women in the car. The conversation became involved, and Stidger leaped into the car as it peeled off into the night.

The next morning, Stidger informed Stockwell that he had been invited to the ladies' home for dinner and was to bring along his friends. Stockwell, Hap Langstaff, and Chief Leu went along with Stidger for a home-cooked meal. The evening was a hit as everyone enjoyed the meal and fellowship. Suddenly, a man identified as the young girl's fiancé arrived at the party a bit irritated, demanding to see his bride to be. Thinking little of the intrusion, Stockwell continued to enjoy himself until the mother, "very mad," asked Tom emphatically to go out to the garden and retrieve her daughter. It seemed the girl was out in the flowers, alone, with Stidger. Tom gleefully went outside and discovered the pair in a rather passionate embrace. Unflappable, Stidger informed the amused Stockwell, "that they would be in shortly." The mother was visibly unhappy but the romantic couple eventually returned to the house and the girl was married the next day.

The squadron frequently threw big parties at the larger hotels where the pilots roomed. They danced and drank the nights away, not just alcohol but also copious amounts of milk. It is no surprise that the pilots often consumed too many intoxicating beverages and paid for it later. One night Chief Leu and George Kross found themselves in sole possession of eight bottles of champagne. The two secreted themselves in their room with the loot and proceeded to empty all eight bottles. The pair awoke the next morning to the expected pounding heads and poor Kross unable to open his eyes. He actually feared blindness and wondered what kind of champagne they had consumed. Chief Leu feared the loss of a good wingman. But like all young men who should know better but do not seem to ever learn, they were at it again that evening, Kross having no trouble in seeing the varieties of beer available.

There were large dances held at the finer hotels in which dozens of servicemen from all branches of service and many different nations would congregate for a good time. Americans, Australians, New Zealanders, and citizens of various other nations of the British Commonwealth rubbed shoulders seeking to forget the war and just enjoy themselves. Marines made a great game of tipping the local bands to play the "Marines' Hymn" at strategic moments. Out of respect, all of the Marines in the room came to attention. This clogged up the dance floor and the aisles between tables, effectively bringing everything to a stop. Sailors would likewise coerce the band to play "Anchors Aweigh," and the sailors would bring everything to a halt by standing at attention. The bluejackets and leathernecks laughed at the frustrated soldiers who could not figure out, for all of their branches and services, a single tune recognized by all.

There were whirlwind romances, addresses were exchanged, and many of the Marines would receive letters over the next few months from newfound friends in Sydney. Some of the pilots would visit the same people on their next liberty after the next six-week tour. No one had expected the time in Sydney to last forever, but they found it over too soon. They tried to fit a lifetime in just a few days, and many bordered on exhaustion due to the long days and longer nights. They had achieved a sort of mental reawakening that enabled them to return to combat. For some, it was their last look at Sydney as they would not be alive when the next liberty came around.

The flight north would be to Espiritu Santo first, via Noumea. Some needed the time to recover from their liberty. It was not only the pilots of Two Fifteen that needed a recovery, as the passengers of one R4D found out. The twelve flyers were idly sitting or standing around their airplane when a flat bed truck pulled up with two obviously recovering drunks reclining on the back. Thinking that someone mistakenly thought they were part of Two Fifteen, Owens mentioned to the aircraft crew chief that they were not any of his pilots. The enlisted man merely smiled and informed the curious Marines that the two were the pilot and co-pilot of their flight to Noumea. Luckily, it was a serene flight after the aircraft's tail wheel was damaged clearing the fence at the end of the runway on takeoff.

RETURN TO THE COMBAT ZONE

After a day on Noumea they flew on to Espiritu. They just missed Thrifty Warner, who had flown out just before they arrived, Doc Neber was still being held and he met the returning airmen. Several of the pilots failed their flight physicals but this was to be expected after a week of liberty. Failing the physical did not keep them from starting their training in preparation for the move up.

In addition to the happy reunion with Neber, the pilots encountered bad news. Jim Neefus, the father of the squadron who had prepared them for battle, was permanently moved to the Air Group Staff. Everyone, including Neefus and Bob Owens, expected that Owens as executive officer would naturally move up to commanding officer. Owens and Neefus had worked hand in hand since the formation of the unit back in Santa Barbara. No one knew the men of the squadron better than Owens. All of the pilots in return knew and trusted Owens. They expected him to carry on as Neefus had. Events proved their expectations to be wrong.

Lt. Col. Herbert H. Williamson, a graduate of Michigan State University where he played football for three years, would be the new commander of VMF-215. Tall and slightly graying, Williamson was thirty years old and had joined the Marine Corps in 1935. After Basic School, he served briefly aboard the cruiser *Houston* before assignment to flight training. He flew with VMF-1 at Quantico, Virginia, until his assignment to the Plans Division of the Bureau of Aeronautics in January of 1942. He left his wife and daughter at home when he sailed for the South Pacific. Saddled with staff positions for over six months, he was eager for action. He had been pushing to get into the fight, and now he was given that chance as the commanding officer of Two Fifteen. Unfortunately he had not flown regularly for nearly two years.

There was a little grumbling from the pilots, but it was quickly quieted when the intense training began. Owens and Williamson developed a good working relationship with the understanding that Owens would take over after the second tour. Williamson agreed that nothing would change in tactics or organization; the divisions would remain the same with only a few changes due to new personnel. Owens willingly continued with the responsibility for day-to-day operations, in addition to the administrative duties of the executive officer, to enable the new commander the freedom to get to know his squadron.

The next few days were spent in updating administrative information, recovering physically from their time in Australia, and looking over the new tactical situation in the Solomons. There was time for a few flights but no time for large-scale tactical training. Larry Smith came down with an appendicitis attack, no doubt painful for the young man, but his condition was termed "normal" in the Unit Diary. Three days later, John Breneman caught up with them after being held at Noumea for an ear infection. He was still unable to fly and spent the next month attached to Group Headquarters.

While at Espiritu, Chief Leu managed to generate a little excitement on a night training mission. Flying around on instruments, Leu received a vector from the local fighter command that indicated an unidentified bogey closing on the field. Back and forth he flew around, banking and turning to instructions from the ground. The cat and mouse game continued for over an hour before Leu broke off due to low fuel. The mystery plane was never found.

The Marines always seemed to be seeking souvenirs or native trinkets. One afternoon Dick Braun, Chief Leu, Hap Langstaff, and Tom Stockwell went to visit a nearby village. Braun had become friends with a native, and they were hoping to meet the chief of the village. Arriving at the village, they were introduced to a "strapping fellow in a lap lap," who the Marines took to be the chief. After their native friend introduced them in the local language, Dick Braun began speaking Tagalog to the man. Unaware that Tagalog was a language from the Philippines, Braun seemed pleased with himself, but the chief was totally perplexed. Finally, in a clipped English accent the chief replied, "I'm very, very sorry, old man, but I can't understand a word you're saying." It seemed he was a graduate of the University of Auckland. The conversation continued in English.

Although he was not an American Indian, Reinhardt Leu went by the moniker "Chief." Author's Collection

The squadron lost several of its more senior, and more experienced, flyers to staff duty while at Espiritu. The "legal eagle" Johnny Downs, former RCAF pilot Gerry Shuchter, and big Bob Johnson said goodbye to the Fighting Corsairs. A new group of pilots arrived from Hawaii to replace those moving on as well as the casualties from the first tour. They were an eager group: shy young George Brewer, who had been inspired to fly by Charles Lindbergh; Samuel Sampler, a serious young man in pursuit of a little adventure; cocky, short Creighton Chandler, who was nicknamed "Spud"; skinny Al Snyder; easygoing Richard Evans; and energetic Kenneth DuVal. Unlike the original members of Two Fifteen who had completed their first tour, each of these pilots would have to fly three, six-week "flights."

Luckily, the majority of the new replacements were a crop of veterans from VMF-214, which was being reorganized. Part of the group included pilots who had only one six-week tour left: Lincoln Deetz, Drury McCall, Jack Petit, Bennie O'Dell, and Otto Williams. These pilots, with six Japanese victims and dozens of combats to their credit,

Tommy Tomlinson started his combat flying Wildcats with VMF-214 before joining VMF-215. USMC Photo

would provide the experience needed to replace losses like Ray Tomes and Don Moore. Also from Two Fourteen were a group of Marines who, like the original members of Two Fifteen, had two more six-week flights to complete. They were also veterans: Texan Ovis Hunter, who already had been credited with the destruction of a *Val* divebomber; tall Thomas Tomlinson credited with one victory; soft-spoken Edwin Hernan, who possessed a devilish smile and carefree outlook on life; and a remarkable young man driven by fierce ambition, Robert Murray Hanson.

CHAPTER NINE

Back in the Saddle

The decisive factor in victory is courage.
—MANFRED VON RICHTOFEN

VMF-215, October 1943
Commanding Officer: Lt. Col. Herbert Williamson
Executive Officer: Maj. Robert G. Owens

Capt. Donald Aldrich

Capt. Richard L. Braun

Capt. John R. Jordan

Capt. Billy K. Shaw

Capt. Arthur T. Warner

1st Lt. John W. Breneman

1st Lt. Roger Conant

1st Lt. Lloyd Cox

1st Lt. Lincoln F. Deetz

1st Lt. David A. Escher

1st Lt. Robert M. Hanson

1st Lt. Ledyard B. Hazelwood

1st Lt. Edwin Hernan

1st Lt. Ovis D. Hunter

1st Lt. Harold A. Langstaff

1st Lt. Reinhardt Leu

1st Lt. Drury E. McCall

1st Lt. David R. Moak

1st Lt. Richard G. Newhall

1st Lt. Bennie P. O'Dell

1st Lt. Jack W. Petit

1st Lt. George P. Sanders

1st Lt. Lawrence M. Smith

1st Lt. Harold L. Spears

1st Lt. Grafton S. Stidger

1st Lt. Thomas D. Stockwell

1st Lt. Thomas M. Tomlinson

1st Lt. Otto K. Williams

1st Lt. Ray K. Wolff

2nd Lt. George W. Brewer

2nd Lt. Creighton Chandler

2nd Lt. Kenneth DuVal   2nd Lt. Richard W. Evans
2nd Lt. Robert L. Keister   2nd Lt. James J. Knight
2nd Lt. George Kross   2nd Lt. Samuel N. Sampler
2nd Lt. Alan J. Snyder   2nd Lt. Raymond H. Wetzel
          Flight Surgeon: Lt. Ernest N. Neber, U.S.N.
          Intelligence Officer: 1st Lt. Robert E. Clark

ROBERT HANSON WAS BORN IN LUCKNOW, INDIA. HIS PARENTS WERE
hardworking Methodist missionaries who worked throughout the northern provinces of India. Hanson lived most of his life in India, coming
home to the United States for the first time in his junior high years.
Although the family home was in Newton, Massachusetts, while in the
United States he spent most of his time on his grandfather's farm near
the small town of Breckinridge, Minnesota, near the North Dakota bor-
der. It was there, near the Otter Tail River, that Bob Hanson first soared
to the heights that would be his military trade years later. On a day off
from farm work, he wrangled a free ride with a barnstormer and became
hooked on flying.

Hanson returned to India and became the light-heavyweight wrestling champion of the United Provinces in northern India. This was an
amazing feat for a young man of eighteen, for though he was muscular
and well-proportioned he was wrestling against all comers, many of
whom had more experience. After graduation from secondary school,
Hanson's parents decided it was best that the young man return to
America to attend college. He agreed but insisted on going to the United
States via Europe, touring the area on a bicycle. While leisurely pedaling
through the Old World, Hanson happened to be passing through Austria
when Adolf Hitler staged his *Anschluss*, the takeover of Austria in March
of 1938. Bob Hanson was one of only a few Americans to see up close
what totalitarian regimes were capable of.

Upon arrival in the United States, Hanson enrolled in Hamline
University, a small Methodist liberal arts college in St. Paul, Minnesota.
Eagerly he threw himself into his studies as well as extracurricular activities such as football, track, and, of course, wrestling. He expanded his
linguistic skills by learning French, Spanish, and German in addition

to the Hindustani he had learned in India. Bob worked part-time on campus at the cafeteria and nights as a bouncer at a local club. His size, athletic ability, and overall physical presence kept trouble at the club to a minimum. During those slow, happy days at Hamline, he also learned to fly, fulfilling a dream he had cherished since his boyhood days on his grandfather's farm. The son of the nightclub owner had an old Luscombe high-wing monoplane, and the two boys spent weekends putting the old plane through its paces.

After the attack on Pearl Harbor, Hanson decided to leave his education behind and get involved in America's war effort. Despite having only one quarter to finish before graduation, he left school after he was accepted for naval flight training in May of 1942. Tough and worldly, Hanson intimidated some of the younger men. The impatient Hanson zealously plunged into the flying program, chomping at the bit to get into action. He received final instruction at Corpus Christi, Texas, and selected the Marine Corps upon graduation. He received his gold wings and second lieutenant's commission on February 19, 1943. He followed a similar journey as previous pilots, via Hawaii, Midway, and Noumea, joining VMF-214, the "Swashbucklers," at Guadalcanal in August.

Hanson was spoiling for a fight, and his aggressive attitude put off some of his fellow pilots. He soon won them over with his success in battle. He scored his first victory on August 4, shooting a *Tony* off the tail of his section leader, future ace Stanley "Chief" Synar, on a mission over the Shortlands. A few weeks later, on August 26, his division joined the Corsairs of Two Fifteen in an attack on Kahili. Suffering supercharger trouble, he lagged behind the formation, which put him in perfect position to down a *Zeke* that tried to sneak up on the Swashbucklers, who only noticed the *Zeke* as it fell in flames to the sea.

The squadron commander, Maj. William H. Pace, was killed in action on August 7, and several administrative problems led ComAirSols to reorganize Two Fourteen at the end of its six-week tour. Those pilots who still had time in theater were transferred to other squadrons and some were sent home. Hanson joined the Fighting Corsairs of VMF-215. The squadron designation VMF-214 would eventually be reorganized and adopt the nickname "The Blacksheep."

BARAKOMA

VMF-215, with its new commander and replacement pilots, was ordered to the new airstrip at Barakoma Point on recently occupied Vella Lavella Island. Barakoma had a four-thousand-foot runway right on the eastern shoreline of the island. Carved out of the jungle by hardworking Sea-Bees of the 58th Naval Construction Battalion, revetments sat opposite the shore. Living quarters, consisting of tents, were well into the trees, separated by a great berm from the interior. Revetments and taxiways encroached into the vegetation. Like Guadalcanal and Munda, slit trenches and bomb shelters were constructed around the living quarters. The Marines were right where they left off. Primitive Barakoma resembled Munda in all respects.

On the very first day they arrived at their new home, Two Fifteen stood runway alerts and standing patrols. The early days on Vella Lavella

VMF-215 Corsairs alongside the coral runway at Barakoma, Vella LaVella, 1943. USMC Photo

served as a good break-in period, allowing pilots who had not flown much in several weeks a chance to get reacquainted with their powerful airplanes. Herb Williamson was able to work his new divisions and sections in basic tactics. New pilots used the time to get to know their new commander as well as the powerful Corsair. Some of the new pilots had only a few hours on the big Corsair and were given priority in flying time. At first, mild-mannered George Brewer was a little apprehensive whenever he took off, but he soon adapted to his new mount, "It was like a whole new world. We'd been flying F4F-3s [Wildcats]. The Corsair was just so much more of an airplane. We loved the Corsair."

George Brewer joined VMF-215 during its second tour in the Solomons and was nearly killed on the same mission that killed Bob Hanson. USMC Photo

The squadron began to mesh as they flew together and rubbed elbows on the ground. Hal Spears had immense fun with the new guys, reveling in their rapt attention to his stories of strange women and long, wild nights of liberty. The newcomers from Two Fourteen provided their own earthy individual in the low-key Ed Hernan. With a sly twinkle in his eye, Hernan would entertain the others with witty tales that ended with deep guffaws. The veterans shared their experiences with the newer pilots, stories of tough dogfights and instructions about basic combat flying skills. Dick Braun and Bob Hanson took the time to teach novices Al Snyder and Sam Sampler the finer points of bridge. The card players also learned to their loss that Jack Petit, one of the new guys from Two Fourteen, was quite a poker player.

Petit, originally from Ohio, had been wounded and also had downed a couple of Japanese planes, a *Val* in April and a twin-engine bomber in July. Considered a skilled pilot by his peers, Petit was known as a dependable leader. O. K. Williams had flown with Petit many times and stated flatly, "I can't think of anyone I would rather have as my wingman."

On October 20, the second day at Barakoma, Petit was part of a local patrol led by B. K. Shaw that included Ed Hernan and O. D. Hunter. All were veteran pilots, having served together in Two Fourteen. The patrol was uneventful, but they were forced to return to Barakoma due to foul weather. Shaw, Hernan, and Hunter all landed at about 1405 in the early afternoon. They noticed Petit was missing as they exited the weather front. Low on fuel, they returned to Barakoma, refueled, and headed back to the area where they had turned around. There was no sign of the missing Marine. A search the next day failed to find any clues to his disappearance. Jack Wardell Petit never returned.

The first offensive strike took place on October 21, a fighter sweep to Kahili. The divisions of Bob Owens, Dick Braun, Don Aldrich, and O. K. Williams flew up to Bougainville in marginal weather. It was part of a new tactic, pure fighter sweeps aimed at enticing the Japanese to come up and fight instead of the Corsairs going down on the deck to strafe the enemy fields. On this particular mission there was no aerial response and they returned home without any loss. The tide had turned. After months of pounding by Army, Marine Corps, Navy, and Allied bombers and

Jack Petit was another former member of the VMF-214 "Swashbucklers" who flew with 215. Unfortunately, he lasted only one mission. USMC Photo

fighters, the Japanese airfields on Bougainville had been evacuated. Japanese airplanes had been removed to Rabaul in anticipation of the Allied invasion of Bougainville. The airfields would only be used by enemy aircraft refueling before attacking Allied bases farther south or by those in trouble and unable to return to Rabaul after such attacks.

Weather was the biggest problem facing the squadron with the lack of aerial opposition. On October 22, Lieutenant Colonel Williamson led his division and O. K. Williams's division on a sweep to check out Kahili and Kara Airfields. There was no enemy opposition but the turbulent air tossed the airplanes around in the sky as if they were weightless. Forced to break formation, they were ordered to return to base.

Bennie O'Dell was caught in one particularly bad downdraft. Flying at twenty-six thousand feet, his six-ton Corsair was struck by a tremendous downward blow. Tossed about as if it were weightless, O'Dell fought for control of the airplane. He was able to finally level out at ten thousand feet. Looking out over his gull wings, O'Dell could see the fabric had been torn off the wing tips. The same weather took one of the new pilots, Ken DuVal. He failed to return from the flight. O. K. Williams took his division up later in the day and circled the area where DuVal was last seen, but there was no sign of the missing pilot and the Unit Diary laconically noted he "is presumed lost."

Luckily, DuVal was not lost. His Corsair was heavily damaged by weather, and he was forced to bail out off the coast of Choiseul. Climbing into his rubber raft, he drifted to the southwest. He tried to row himself to the nearby island but the current was too strong, which proved fortunate. He learned later that area where he would have landed was infested with Japanese troops. For five days he drifted in the little rubber boat, at the mercy of the wind and the water. Ever resourceful, he used his jungle pack rations and then fish that he caught with a small pail. It was just enough to sustain him for five days. DuVal was in good condition when he was rescued by the fleet tug USS *Apache* fifteen miles from Vella Lavella. Amazingly, he still had two swigs left in his canteen when he was picked up. He arrived back at Barakoma on October 30.

The mission on the 22nd involved Army P-39s, Navy F6Fs, and eight Corsairs from Two Fifteen. Drury McCall and Hal Spears were unable to join up on the SBDs and TBFs and Jack Jordan led the remaining six Corsairs to Kahili. The divebombers and torpedo planes bombed the nearly deserted runway and then turned south through desultory anti-aircraft fire.

Dick Braun, with Al Snyder and Dave Escher on his wings, headed home at ten thousand feet. Braun spotted two planes behind, closing slowly. One of the unidentified planes rolled and headed into the clouds. In the split second he saw the plane, Braun saw square wings that indicated it was a Navy Hellcat. The other plane continued and passed underneath the trio of Corsairs; its elliptical wings indicated it was a *Zeke*. Braun slid in behind the enemy plane and opened fire. The fire from Braun's guns tore pieces off the enemy aircraft, but the *Zeke* pulled up in a loop. The Corsairs could not follow the Zeke at the steep angle of its climb, and Braun broke off to prevent stalling.

The *Zeke* finished its loop and rolled out behind Escher. The Marine realized the danger and went into a steep dive before the *Zeke* could open fire. The heavier Corsair easily outdistanced the *Zeke*, and Escher returned to Vella Lavella shortly after Braun and Snyder. The short encounter, one of the few aerial combats that Two Fifteen would be involved in during its second tour, illustrated the different characteristics of the American planes and Japanese. The *Zeke* was highly maneuverable and able to outclimb the heavier Hellcats and Corsairs due to its lighter construction. The Corsair, with its powerful engine and great size, could outrun a *Zeke* in level flight and in a dive.

The Corsairs used by Two Fifteen in October of 1943 were the initial combat version of the aircraft, referred to as the "birdcage" model. It derived its nickname from its poorly designed cockpit canopy. The sliding hood of the canopy was framed with small panes of glass that decreased the already poor visibility of the long-nosed Corsair. In addition, the planes used by Two Fifteen at Barakoma were hand-me-downs, planes used by many different squadrons previously with many hours of use on the engines and airframes. The aircraft were in a poor state of repair due to overuse and a lack of trained maintenance personnel. There were never enough experienced ground crewmen or spare parts. The few school-trained ground crewmen were overworked and suffered from lack of sleep and poor nutrition.

Coral dust seeped into every nook and cranny of the machines. Tape was used to cover the seams on the leading edges of the wings, rudder, and stabilizers. The six gunports were taped over to prevent dust buildup in the barrels of the .50-caliber machine guns. When fighters returned from a mission, it was easy to tell which aircraft had seen action. The tape was shot out with the first burst of fire. The fuel tank located in front of the pilot often leaked dangerous or irritating fumes, resulting in the seams on forward fuselage also being taped over. Being naval aircraft, the Corsairs had folding wings to help with storage on aircraft carriers. The land-based Corsairs did not have the space limitations found on aircraft carriers, so the hydraulic lines that worked the wing-folding mechanisms were drained and capped as they frequently leaked.

The paint on the upper surfaces of the planes faded due to the intense sunshine, wind-blown coral dust, and hours of flying. The propellers blew dust into the engines that drastically cut down engine life. In addition to major problems, there seemed to be an endless number of small things that did not work. Lightbulbs for the reflector gun sights burned out, microphone cords became frayed and wet, oxygen masks cracked and split. Guns often jammed due to improper loading or cleaning, leading pilots to kick themselves as promising targets escaped.

Before taking off, pilots must run their checks. One of them involves the two magnetos, the parts of an aircraft that ensures ignition of fuel in each cylinder. Running a magneto check one morning before takeoff, Tom Stockwell noticed a 600-rpm drop when set on "both." Knowing the drop should be no more than 125 rpm, Tom sought the advice of Bob Owens. The "Big O" laughed and shook his head. Tongue in cheek, he sarcastically informed the young Marine that he had once taken off with a bird that had a 1,200-rpm drop! Whether he was pulling Stockwell's leg or not, Owens illuminated a problem with the maintenance of the planes. Many of the ground crewmen were not trained on single-engine aircraft or not on the Corsair. Some had never trained on airplanes at all and were just good auto mechanics or men with an aptitude for fixing things pressed into service by their units. Navy CASU (Carrier Aircraft Service Units) detachments did their best when Marine ground crews were unavailable. Luckily, more new aircraft were arriving in theater. Pilots looked forward to the trip back to Guadalcanal both for rest and the chance to pick up a new, replacement aircraft.

The fresh planes had the newer canopy, the so-called "blown hood." It was seven inches higher, allowing the pilot better all-around vision. The glass had only two braces across its top, reducing visual obstructions. The seat was raised nine inches to help the pilot see over the long nose. The tail wheel was also raised, pushing the nose down to give a better line of sight on takeoff and landing. Armor was added to the headrest, and the control column was lengthened for easier use. Pilots eagerly hoped they would get one of the new planes after drawing their assignments for the next mission. Rank had no privileges, and Owens often lamented his assignment when saddled with an old, beat-up Corsair for a mission.

The Japanese attempted to disperse their aircraft, placing them on smaller airfields or staging them through Kahili only briefly. One of the small airstrips was Kara, located in the jungle about five kilometers east of Kahili. Bob Keister and Dave Moak were assigned with three pilots from VMF-221 to strafe the field to get a group of Japanese staging through the base to attack Allied positions farther south. Moak experienced engine trouble and was unable to accompany the others.

Weather was fair as they passed over the east coast of Bougainville and swung southwest to attack Kara from the north. They were able to surprise the Japanese, but they were also surprised as there were over forty Japanese planes packed together on the runway and in the run-up areas. The three Two Twenty-One pilots attacked first, online with eighteen .50-caliber machines spraying the enemy planes. Keister followed, greeted by the sight of flames and smoke from the other planes' guns. Keister gulled down to seventy-five feet and picked a group of undamaged planes parked off to the side. His bullets struck the parked planes, ripping through them. Other bullets struck the ground and flew off into the air like some excited fireflies. Mission accomplished, he climbed and joined the others, leaving behind red, orange, and yellow flames rising into gray and black clouds above the jungle. Intelligence photos would show that twenty Japanese aircraft were destroyed, and Bob Keister was credited with six of them.

The rest of the month of October was spent in attacks on the Japanese in the Bougainville area, combat patrols over the invasion force at Treasury Island, escort missions with Army, Navy, or Marine Corps bombers, and combat air patrols over Vella Lavella. There was plenty of flying and shooting, but there was little in the way of air combat. The Japanese were husbanding their strength at Rabaul to defend Bougainville when the Allies chose to invade that island.

One mission, on October 29, was a little unusual. Three divisions escorted a B-25 mission to Buka, a small island just off the northern coast of Bougainville. There was no aerial opposition, and the Army bombers dropped their parachute bombs effectively. The Corsairs strafed Japanese positions, but there were few worthwhile targets. Don Aldrich shot up a couple of floatplanes hidden in the jungle, and Ray Wetzel killed a poor Japanese soldier who was fishing. There was very little antiaircraft fire, and all of the planes returned safely, except Jake Knight.

Knight headed south with the rest of the formation, and everything appeared to be fine. Passing Choiseul, oil began to seep from the cowling of his engine. The oil leak grew worse as the Corsair neared Vella Lavella, making it less likely that he would be able to land safely. The engine seized up before he could join the landing pattern, and he decided to land in the water. Three miles from Barakoma, he set the fighter into the water and quickly leaped into his life raft. A small boat was already on its way from shore, and he was rescued within a few minutes. Owens gave the bedraggled young airman a cigar to celebrate his return.

Jake Knight gets a cigar from Bob Owens after being rescued on October 29, 1943, after his Corsair suffered an oil leak and he was forced to ditch. Doc Neber and Herb Williamson look on. USMC Photo

INVASION OF BOUGAINVILLE

The squadron spent November 1 covering the long anticipated Allied invasion of Bougainville. The invasion force landed at Cape Torokina, about midway down the west coast of the island. The primary Japanese airstrips were on the southern and northern tips of Bougainville, but their planes had been withdrawn several days before. The pilots of Two Fifteen spent the day in constant patrols over the beach; the first patrol took off before dawn and the last returned just after dark that evening.

Taking off in the dark at 0445, the first patrol consisted of the divisions of Herb Williamson and Don Aldrich. Williamson's four planes made it off using only direction lights and the exhaust flames of the plane ahead of them, followed by Aldrich and Bob Keister. For some reason a pilot of VMF-212 took off at this time and lost control of his plane, crashing into a PV-1 twin-engine patrol bomber. Both planes erupted into massive flames that lit up the entire area. At the same time that the Corsair and Neptune blew up, an explosion was seen three to five miles off the end of the runway. Adding to the confusion, a Japanese plane used the light of the fire to attempt to bomb the well-lit airfield. All six bombs landed harmlessly in the water. The rest of Aldrich's division climbed off to join the patrol over Torokina. Bob Keister didn't join up and was not seen when they arrived over Empress Augusta Bay off Cape Torokina.

Reinhardt Leu spotted nine *Val* divebombers as they finished dropping their bombs. Leu set off in hot pursuit as the Japanese turned and headed for Buka Passage. Excited by the prospect of gunning down several of the slow Japanese bombers, he poured on the coals. Lining up the last plane in line, Leu noted the rear gunner energetically firing at him. Leu closed in and opened fire at point blank range. After a few bullets, all six guns were silent. Leu charged his guns again and again but couldn't get them to fire. He returned to base fuming about the missed opportunity.

The remainder of the day was spent in two-hour patrols over the beachhead. ComAirSols tried to keep at least thirty-six fighters over the invasion force at all times. VMF-215 provided at least one division for each of the two-hour rotations. Only Thrifty Warner's division had any aerial action, downing five Japanese in their afternoon flight. (The fight was described in detail in the introduction to this book.) Three aircraft were reported missing that day. Kross arrived an hour later than his flight, unhurt and undamaged. Hanson was shot down but his rescue was reported within a few hours.

Robert Louis Keister never did return; he was reported missing in action after that predawn takeoff. After talking to Don Aldrich, who had been Keister's section leader, and using a little conjecture to piece together the facts, Owens and Bob Clark determined the explosion seen by observers that morning had probably been the crash of the well-liked Keister. It was a frustrating combination of things: darkness, lack of night flying and instrument experience, as well as the blinding explosion that took place just as Keister took off, that resulted in the accidental death. The official cause of death was vertigo, but it also must be attributed to an aircraft in a poor state of repair due to overuse and lack of trained maintenance personnel.

A "boneyard" of damaged or derelict aircraft grew up at the end of the flight line. Some of the planes could be repaired, and those that couldn't were used for spare parts. Predawn strikes contributed to many losses, but poor visibility in the darkness produced at least one comical episode.

Tired and still half asleep, Tom Stockwell was assigned to an early morning mission: "One morning on one of our pre-dawn takeoff hops the driver of the truck delivering us to our planes dropped a plane captain and me off in front of a dim shape in the darkness. We walked over to the plane where I proceeded to climb into the cockpit and fumble with the light switches while the mechanic climbed on to the wing and groped for the door to the starter firing chamber. None of the switches were producing any light and I was cussing a dead battery when the mechanic called out, 'Lieutenant, this plane ain't got no engine!' We were in the boneyard."

The rest of that first week of November was spent in much the same way, divisions rotating above the invasion fleet and local patrols. There was no aerial opposition for Two Fifteen, although other squadrons intercepted several Japanese attacks. The only losses were due to the early morning takeoffs.

On November 3, Bob Owens and Jack Jordan were assigned the early takeoffs with their divisions. The airplanes took off using only formation lights. Unfortunately, the lights of trucks and jeeps off the airfield often distorted the shape of planes and the dimensions of the runway. In Owens's division Dick Newhall became disoriented and lost control of his Corsair, veering off the strip and back on. His plane was only slightly damaged, but it needed repair and he was scratched from the mission. Newhall complained that the lights of the vehicles around the field caused him to lose the edge of the runway.

Handsome, steady Jack Jordan led his division into the air, heading toward the brooding hills just to the north of the strip. His plane lost power and he was unable to clear the hills, clipping the trees about a mile off the end of the runway. The plane broke up on impact and spread fiery pieces over a wide area. Jordan's body was badly burned. Early morning takeoffs had killed their second Two Fifteen pilot in two days.

The rest of that day was spent with the fighters flying up to Bougainville for their rotations. Doc Neber was detailed with the gruesome task of retrieving the remains of John R. Jordan. Jordan's service watch was still intact, forever stopped at the time of death, 0445. Returning from the afternoon's first patrol, pilots of Owens's division were shocked to find Doc Neber on their truck with their dead comrade's remains. Jack Jordan had been a family man. An excellent flyer and a respected leader, he was one of the original Santa Barbara pilots, and his death was a terrible loss to the squadron. Roger Conant was shaken when Doc Neber reported he had found a pair of baby's booties dangling from the gun sight in Jordan's mangled Corsair. Conant was so affected by the symbol that he vowed he would never fly again with personal items on him or his aircraft. Jordan had always kept his wife's picture prominently displayed in their tent. Young pilots admired the photo and what it represented, the hope and promise of life after the war. Now these same men avoided looking at the picture and viewed it as almost an obscenity. They had suffered a blow to their future hopes in Jack Jordan's death, and the picture's absence was appreciated when Jordan's personal effects were finally inventoried.

George Kross was shot up over the Shortlands by Japanese anti-aircraft fire on a strafing run after one of the air patrols but returned unhurt. On another return flight from Cape Torokina, Thrifty Warner and his division strafed Kahili on their way to Barakoma. There were no worthwhile targets on the field, and bullets were just wasted as they swept down the field in line astern. They found a seventy-foot vessel just off the coast, and it was loaded with troops. They attacked the small lugger, and

Lloyd Cox noted that their bullets "tore them to pieces." It was a sight that would haunt him for the rest of his life. Strafing nearby antiaircraft batteries, Warner noticed more than fifteen barges tied up under camouflage along the shore. When the four Corsairs were finished, eight of the barges were sinking.

Air operations were not only dangerous to pilots but also to those working on the ground. Returning from an escort mission to Bougainville on November 7, Hal Spears and his division "pancaked" (landed) at Barakoma at 1535 in the afternoon. The first three planes landed without incident, but Jake Knight had a brake problem. His left brake went out, and the plane ground looped. His left wing struck a nearby truck and killed SSgt. Axel Larsen of VMF-222.

On November 11 the squadron was given an unusual assignment: protection of a carrier task force. The carriers' own fighters were escorting air strikes on Rabaul and the land-based Corsairs protected the fleet in the absence of their own fighters. The twelve Corsairs of Owens's, B. K. Shaw's, and Hal Spears's divisions provided cover for the carriers in the morning, just missing a massive Japanese attack on the task force around 1400.

That same day, Dick Newhall left for Guadalcanal with a severe skin infection. Pilots flew with all sorts of minor skin problems and that ever-present enemy, dysentery, but "Tripod" Newhall would not serve with VMF-215 again. Small physical infirmities could be the difference between life and death.

Despite the lack of aerial action, there was constant flying. Pilots looked for targets of opportunity and hoped to find a barge or a few planes on a Japanese airfield returning after their patrol over Torokina. After one of these combat air patrols, Dick Braun's and Hal Spears's divisions headed home via Kieta, the Japanese airdrome on the east coast of Bougainville. Spears had a severe head cold and was grounded, so "Ledge" Hazelwood, one of the Two Fourteen transfers with only six weeks to go, led his division. Passing by the airfield a lone 20mm gun opened fire on the planes. Braun turned the formation and led them in a column to take out the gun. As the planes turned, Jake Knight noticed that Hazelwood's plane banked much steeper than the others and suddenly did a sharp wingover into the sea. The remaining seven fighters tore the gun and its crew to pieces. Ledyard Hazelwood, a Princeton man who enjoyed playing acey-deucey, was declared missing in action, but the pilots who saw his crash knew he didn't survive.

INTERIM

When not playing cards or writing letters, there was little to do in the way of recreation. Special Services provided odds and ends of sports equipment, but the pilots made their own fun. Like most young Americans, these college-age men enjoyed competition, and if they could get a volleyball game going, it could be a fierce contest. Often they were provided with athletic shoes to wear instead of their boondockers, and this always led to a reference back to an incident involving Ray Wolff back on Guadalcanal. The pair of shoes provided to "The Kid" Wolff was so small that he spent much of a volleyball game hopping around. Reinhardt Leu laughed and said it looked like some Indian dancing at a powwow and the nickname "Chief" stuck, not to Wolff but to Leu!

On this second tour, the Marines were adept at begging, borrowing, or stealing anything they could use to have fun. Those not engaged in competition, like Bob Hanson who played a mean hand of bridge, were involved in more relaxing activities. Swimming required no special clothing and the ocean was always close by. More daring pilots, like Hanson and his wingman Sam Sampler, enjoyed diving into the more treacherous, deeper waters in search of exotic seashells. Sampler often found himself anxiously watching as Hanson went under the wrecks of Japanese barges that might swing with the tide and crush the adventurous former wrestler.

During one Japanese raid, Ken DuVal was stung by a scorpion. When the all clear sounded, some of the Marines noticed DuVal in obvious agony. In the darkness it appeared as if DuVal had been wounded by a bomb fragment. Doc Neber was called, and he made the correct diagnosis and provided the best antidote. DuVal was back in the air a few days later.

George Sanders managed to wrangle a ride on an LCVP to Boga Island, where a Japanese plane had wrecked. He invited "Spud" Chandler, Hanson, Sampler, and several of his old friends from Two Twenty Two to join him. The small party of flyers returned later that afternoon in jaunty spirits with brass binoculars, compasses, parts of a Japanese sailor's uniform, and a gruesome, blackened skull.

Despite the knowledge that "he could pick me up and put me down with one hand," Roger Conant was not adverse to tangling with Hanson. It was quite a sight, the 200-pound former wrestling champ of northern India being accosted by the 145-pound former collegiate grappler. The two were opposites, Hanson grinning with a huge, honest smile while Conant was grimly serious, unable to bring the bigger man down. There were also unwelcome contests that found Hanson seeking out his diminutive friend, who would run and hide if possible. The contest between the two always was a sight to see, and both the participants enjoyed, Conant reluctantly, it as much as the onlookers but the outcome was invariably the same.

Doc Neber described a poker game that seemed strangely familiar: "The identical same game with same participants was being played and this time I caught 4 10s. The betting went along the same—3 raises, table stakes, pot limit, and when I was doing most of the raising Aldrich sadly remarked that it reminded him of a previous game and that it had never better happen again. When over and hands turned over Aldrich stated—'You had to have cheated!' He rapidly apologized and the game stopped as far as he was concerned for quite awhile. Naturally, I was surprised as he having had 2 4s of a kind. He finally got over his 'mad on' & went back to winning his small amounts. I must admit these hands feathered my nest quite well and, being rather adept with a needle calmly stitched a faintly longer seam into the lining of my green Navy jacket for future use in Australia!"

NO CONTACT

On November 17, Fighter Control vectored seven Corsairs under Dick Braun to a burning ship. They were to search for the divebombers that had struck the vessel. The courses that they followed sent them scurrying around the sky, but there was no sign of the enemy. After a few more minutes circling Empress Augusta Bay, it was time to go home. As the F4Us banked into their turns to the south, "Chief" Leu spotted two *Val* divebombers pulling out of their dives after attacking Allied shipping. Leu and his wingman, Al Snyder, had no trouble catching the obsolete old bombers with their fixed landing gear. Leu fired a quick burst, but his target slipped out of his sights. Moving in closer, he pressed the trigger again but nothing happened! His guns were jammed, and he quickly recharged them but it was too late. The stubby old divebombers escaped into nearby clouds.

Snyder became separated as they entered the clouds. Heading home, Snyder heard a call over the radio indicating *Zekes* were strafing the beachhead. Throttle forward, Snyder headed back to Cape Torokina just in time to see four *Zekes* at high speed to the north. Snyder poured on the coals and attempted to catch the little enemy fighters even though they had a good head start. The F4U slowly closed the distance, and the jungle of Bougainville swept by at a tremendous speed. Looking down, Snyder was dismayed to see he was nearing Buka on the northern coast of Bougainville. He wouldn't have enough fuel to return to Barakoma! He would be lucky if he could make it to Torokina.

Nearing Laruma Point just north of Empress Augusta Bay, he decided to make a water landing. Trimming the aircraft, he jettisoned the hood and made a perfect landing. Removing his harness, he tossed out his life raft, and plunged into the rubber boat. A boat quickly rescued him, and a PBY flew him back to Vella Lavella the next day.

AUSTRALIA, AGAIN!

The rest of November passed with continued Torokina patrols. Larry Smith returned on the 20th after recovering from his appendicitis. A week after he returned, the pilots boarded a SCAT transport and flew to Guadalcanal in preparation for the squadron's second trip to Sydney. From the 'Canal they flew to Efate in the New Hebrides to store their gear and ready for the return to Australia. The wait seemed long, just a few days, but Doc Neber managed to stay out of trouble to make sure there was no repeat of his ruined first liberty. His money belt was crammed full of poker winnings, and he managed to wrangle a few extra days in Sydney. He would not rejoin the squadron until the first week in January of 1944. The second liberty trip was even better than the first, as

Awards photo at Vella Lavella, November 20, 1943. Left to right: 1st Lt. Robert E. Clark reading the citations, Major Robert G. Owens, Jr., Major James L. Neefus, Lt. Col. Herbert H. Williamson, 1st Lt. Lincoln Deetz (Gold Star), 1st Lt. Bennie P. O'Dell (Air Medal), 1st Lt. David Moak (Air Medal), Capt. Don Aldrich (Purple Heart), 1st Lt. Drury McCall (Air Medal), 1st Lt. Robert M. Hanson (Air Medal) bandaged after suffering a burn on landing, 1st Lt. Thomas M. Tomlinson (Air Medal), 1st Lt. Otto K. Williams (Air Medal), and 1st Lt. Grafton S. Stidger (Purple Heart). USMC Photo

most of the men had names and addresses they had gathered on the first go-round or they had names and addresses from other pilots of other squadrons. The new men stuck close to the veterans, and they learned the ropes easily. All agreed that Sydney was "delightful"!

When the men of Two Fifteen returned from Sydney, with Roger Conant and Larry Smith in fancy leather walking shorts, there would be another reorganization. Herb Williamson moved on to a staff position; he had proved competent enough but never really connected with his pilots. The men who had flown two tours with Two Fourteen were gone, going home. B. K. Shaw moved up to Air Group Staff, joining Two Fifteen's mentor, Jim Neefus. Enterprising Ken DuVal was also gone to a non-flying billet. Intelligence officer Robert Clark left, to be replaced by Lt. James Tyler. Among the new faces was another Williams, Gerard Maurice Haralson Williams, born in Nice, France. Another was Patrick Gildo Santin, intent on surviving the war to become a priest. These new faces were absorbed into the ranks with little trouble, for the intense training that began immediately broke down any social or cultural barriers. The new pilots were fortunate to join Two Fifteen. They were flying with a veteran squadron led by capable men. They would need that, for the squadron was about to join in a ferocious and dangerous battle for the biggest prize in the South Pacific: Rabaul.

CHAPTER TEN

First Shot at Rabaul

*Rabaul was really something, there was only one way to think of that
target. Rabaul would really shake you up whenever you went up there
to try your luck. It was rugged, real rugged. Those Japanese were some
damn fine flying people.*

—B-26 PILOT JOHN EWBANK

VMF-215 January 1944
Commanding Officer: Maj. Robert G. Owens
Executive Officer: Capt. Arthur T. Warner

First Division	Second Division
Maj. Robert G. Owens	Capt. Arthur T. Warner
Capt. Ralph E. Robinson	1st Lt. Lloyd E. Cox
Capt. Ray K. Wolff	1st Lt. Robert M. Hanson
1st Lt. Richard W. Evans	1st Lt. Samuel M. Sampler
2nd Lt. Patrick G. Santin	2nd Lt. John J. Fitzgerald
Third Division	Fourth Division
Capt. Donald N. Aldrich	Capt. Richard L. Braun
Capt. John W. Breneman	Capt. Thomas D. Stockwell
Capt. Larry M. Smith	1st Lt. George P. Sanders
1st Lt. John K. Burke	1st Lt. Alan J. Snyder
2nd Lt. John J. Knight	2nd Lt. George L. Gilman

Fifth Division
Capt. Harold L. Spears
1st Lt. Ovis D. Hunter
1st Lt. Edwin J. Hernan
1st Lt. Creighton Chandler
2nd Lt. G. M. H. Williams
Seventh Division
Capt. Roger A. Conant
Capt. Grafton S. Stidger
1st Lt. John J. Knight
1st Lt. Raymond Wetzel
2nd Lt. Richard V. Bowman
2nd Lt. Earl N. Moore

Sixth Division
Capt. Harold A. Langstaff
Capt. Reinhardt Leu
1st Lt. George W. Brewer
2nd Lt. George Kross
2nd Lt. Richard K. Samuelson

Flight Surgeon: Lt. Ernest J. Neber,
USNR
Intelligence Officer: 1st Lt. James E.
Tyler

FORTRESS RABAUL

The pilots of VMF-215 returned to Barakoma on January 6, 1944. It was a new year and a new war, focused on the reduction of Rabaul on the northeastern tip of New Britain Island. For the pilots eager for action, the war would prove more active than they bargained for. The Japanese fighters would be both plentiful and aggressive.

Rabaul was the principal objective of Allied efforts in the South Pacific. Before the war it was a small town of about three hundred structures with ten thousand people, mostly natives and Chinese. Captured in February of 1942, by 1943 it was surrounded by over 260 antiaircraft guns, protected by two divisions of infantry, and its harbor was capable of handling at least 20 twenty-thousand-ton warships at a time. It stood as one of the greatest bastions of Japanese power outside the home islands. It was spoken of in almost reverent tones in the various Allied headquarters, and comparisons with the British bastion of Gibraltar crept into conversations about the airfields and harbor nestled in a rugged country of jungle and mountains. Rabaul was also in perfect position to threaten any Allied moves in the South Pacific, situated only 525 miles from Guadalcanal, 445 miles from Port Moresby on New Guinea, and about seven hundred miles from the main Japanese fleet base at Truk in the Caroline Islands.

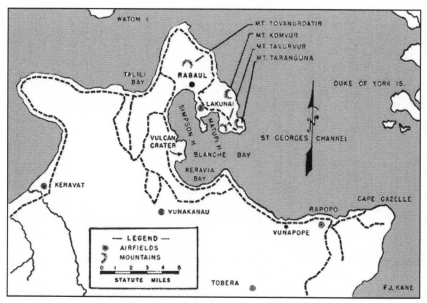

Map of Rabaul and its fields. From Wesley Frank Craven and James Lea Cate, *U.S. Army Air Forces in World War Two, Volume IV: The Pacific: Guadalcanal to Saipan, August 1942 to July 1944*, Office of Air Force History, Air Historical Group, USAF Historical Division, Chicago, University of Chicago Press,1948–1958, 313.

Originally the Allies had intended to capture the Japanese base, but by the summer of 1943 Allied leaders had decided that a ground attack on Rabaul would be difficult and costly. Rabaul would be isolated and allowed to wither. A landing would be made on New Britain's less defended southwestern tip, opposite Rabaul, on Cape Gloucester. On December 26, Marines landed at the cape and took the Japanese airfields there. The air attacks by the Allies from New Guinea and the Solomons, as well as periodic carrier air strikes, would neutralize Rabaul without ever having to actually occupy the fortress.

The town of Rabaul was on the plantation-strewn Gazelle Peninsula that covered the northeastern fifth of New Britain. Simpson Harbor, where most visiting vessels docked, lay next to Rabaul Town as part of larger Blanche Bay. Two other inlets in Blanche Bay, Karavia Bay and Matopi Harbor, allowed space for smaller vessels to tie up. Several volcano craters and a family of mountains, Mother, North Daughter, and South Daughter, formed a half circle around the settlement to give an amphitheater effect. It was not the town but the airfields nearby that gave it importance.

After the small Australian garrison was forced out in the first month of the war, the Japanese moved quickly to improve the existing port facilities and the adjacent airfields to support further Imperial expansion to the south. By early 1944, there were five operating airstrips in and around Rabaul.

A former Royal Australian Air Force field, Lakunai sat between the southeast end of Rabaul Town and Rabalankia Crater. It was also known as Rabaul East and served primarily as a fighter strip. Another former RAAF field, Vunakanau was situated in kunai grass and brush about eleven miles southwest of Rabaul Town. This airfield was the largest of the Rabaul airfields. Its aircraft revetments, dispersal areas, shops, and taxiways covered well over two square miles.

At Rapopo was the longest of the Japanese runways, a bomber field running north to south approximately six thousand feet. This field was located about fourteen miles southwest of Rabaul Town and five miles west of Cape Gazelle. This large field, like most of Rabaul's fields, made use of the evenly spaced coconut trees of plantations to hide its staging areas and revetments. Tobera was another of those strips carved from a plantation. It was the farthest to the south, lying southeast of Vunakanau and southwest of Rapopo.

The last of the airfields around Rabaul was located at Keravat on the western coast of New Britain, twenty-six miles southwest of Rabaul Town. Because of nature and engineering problems, the Japanese were never able to use this field for anything more than emergencies or temporary staging. In all, the fields, run-up areas, and revetments were capable of supporting hundreds of planes. At times the Japanese had over three hundred aircraft stationed there or transiting through to other areas.

Japanese shipping was driven out fairly easily; most of the large naval units left after fierce raids by aircraft carriers and the Fifth Air Force out of New Guinea. Getting rid of the Japanese air units proved a bit more difficult. Despite raids by the Fifth Air Force, air strikes from the carriers, and the campaign of Allied bombers from the Solomons in late 1943 and into 1944, the Japanese would always maintain over one hundred airplanes on their airfields.

The principal Japanese aviation unit at Rabaul was the Navy's 11th Air Flotilla. Since August of 1942, these Japanese aviators had been fighting the Allied advance up the Solomons and now faced daily raids by the Allies designed to destroy any offensive power, aerial or naval, that Rabaul might have. Occasionally additional navy planes from aircraft carrier squadrons would reinforce Rabaul. In addition to the navy's planes, the Japanese army frequently contributed their planes to the effort to defend the Japanese Greater East Asia Co-Prosperity Sphere in the Solomons. Some of the greatest Japanese fighter aces were stationed at Rabaul at one time or another. Men like Saburo Sakai, Tetsuzo Iwamoto, and many of Japan's prewar veterans flew out of Rabaul.

ACES

The campaigns in the South Pacific had revived a romantic notion surrounding those pilots who were particularly adept at shooting down their opponents in aerial combat. Since World War I, the first major war involving airplanes, flyers were judged on how well they killed other flyers. Tallies of aerial "kills" were measures of the effectiveness of a pilot in combat. During the Great War a mystique grew concerning those famous aviators. The famous Red Baron and his Flying Circus, Billy Bishop of Canada, Georges Guynemer of France, "Mad" Mick Mannock of Britain, and Eddie Rickenbacker of the United States were legendary characters who were called "aces" in reference to downing five planes in air-to-air combat. The custom continued in the Second World War.

In the battles over Guadalcanal, several Marines had shot down great numbers of Japanese planes. Media attention highlighted their actions as a way to energize public support back home. Marine Capt. Joe Foss shot down a total of twenty-six enemy planes before returning to the United States in March of 1943. This matched the highest score of World War I's Eddie Rickenbacker. Foss's picture appeared on the cover of *Life* magazine. Newspapers and radios focused on his score, and every fighter pilot in the US armed forces wanted to beat that number. When Two

Fifteen arrived back in action at the beginning of 1944, Maj. Gregory Boyington of VMF-214 was chasing that score. He claimed nineteen Japanese with 214 and six more as a Flying Tiger before the US entry into the war.

Pappy Boyington was shot down and reported missing in action on January 3, 1944, and his fellow pilots reported that he had downed one more plane on his final mission for a total of twenty, or twenty-six if he included his claims with the Flying Tigers. (After the war, Boyington claimed *three* enemy victims on that last flight, giving him a Marine total of twenty-two. Adding in his six claims as a Flying Tiger, his total would be twenty-eight.) Instead of instilling caution in the young fighter pilots, as both Boyington and his wingman were shot down on that final mission, the loss of the highest scorer in the theater only encouraged competition. Many Marines wanted to break that magic score of twenty-six aerial victories. Most senior leaders tried to downplay the individual scores, because too much attention to the number of kills seemed to lead to an unhealthy individual attitude toward battle with the more maneuverable *Zekes*. In most cases the advice fell on deaf ears. Boyington's loss did not instill any caution in young, aggressive pilots like Hal Spears and Bob Hanson. The eager young pilots were not deterred by the threat of being shot down, as the chances for rescue were good. Some of the Corps' best flyers—Marion Carl, Jefferson LeBlanc, Jimmy Swett, Bob Galer, and Ken Walsh—had been shot down and later returned to duty. Bob Hanson and Al Snyder had each survived a water landing and returned to duty. Perhaps even Pappy Boyington might return.

RETURN OF VMF-215

VMF-215 joined the campaign against Rabaul with a new command structure. Tough, honest Bob Owens finally assumed the command he had been training for since the first days at Goleta. He had shown that he could get the most from those under him and he would continue to do so. The new executive officer was Thrifty Warner. The two Marines were close friends and made an excellent team that evoked confidence in the men they commanded. Owens found that many of his pilots were affected by the scoring contest epitomized by Boyington. The "Big O" wanted his men to fly as a team and feared that those wanting to get big scores would lose sight of all the tactics they had worked on up to this time. He worried that individual, selfish tactics would get pilots killed. But it was difficult to fight all the publicity surrounding the aces, and the pilots talked openly of getting *Zekes* and running up scores. Don Aldrich and Bob Hanson had each downed five Japanese and attained the status of ace, making it even more difficult for Owens and Warner to emphasize section and division tactics.

On January 6, the squadron received a briefing on their new area of operations, with New Britain and New Ireland covered in depth. New Ireland is a long, mountainous, and jungle-covered island that shielded Rabaul's northeastern approaches. The Japanese had observers on the island as well as a naval base and air station at Kavieng on its northern tip. At the southern end of the island was a radar station located near an old lighthouse at Cape St. George. The pilots were issued new strip maps to cover the Bougainville-Rabaul area, and there was a quick session on escort tactics in use at the time. The raids on Rabaul and its environs were larger than the missions they had been running in the lower Solomons. The next morning would be their first go at the enemy at Rabaul.

First Mission Over Rabaul

At 0600, Major Owens led three divisions to provide high cover for an SBD strike on the Rabaul area. This day would set the pattern for the rest of their missions against the Japanese fortress. The squadron sent planes as part of the strike escort as well as scramble alerts at both their home field of Barakoma and the new field near Torokina Point on Bougainville, codenamed Piva Yoke. Owens took his division and those of Don Aldrich and Dick Braun. Hap Langstaff's division covered Torokina, and Hal Spears sat strip alert at Barakoma with Sammy Stidger. The assignments for the next month would vary little. The divisions rotated missions, and the members of each division shared the various assignments. The number of aircraft available dictated how many pilots flew, no one had personal aircraft, and they flew the plane assigned to them by Don Aldrich, the operations officer. Some divisions had five pilots, forcing

VMF-215 flew cover for the invasion that captured Torokina Airfield and would operate from this airstrip, or nearby Piva Yoke, a fighter strip in their raids over Rabaul. USMC Photo

some pilots to sit out missions when their division flew. Pilots rarely flew to Rabaul without a wingman; to fly alone invited disaster.

At 0715, Owens's flight landed at Torokina. They received a mission briefing, their planes were refueled, and they ate a breakfast if they wanted it. Owens and his Corsairs took off at 0855 to join the other fighters heading north. To the men of Two Fifteen, who had become accustomed to eight or ten escorts for a few bombers attacking Kahili during their last tour, this raid was an eye-opening experience. The formation they joined included twenty-one SBDs, eighteen TBFs, more Corsairs from VMF-211, New Zealand P-40s, and several divisions of Navy Hellcats from VF-40.

Forming up north of Torokina, the pilots of Two Fifteen were introduced to the new tactical organization of the raids on Rabaul. With so many fighters available, the escorts were set up in layers with different assignments. Prior to the mission, Fighter Command assigned each squadron its position in the formation. The individual squadron would then assign as many pilots and planes to fulfill their responsibility, considering they might have assignments elsewhere. High cover was free to weave above the bombers and look for enemy planes to attack at will. Medium cover patrolled between the high cover and the bombers. Close cover had the toughest task of all, staying with the bombers throughout their run, fending off Japanese attackers, and then returning alongside the formation. Low cover took care of any Japanese attacking from below. The three lower layers were required to stay with the bombers and not stray too far in pursuit of Japanese planes.

At ten thousand feet, the Allied bombers passed New Ireland on their right and turned west to cross the New Britain coastline at Kabanga Bay. From their position as medium cover, Two Fifteen's pilots got their first look at the sinister harbor of Rabaul and its defenses. Six Japanese army *Tony* fighters dived on the bombers but only released bombs, the dark shapes exploding into showers of phosphorous at about 13,500 feet. The bombs had no effect on any of the Allied planes except to increase a few heartbeats in the aircrews. Approaching Rapopo Field, the first *Zekes* approached the bombers. About fifty in number, the Japanese looped and rolled around the formation of Allied planes. After a few minutes of wonderfully executed aerobatic maneuvers, the first attacks began. The *Zekes* came in waves of six, flying straight at the SBDs or TBFs and then pulling up at the last minute in an effort to draw off the fighter escort. The *Zekes* swooped in, then broke away as the nose of a weaving P-40, F4U, or F6F faced them.

It had been over six weeks since the last combat action for the men of the squadron. Four of them had never been in an aerial fight, yet they managed to stay in their weaves, constantly turning into their attackers. The Allied fighters fired only when a *Zeke* pulled in too close to the bombers. A single Japanese plane would swing in close and slow down, offering a lucrative target. As soon as a pair of Corsairs, Hellcats, or Kittyhawks went after the single enemy plane, six or seven *Zekes* would pounce from above. If the Allied fighters rejoined the formation, the Japanese climbed away. The antiaircraft fire was weak and inaccurate, posing no serious threat to the attackers. The divebombers and torpedo planes, acting as glide bombers in this role, made their runs relatively unmolested and headed for home. It was then that the Japanese got a break.

Dick Braun swung a little too wide in his weave, and three Japanese quickly latched onto his tail. The lanky Marine saw 20mm and 7.7mm fire streaking past his wings and instincts took over. He put the Corsair into a dive and easily outran the Japanese into a cloud before they could inflict any damage. Pulling up through the scattered clouds, Braun was surprised to find himself sitting dead astern of a Japanese plane obviously unaware of his presence. A .50-caliber bath and the *Zeke* blew up in bright flames and crashed into the sea. Braun saw his victim hit the sea, but he had no time to gloat. Three enemy planes jumped him and opened fire. Despite a few minor hits on his wings, Braun played nip and tuck in the clouds, and the Corsair gradually pulled away from its pursuers. Two of the Japanese broke off after only a few moments, but one chased him for over thirty miles south of New Britain before it gave up the chase. Relieved and a little shaken, Braun wrote in his after-action report: "I was set at 2700 rpm, with 53 inches, and 260 knots indicated and I drew away from him very slowly."

Good teamwork and flight discipline enabled Two Fifteen to return without loss. Even though Dick Braun was the only pilot to shoot down an enemy plane, the fighters had protected the bombers so well that not one *Zeke* was able to penetrate their protection and attack the SBDs and TBFs. Only Braun's plane was damaged, and the War Diary reported, "The effectiveness of the violent two plane weave cannot be overemphasized."

ROUTINE OPERATIONS

The next day, Thrifty Warner was scheduled to escort a mission with the divisions that had not flown the day before: Spears, Langstaff, Conant, and Warner's own. It was a big raid; all of the future missions would be big compared to those the previous fall, with two-dozen B-24s flying to Rabaul to hit Lakunai Airfield. Weather was terrible and it delayed takeoff from 0830 to 0930, which meant the Corsairs would not leave their stopover at Torokina until after 1130. John Fitzgerald started down the runway with the others, but his Corsair's torque got the best of him and he hit a stump. He did not make the flight. Thrifty Warner, Chief Leu, Ray Wetzel, and Hal Spears all experienced mechanical trouble and stayed behind.

Volatile Hal Spears was upset about missing out on a chance to get a crack at the Japanese after sitting on strip alert the day before. He need not have felt any disappointment as the rest of the squadron returned not long after taking off from Torokina. The bombers had just about reached the coast of New Ireland when the fighters caught up with them to escort them the rest of the way. It was at that point that the mission commander chose to call off the flight due to poor weather.

The pilots returned at 1615 that afternoon, pulling off their flight gear and heading for the squad tents they called home. Chow was the usual lackluster fare they knew so well, that ubiquitous meat Spam. After the evening meal, Bob Owens briefed the squadron on a meeting he had attended that day, a staff conference that had included praise for the efforts of Two Fifteen on its first mission to Rabaul. Owens also outlined an upcoming change in operations. VMF-215 had thirty-six pilots but rarely had more than sixteen fighters assigned to them (a Marine Corps fighter squadron was usually assigned eighteen planes in its table of organization). Owens worked out a plan with Maj. Hugh Elwood of VMF-212 to combine the strength of assigned aircraft for each mission. Each squadron would fly every other day, giving one squadron a possible number of thirty-six aircraft. Two Twelve would use all of the planes one day, Two Fifteen the next. Due to maintenance, wear and tear, and battle damage, there would only occasionally be more than thirty planes, but it did give more pilots a chance to fly with their own squadron.

The new system started on January 9, 1944. VMF-212 took all available planes north; and Two Fifteen did test hops, familiarization flights, and engine run-ups. Many of Two Fifteen's pilots had not been up to Rabaul yet, but the day was treated as a day of rest with thoughts of Rabaul and its *Zekes* put away for a few hours. Owens told those not involved in any regular duties to take the day off. Lloyd Cox was maintenance officer and had to make sure the ground crews, a hodge-podge of various units, were doing their jobs. With most of the planes in the air with Two Twelve, there was little the ordnance officer, radio officer, oxygen officer, or any of the other additional duty officers could do.

Some pilots played volleyball on a net strung between two tents. Several pilots walked to the nearby beach. Some read books or technical manuals and others caught up on their mail. Some had dozens of letters. Cox had sixty-three letters waiting for him when he returned from Sydney. Mail tended to back up as ships sailed with batches of mail and planes waited for a full load of mail before carrying it to the squadron's next stop. Some of the mail for new pilots had traveled around the South Pacific, and former members of Two Fourteen had mail forwarded from their old squadron that was several months old.

Hal Spears enjoyed kidding those members of the squadron that were married or romantically involved, joking about the 4F men back home having fun with their women. Bob Hanson, who had once been a thorn in the flesh of those receiving love letters, was not joking about those letters from home. During the last trip to Sydney, Hanson had met a very nice Australian girl and now he spent time reading her letters. Laundry was hung from a line between trees and money changed hands in quiet card games.

Their next mission proved to be a repeat of that on the 8th. The strike force turned back at Cape St. George due to poor weather. A big difference was that Two Fifteen put twenty planes in the air, more than any mission before, thanks to the sharing system worked out with Two Twelve. The following day was another day off, with only Dick Bowman flying a short familiarization hop. The pilots of Two Twelve came back with glowing reports of fierce combat, claiming to have downed nine of the enemy. Mouths watered as Two Fifteen's Marines anticipated the chance of getting a victory over Rabaul, although some pilots probably felt apprehension at the prospect of combat. They were sure the next trip north would be a tough one.

After three days of relative inaction, the luck of Two Fifteen changed with a B-24 strike against Lakunai. Because of the arrangement with Two Twelve, Owens was able to put six divisions into the air from Barakoma at 0600. Unfortunately, Sammy Stidger and Jack Knight were unable to proceed after refueling at Torokina. Knight's Corsair was damaged when he put it on its nose to avoid colliding with a Corsair from another squadron that ground looped in front of him. Stidger had engine trouble. The rest of the squadron took off at 0920. The Corsairs joined up with the

B-24s and the rest of the escort: a quartet of P-38s from the Treasurys, F6Fs from Vella Lavella, and twenty additional Corsairs from Torokina.

The Corsairs weaved to counter enemy attacks and also to keep their speed up despite staying with the slower bombers. Over New Ireland the first enemy planes appeared, dropping phosphorous bombs that Thrifty Warner called "the largest I ever saw." At this point, Dick Evans had an engine fire, unrelated to the phosphorous bombs. Forced to turn back, Evans nursed his plane back to Torokina with Bob Owens, his wingman, escorting him.

The bombers found that Lakunai was too overcast for effective bombing and dropped their loads on the taxiways and revetments of Vunakanau. Turning for home, the weaving Corsairs were confronted by forty green and brown Japanese interceptors. Flying high cover at twenty-eight thousand feet, Aldrich swung wide in his weave to allow his division a better chance to engage the approaching *Zekes*. Aldrich and his wingman, John Burke, eased behind three enemy fighters preparing to attack the bombers, who seemed unaware of the Corsairs. John Burke thought to himself how easily Aldrich had set them up for a shot. Both pilots opened fire at the same time, with the same results. Flaming wrecks, the two targets fell from the sky. The third enemy plane pulled up into the clouds. Climbing back up to rejoin the bombers, Aldrich looked about and noticed Burke was no longer with him, lost in the scattered clouds below.

John Burke's oxygen system failed at the moment he triumphed over his Japanese adversary. The Marine was forced to go down to ten thousand feet; and now alone, he decided to go home. Flying in and out of the haze, he caught sight of a single B-24 with one engine out and a pair of pesky *Zekes* pouring gunfire into the crippled plane. As Burke dived into the attack, he quickly checked his tail. He spotted two *Zekes* moving into position behind him. As 7.7mm bullets struck his Corsair with metallic snaps, Burke dived for the deck, leaving the slower *Zekes* behind. He returned to Torokina alone.

Aldrich and his remaining fighters fought off several more attacks on the bombers. One of the *Zekes* failed to turn away in time, Aldrich latched on to it, and streams of .50-caliber bullets set it afire. His division watched as the *Zeke* splashed into St. George's Channel. The three Marines returned without further incident.

The problems for the pilots were not always the Japanese fighters or, as on this day, deadly and accurate antiaircraft fire. The intense mental concentration and physical effort required to fly escort on the bombers long hours over the ocean, maintain position in the weave, and take potshots at intruding Japanese was exhausting. Just flying the airplane—monitoring prop settings, mixture, throttle, and engaging in aerobatics—took a toll on the flyers. Most were near exhaustion when they returned, bathed in sweat.

Fatigue caused pilots, especially those who were inexperienced, to make little mistakes. Roger Conant's wingman, boyish Ray Wetzel, turned a little too tight in the weave resulting in a spin. The Corsair was notoriously unstable in a spin, and Wetzel fought desperately for control as the big bird twirled through the clouds down toward the ocean. He finally broke through the clouds and regained control of his plane safely above the ocean. But his troubles were not over as he glimpsed the shape of a dark green airplane closing in on him from directly astern. Wetzel quickly pulled back up into the clouds and lost the *Zeke* before it could fire. He made it back to Torokina shaken but without further trouble.

Everyone returned safely, now blooded over Rabaul. They would rest the next day. One new pilot spoke aloud of an idea he had formulated about a single Corsair going down on the deck and strafing a Rabaul airfield. He reasoned that one Corsair flying on the deck all the way would be able to avoid spotters and radar. More experienced hands, remembering those awful days strafing Kahili, and the loss of Ray Tomes and Charles Lanphier, approached Owens and requested he tell the young pilot to knock it off before someone on the staff caught the idea. The pilots felt that Owens always had their welfare uppermost in his mind. He quietly took the eager Marine aside. He put a friendly arm around the youthful flyer and advised the enthusiastic Leatherneck that it was not a good idea to talk so loudly about his Rabaul idea. He also suggested that the pilot shelve his plan. The incident was not easily forgotten, and the rest of the squadron enjoyed chiding the young man for days afterward.

Jack Knight returned from Torokina by TBF that same afternoon. His Corsair remained on Bougainville to get a new propeller and engine. Owens learned from Knight that Sammy Stidger was still trying to get his F4U in the air to fly back to Barakoma. Unfortunately, every time the mechanics thought it was fixed, a test flight proved them wrong. Twice he attempted the flight to Vella Lavella but was forced each time to return to Torokina. Finally he decided to wait until the next mission arrived at Torokina and then join them as they went on to Rabaul.

CHAPTER ELEVEN

Just Another Mission

Always carry through an attack when you have started it. Fire only
at close range and only when your opponent is properly in your sights.
— OSWALD BOELCKE

JANUARY 14, 1944, WAS AN OCCASIONALLY HAZY, YET SUNNY, DAY AT THE
port of Rabaul. Due to cumulus conditions and the intermittent haze, visibility was zero at times along the day's route from Torokina to the target
at Lakunai. The Corsairs of VMF-215 were providing escort for a strike
of eighteen TBF Avengers out of Munda loaded with five-hundred-
pound bombs. After a predawn takeoff from Barakoma, the twenty-four
Corsairs landed at Torokina at 0715 for their last-minute briefing and
a bit of breakfast. The first problem of the day happened at this time,
when unlucky John Fitzgerald continued an individual string of bad
fortune through no fault of his own. A New Zealander who was also to
accompany the strike landed, lost control of his Kittyhawk, and crashed
into Fitzgerald's waiting Corsair. The noise of the collision turned heads
all around the runway, but Fitzgerald could only stand helplessly and
watch as the tail section of his plane was demolished. The Kiwi pilot was
unhurt.

Sammy Stidger, his plane repaired and ready to go, would take Fitzgerald's spot in Warner's division. Planes fueled, the pilots filed out to
the flight line slowly with their seat-pack parachutes awkwardly banging
against their buttocks. Some were dressed in their khakis while others

wore dungarees. Despite publicity shots of them in shorts, the pilots wore long trousers to cover themselves in case of fire. All carried .38-caliber or .45-caliber pistols, and many had Marine Corps issue KABAR knives. Bob Hanson wore a camouflage jacket he had traded for with some mud Marines as the flyers referred to the infantry and other ground troops. The aviators made flippant comments to each other as they made a last minute preflight check on their birds. The barely blue Corsairs appeared as submissive medieval chargers awaiting their twentieth-century knights. Roger Conant climbed up the right side of Corsair #590 and lowered himself over the cockpit sill. Even with his parachute and flight gear, he was amazed at how spacious the cockpit seemed. Not far away, George Sanders and Jack Knight traded last-minute thoughts as they proceeded out to their mounts. Having just devoured his usual light meal of fruit and salad, Bob Hanson fairly leaped into the cockpit. He felt that a more substantial meal made him sit too heavy and uncomfortable in the seat. He tried to get lighter fare when available. After months of rarely having enough planes for the squadron, it did Bob Owens's heart good to see so many airplanes with Two Fifteen pilots ready to get into the air at one time.

After checking harnesses and straps, the pilots started the big Pratt and Whitney engines. All of the senses were pleasantly engaged by the familiar preparations for flight. The mixture of smells from oil, fuel, and hydraulic fluids filled the nostrils of pilots as they settled in. The static of the radio was nearly drowned out by the pleasant roar of 2,000-horsepower engines. Dozens of aircraft could be seen queuing up in preparation for their turn to take off. The dull green Kittyhawks of the New Zealanders and the various shades of blue of the American aircraft were nearly hidden by clouds of smoke and dust. Propeller blades danced back and forth, moving around in one direction but appearing to reverse direction or even remain stationary as the pilots did their preflight checks. Mouths were dry in anticipation of the mission, and gritty dust coated the lips of the pilots in their open cockpits. Gloved hands trembled as the vibrations of the engines were passed through the control columns and throttle quadrants.

The Corsairs waddled out by section in their distinctive bent-wing gait and turned to take off. The thundering noise of the Corsairs' engines mixed with the Allison engines of the P-40s and Wright Cyclones of the Avengers in a loud cacophony announcing their departure. Planes rolled down the runway, canopies open to the engine sounds and the screaming wind. Picking up speed, pilots kept the stick back and the tail wheel down until the rudder took to the wind. Slowly, they let the tail wheel leave the ground and lifted off the runway as speed reached about 90 knots. Speed increased as the gnarled jungle passed behind them and they reached the coast. Gear up, drag decreased and canopies slipped forward, leaving the pilots alone in a sky full of airplanes.

One by one, the Fighting Corsairs began to form up over the water with the other squadrons. Sammy Stidger reported his engine was again giving him problems and he was returning to Torokina. The Corsair "mushed" as it approached the airfield, low on the water. Members of Two Fifteen's ground echelon, servicing all units at Torokina, thought that Stidger was attempting a water landing. Instead they watched, as did Al Snyder and other pilots awaiting takeoff, as Stidger's Corsair hit a log on the edge of the runway and crashed in flames. An original member of the squadron at Goleta, Stidger was a favorite with all members of the squadron, new and old. Capt. Grafton S. Stidger of West Virginia, the only man Bob Owens considered completely without fear, died in a mass of flames on the stinking island of Bougainville.

Adding to the heart-wrenching loss of Stidger, a less fatal engine problem kept Larry Smith from continuing from Torokina. The builders of those engines had not intended them to be used daily and hammered with coral dust and sea water without proper maintenance.

Just north of Bougainville, the fighters and bombers sorted themselves out in the formation that would attack Lakunai. Despite the apparent orderliness, sometimes the formations appeared disorganized due to one or more squadrons not maintaining their position. Roger Conant sarcastically termed a Marine Corps formation as "anytime the airplanes are heading in the same direction." There was organization to this group of planes. Owens and Dick Braun were with their divisions at high cover at eighteen thousand feet, Thrifty Warner's and Roger Conant's planes were at sixteen thousand as medium cover, and Don Aldrich and Hap Langstaff were flying low cover. The New Zealanders flew close cover on the Avengers at thirteen thousand feet. The entire formation was just a few minutes behind a similar formation of SBDs and their escorts.

After crossing East Cape on New Ireland, several *Zekes* appeared at nine o'clock, flying above twenty thousand feet. The Imperial Eagles slowly circled the Allied planes, adding constantly to their numbers and performing impressive aerobatics. Though a mystery to the Allied flyers at the time, it was learned later that many Japanese pilots removed their radios, unreliable for the most part anyway, to conserve weight. The aerobatics were often used to pass signals between leaders and their sections, as well as organize for different kinds of attacks.

By the time the bombers were off the coast of New Britain, they were facing about seventy Japanese interceptors. The *Zekes* were no longer content with mere aerobatics, and some of them streaked in to pelt the bombers with machine-gun and cannon fire before breaking away. Just as the Japanese were unable to get in a good shot before the Allied pilots turned into them, the Kittyhawk and Corsair pilots were frustrated by these harassing tactics. The darting and diving Japanese avoided attacking the mass of the formation and concentrated on stragglers or tail end aircraft. The Japanese climbed away when faced by massed gunners or the nose of a fighter aiming at them. Crossing the coastline, the bomber leader decided Lakunai was too obscured and ordered the bombers to bomb the few unfortunate vessels caught in Simpson Harbor. Each fighter division faced the enemy independently and, eventually, as sections and individuals.

OWENS'S DIVISION

The Avengers went into their shallow dives, and the escorts lost altitude with them. Bob Owens, flying top cover, noted with pride the way that the fighters clung around the bombers. Slashing attacks were met by weaving fighters, and the *Zekes* zoomed up and away to avoid confronting the Marines. One enemy plane tried to get into the sprawling formation but pulled up too late, presenting "O" with an easy target. Owens fired a long burst, and the *Zeke* blew up in dazzling flames, and blazing pieces of wreckage crashed into the shoreline of Simpson Harbor. Several pilots confirmed the kill later when they returned to Torokina. Owens took this moment to size up the situation, counting ten planes from both sides going down as the bombers finished their bomb runs.

Ralph Robinson, a new captain who had joined the squadron at the start of the third tour, was the second section leader in Owens's division. At the same time Owens was knocking down his target, another *Zeke* tried to slip in behind Owens. Robinson's guns hammered the plane's cockpit, and the fighter flew away erratically, as though the pilot was injured. Rejoining his division, Robinson encountered a second *Zeke* on its back, looping to avoid the turret guns of the Avengers. He fired a short burst that set the enemy plane afire.

A swarm of ten *Zekes* stalked the bombers after they made their break for home. Robinson picked one of them out as it closed in on the Avengers, making a head-on run. His guns struck the enemy fighter repeatedly, but he was frustrated when the little fighter refused to burn. He continued to fire and his effort finally bore deadly fruit. Robinson passed the *Zeke* and took a quick glance. He saw the enemy plane on its back, out of control, and going into the drink.

Dick Evans, Robinson's wingman, faced another *Zeke* head on. He fired until the two fighters nearly collided. The Japanese plane seemed to be smoking, but there was no time for Evans to note the results of the battle as the two planes passed at a closing speed of over seven hundred miles per hour.

Out to the rally point, Owens, Robinson, Evans, and Ray Wolff continued firing quick bursts at intruding Japanese. After the bomb run, low on the water, Evans had a quick look at the targets of the TBFs and counted twelve small coastal craft destroyed and pieces of debris scattered on the surface of the harbor.

DICK BRAUN'S DIVISION

George Sanders was weaving with Jack Knight over the harbor when he noticed his wingman moving away from him. Sliding over to follow, the last Sanders saw of big, jolly Jack Knight was his Corsair drifting into a cloud over Duke of York Island. He was not seen by the pilots of Two Fifteen again.

Sanders joined the rest of his division, Dick Braun and Earl Moore, about five miles from the New Britain coastline. A *Zeke* swooped in and tailed Moore, firing both machine guns and cannon. In attacking Moore, the *Zeke* placed itself directly in front of Sanders, who immediately opened fire. The *Zeke* sprouted flames and fell off on a wing, headed for the sea. Unfortunately, it was all too late for Earl N. Moore. His Corsair burned at the base of the bent wings, and the F4U went into the sea without a sign of a parachute.

Dick Braun saw Sanders's target *Zeke* go in, and he also saw Moore crash. His two Corsairs followed the Avengers into their dives and pulled out over Simpson Harbor. A *Zeke* tried to attack the retiring TBFs but in doing so swept across the front of Braun's F4U. Dick Braun, steady despite the action around him, easily positioned himself for a stern shot and opened fire on the unsuspecting Japanese plane. A small flame appeared, and the *Zeke* slowly lowered its nose and crashed into the water.

THRIFTY WARNER'S DIVISION

Thrifty Warner's division broke while weaving through the clouds. Lloyd Cox, Okie Bowman, and Bob Hanson seemed to disappear, leaving Warner alone at the extreme tail end of the bomber formation. From his vantage point, Warner saw various Japanese attacks and several *Zekes* dropping phosphorous bombs that failed to hit anyone. He could see the formation as a giant telescope, the bombers and escorts at the front, slowly thinning out through various combats and stragglers until it reached his single Corsair at the end. It was a lonely spot.

Warner passed over Rapopo Airfield and spotted a *Zeke* moving in for a high side run on a group of TBFs. The Japanese pilot fired, and the Avengers gamely returned the fire from their turret guns. Pulling up, the *Zeke* pilot reversed course to attack again but found himself facing Warner. The Marine was quicker to the draw and fired a long burst that shattered the engine of the Japanese plane. Flames sprang from the black cowling as the *Zeke* flashed by.

Witty and quick thinking, Arthur Warner was nicknamed "Thrifty" because of his background as a salesman. He was given credit for eight enemy aircraft destroyed. USMC Photo

Climbing, Warner attacked another *Zeke* encroaching on the bombers' formation and set it afire. This time he was able to see the flaming wreck, wrapped in smoke, hit the water. Other Japanese planes broke off their attacks as soon as they spotted Warner's Corsair.

The bombers made a wide turn and headed for home, slowing just enough that Warner's Corsair passed over them in his turn. A *Zeke* dived toward the bombers but zoomed high when the Corsair turned into its path. Next to attract his attention was a *Zeke* trailing the formation below the Avengers. The enemy pilot had target fixation, too intent on the TBFs to see Warner move into position on his tail. Warner fired a couple of long bursts, and the *Zeke* crashed just east of Cape Gazelle. At the rally point, a Corsair swept by, pursued by a lone *Zeke*. After the two planes passed overhead, less than two hundred feet away, Warner banked around and fell in behind. Firing a single burst, the Mitsubishi showed flames and was last seen heading for the water.

Lloyd Cox tried to follow a *Zeke* that zipped past him and climbed away. Too steep for the Corsair to follow, Cox was forced to level off to keep from stalling. The *Zeke* did a quick wingover and latched onto the Corsair's tail. The Japanese fighter began firing when in range, and as Cox slipped and skidded to avoid the fire, he thought, "He's got me bore sighted!" Cox put his big fighter into a dive hoping to strip away his pursuer in the layers of clouds stretched out below. The Corsair gained speed rapidly, and Cox felt relief as the trailing enemy plane proved unable to catch him. The last he saw of the *Zeke* it was being attacked by a New Zealand P-40. Cox joined the retreating TBFs and formed up with several F6Fs at the rally point.

Cox lost the F6Fs when they chose to go through a cloud and he went above it. Cox felt lonely, even though everywhere he looked there were airplanes. A single F4U flew by, and Cox joined on its wing. A *Zeke* looped up and rolled level into an attack on the other Corsair. Cox fired a few rounds, and the enemy pilot responded with a dive to the right. Cox followed and opened fire from long range. The little fighter burst into flames; it fluttered like a falling leaf through the dozens of combatants. Cox watched it fall but lost it just before it hit the water.

The Corsair that Cox had rescued, the number 92 on the fuselage indicated it was from VMF-211, joined on his wing and the two set course for Torokina. The number of Japanese aircraft diminished as they left the rally point but occasionally a Japanese plane would attempt one last assault. Two *Zekes* attacked a Corsair below Cox and his new wingman, prompting a diving attack by the pair of F4Us. Cox fired at the nearer of the enemy planes, and it flipped on its back to dive away. The other Japanese plane disappeared as the two Corsairs continued for home. Cox thought that the *Zeke* he shot at pulled out at about twelve hundred feet, but a report from VMF-211 after landing stated that the frantic Japanese was unable to clear the hard surface of St. George's Channel.

Hanson and Bowman stayed with a single TBF as it made its bomb run. Unlike divebombers like the SBD Dauntless, TBF Avengers were built to drop torpedoes in level runs a few feet off the deck. The Avengers made shallow dives that the Corsairs could easily follow.

The trio of planes, two Corsairs and the Avenger, pulled up at two thousand feet and headed for the rally point, avoiding the heavy antiaircraft fire at lower levels. Approaching the rally point, they encountered a giant dogfight of SBDs and Corsairs hounded by scores of Japanese. The lower altitudes were swarming with *Zekes*, and Hanson calmly noted that they all seemed to be cruising at less than 180 knots. Using a cloud for cover, Hanson and Bowman maneuvered toward the Dauntlesses under attack, picking out a pair of *Zekes* strolling along at fifteen hundred feet. Sneaking up, if that is possible in an airplane weighing over six tons, thirty-three feet long, and having a wingspan of forty-one feet, the pair of Marines moved into an excellent firing position before the two Imperial Eagles realized the danger. The first the Japanese knew of the Corsairs' presence was when .50-caliber rounds struck their airplanes. Hanson's target erupted into flames and headed for the water, pieces of flaming metal and debris trailing as the *Zeke* took its last plunge. The Mitsubishi that Bowman attacked proved more difficult, absorbing scores of bullets before making it into a cloud. Bowman went into the cloud to follow, while Hanson stayed out of the cloud to try to get the Japanese aircraft when it exited. The *Zeke* did leave the cloud, in flames and headed for the earth, indicating a successful attack by Bowman.

Two more *Zekes* appeared out of the cloud, and Hanson fired at them from six o'clock. The *Zekes* broke, as one went up and away while the other mistakenly tried to outdive the Corsair. The U-bird easily followed, and the *Zeke* finally had to pull up at three hundred feet with Hanson right behind him. The two planes had built up speed in the dive, and the *Zeke*'s great maneuverability was no good at such velocities. Stick forces kept the *Zeke* from out-turning the Corsair, and fire from Hanson's guns blew the sluggish Japanese plane into little pieces.

Using clouds for cover, Hanson regained altitude and used the height to jump two *Zekes*. The Japanese turned the tables on Hanson and pulled up into the same clouds that Hanson had used to hide. Using the sparse clouds for cover, he spiraled up past three thousand feet, his head on a swivel looking for the pair of enemy aircraft.

His eyes were attracted to two shapes below him at about twenty-five hundred feet. A couple of enemy planes were turning away from him along the edge of wispy clouds. Hanson opened fire on one of the *Zekes* and set it aflame. Before the other *Zeke* pilot could react, his Corsair zoomed up and away. The burning *Zeke* fell away in a dive toward the sea.

Hanson continued climbing and turned away from Rabaul. A single Japanese fighter approaching the rally point drew his attention. It was flying just above him, and he noted the light gray belly stood out against the blue sky. Pulling the nose of his Corsair up ever so slightly, he let go with his six .50-caliber machine guns, and the *Zeke* showed flames along the fuselage. The Japanese plane fell off toward the sea, flames licking at the metal skin, inspiring Hanson to note in his after-action report: "I think that's the best way to shoot them: from astern and below—the belly seems to be the most vulnerable point." Marine pilots were learning that to their six heavy machine guns, all parts of the lighter Japanese fighters were vulnerable.

Several more *Zekes* slid through Hanson's Mark 8 gun sight, but they quickly zoomed up away from him. He turned toward Rabaul to see if he could find any action over Lakunai or Vunakanau. He caught one Japanese plane returning to base. The pilot was flying straight and level, probably thinking that the Allied planes were gone and the danger had passed. Unfortunately for that pilot, Hanson pounced from three thousand feet above and opened fire. It took only a few seconds until flames appeared at the wing roots, and the *Zeke* plummeted toward the ocean.

Crossing over New Ireland, two *Zekes* moved in to cut him off. Low on fuel, he pulled up into a cloud and turned to circle the harbor and then head south. The two enemy pilots realized they were between Hanson and home and stalked him as he went in and out of the clouds. If he turned south, they would immediately be on his tail. As it was, they flew around the clouds keeping pace with him. He headed for a cloud, allowing the Japanese to close in on him. Hanson entered the cloud, carefully watching the tail of his plane. As soon as the Corsair's rudder became enmeshed in the wispy cotton-like cloud, he pushed hard on the right rudder pedal and banked hard to reverse course. The two *Zekes* disappeared into the cloud. Hanson set course for Bougainville, diving toward the deck to build up speed and opening up the throttle to allow the eighteen cylinders to pull him away from the Japanese. He "beat it" for home without meeting any other enemy aircraft.

Pilots leaving the combat area experienced a physical as well as psychological relaxation. Sweaty palms, dry throats, and nervous fidgeting were byproducts of aerial action. For Bob Owens, no matter how cold it was at high altitudes, his gloves seemed to fill with moisture during a fight. Bob Hanson chain-smoked in the cockpit during combat flights. For each pilot it was different, just as each encounter was different.

ROGER CONANT'S DIVISION

At the same altitude as Thrifty Warner when they passed Duke of York Island, Roger Conant's four planes frustrated several enemy attacks by merely turning in their direction. Conant fired at one *Zeke* that swerved in from above but was frustrated by his lack of observable results. His guns, normally loaded with one to five tracers, did not seem to have any tracer ammunition. His wingman, Ray Wetzel, could see hits on the *Zeke* and smoke each time Conant fired. It was obvious to all in the division, save Conant, that the Japanese plane was being hit. It finally caught fire and fell toward the sea. Conant test fired his guns and found they had apparently been belted wrong in the first part of the load. Finding himself low on the water above Simpson Harbor at 300 knots, Conant decided

Roger Conant, Okie Bowman, Larry Smith, Ray Wetzel, and Jake Knight in a lighter moment between missions on Bougainville. VMF-215 shared its planes with VMF-212. Author's Collection

to strafe Rapopo. Firing into revetments and run-up areas, he glimpsed a *Betty* bomber under camouflage netting but was going too fast to adjust his fire and pulled up without attacking the twin-engine aircraft.

HAP LANGSTAFF'S DIVISION
Flying bottom cover were Hap Langstaff's and Don Aldrich's Corsairs. Langstaff's Marines were relatively unmolested. Being close to the Avengers gave some protection from their turret guns, and the Corsairs turning in to incoming Japanese fighters provided some protection for the Avengers. Langstaff had been Ray Tomes's prime tactical pupil. Hap reflected that training by keeping his division close to the bombers. There were plenty of Japanese flying around, looking for any opening—an American plane by itself or a Corsair swinging wide in its weave. Passing Duke of York, one *Zeke* tried to attack a Corsair, and Langstaff used a liberal dose of .50-caliber to drive it away, damaged.

The Corsairs did not encounter any other targets as they followed the Avengers out to the rally point. Once the tubby bombers headed for home, Langstaff turned to give the Japanese a parting shot. Earlier he had spotted a small coaster in the outer harbor, and he chose the vessel as his target. Despite heavy antiaircraft fire, he dived on the ship and opened fire, sending showers of debris into the air in the midst of fountains of spraying water. One pass was enough, and Langstaff led his division home.

Langstaff turned in a slow, vertical turn exiting Simpson Harbor when a *Zeke* plummeted out of the sky and pounced on his wingman George Kross. The *Zeke* pounded Kross with 7.7mm and 20mm fire before the other three weaving Marines drove it away. His body struck hard by shrapnel, Kross took a look at his plane and was appalled by what he saw. The U-bird had at least fifteen small bullet holes in the wings and two big cannon holes in the right wing. He had no idea how many holes were in the fuselage and tail. Most of the fabric on the outboard section of the right wing had been torn off, damaging the control surfaces considerably. His attention was drawn to the center of each wing where the doors to the ammunition bays had been blown off by the explosion of .50-caliber cartridges. He could see the ammunition pans aflame with burning .50-caliber rounds, occasionally sparkling as the shells cooked off. Fire licked at the crippled airplane, making the damage, as bad as it was, appear worse. Pulling up, Kross flew through a cloud. The moisture and change of altitude put the fire out. Kross turned his thoughts to making it to Torokina.

Exploding ammunition and torn fabric had reduced the lift in the wings, and Kross nervously watched the badly damaged right wing fearing it would buckle at any moment. Drag from the damaged portions of the aircraft increased as the distance to Torokina decreased. Speed dropped, and whenever airspeed approached 160 knots, the crippled Corsair would make an abrupt, diving right turn. He babied the big bird along, occasionally nosing down to get all the airspeed he could. Buka finally passed, and Bougainville filled his windshield.

He passed Cape Moltke, but the F4U just could not make it. He had traded too much altitude for speed and now the plane was becoming uncontrollable. Bailing out was his only option. Nearing Empress Augusta Bay, Kross trimmed up the faithful but doomed Corsair the best he could and stood up, fighting the stream of air that tried to pin him in the cockpit. Just short of the beachhead, he succeeded in getting out and parachuted clear of the dying Corsair. Shore parties jumped into landing vessels and quickly retrieved the worn-out pilot. He was jeeped immediately to the field hospital. Though his wounds were not incapacitating, he would not fly again until February 7.

DON ALDRICH'S DIVISION

Right behind Langstaff were the four planes of Aldrich's division. The Corsairs didn't have much action following close beside the bombers, and there was relatively little aerial action until the bombers nosed over into their shallow glides. Watching the bombers start their runs, Aldrich felt a presence, a sensation more than a tangible feeling. He glanced up. A dark green shape loomed less than three hundred feet above his Corsair. Easing back on the stick, Aldrich fired a burst and the *Zeke* flew right into the bullets. The Japanese pilot snapped into a wingover and dived away, watched by the amazed members of Aldrich's division.

At two thousand feet the bombers leveled out and then slightly turned to exit the harbor. An unfortunate *Zeke* chose that moment to attack the TBFs, placing itself right in front of the four Corsairs. Don Aldrich did the honors. The doomed Japanese plane had no chance of escape as the .50-caliber shower started an immediate fire. The *Zeke* leveled out slightly just before diving into the sea with a burning pool of oil and fuel marking the grave of another Imperial airman.

With the bombers safely exiting the target area, Aldrich turned his attention toward the Japanese in the harbor, picking out a transport vessel close to shore as a strafing target. Coming in to attack just off the water, he could see the vessel was close to five hundred feet long and it seemed alive with bright sprinkles indicating antiaircraft fire. Rapopo Field was just behind the target, and gunfire from around the airdrome added to the conflagration, filling the air with tracers and puffs of smoke. Aldrich led the column of Corsairs, his bullets running up the side of the hull into the superstructure. The rest of the division followed with "Gizmo" Gilman bringing up the rear. The Marines were impressed by the amount of return fire and were surprised that no Corsair was hit. Small fires burned aboard the ship but the volume of antiaircraft fire from Rapopo served as a reminder not to strafe the airfields.

TOROKINA AND BARAKOMA

Thirty Corsairs settled down on the strip alone, in pairs or, on a few occasions, divisions of four aircraft. Disorganized gaggles of aircraft split up to land on the main strip or Piva Uncle. Ground guides taxied the planes to the various shops and the refueling area. With all switches off, the pilots wearily unfastened their harnesses and exited their aircraft. Several gave an affectionate or reassuring pat to the big flying machines, a muted "thank you."

Lloyd Cox was not surprised when a ground crewman announced that he had returned his Corsair with thirty-two 7.7mm holes and a single 20mm cannon hit. Bob Owens met the pilot of a Corsair he'd rescued. The man, from VMF-211, said the *Zeke* that Owens had shot off his tail went into the water off Rapopo. Not all of the news was good. Sammy Stidger's loss had been a hard blow; Kross, Jack Knight, Moore, and Hanson were still overdue.

Slowly, the picture improved. Hanson landed twenty minutes after the last of the others. Mechanics discovered his Corsair had seven bullet holes in it, less than twenty gallons remaining, and less than four hundred rounds in his ammo trays (the Corsair's full load is normally 2,350 rounds). Owens received word that Kross was in the nearby hospital, being treated for minor wounds and shock. Knight and Moore would never return.

At Barakoma, Doc Neber put his magic skills to use. The mysterious medicine bottles restored spirits and his clever, sometimes biting remarks did much to bring the exhausted men around. Jim Tyler, the intelligence officer, debriefed the returning pilots, the young flyers telling the story of the day's mission with serious, tired voices and grand hand motions. By next morning the cold statistics were reviewed: Bob Hanson claimed five Zekes, Thrifty Warner four, Ralph Robinson two and a probable, Owens and Cox two each. Don Aldrich, Okie Bowman, Roger Conant, and Dick Braun all received credit for one enemy plane for a total of nineteen enemy planes. In addition to the kills claimed by the various fighter squadrons, the Dauntlesses and Avengers claimed six victims.

There was no celebration that evening. The nineteen claims were offset by the losses of Moore, Knight, and the irreplaceable Sammy Stidger. Sammy's death was a crushing blow to many of them. He had been with the squadron since the first days in California, and his free spirit and cheekish humor always livened up those around him. Many had shared his postwar dreams of parleying their military acquired flying skills into a charter or airline business. The death of Grafton S. Stidger was a blow to their dreams of what would happen after the war.

Major Owens was not impressed with the stark, emotionless numbers of enemy planes shot down. Instead, he took great pride in the way the Corsairs of Two Fifteen had maintained their weaves to stay alongside the bombers. Only after the bombers had cleared the harbor did the Corsairs go after Zekes or ships. Their tactics had been simple, yet effective. The Marines attacked the enemy, made excellent use of deflection shooting skills, and broke off individual combat when the odds were unfavorable. Ultimately they stayed alongside the TBFs instead of hunting the enemy until the bombers were safely on their way home.

The months of tutelage under Jim Neefus had paid off. Owens noted in his aircraft action report: "We were fighting all the way to the target and fighting all the way out. We were getting an occasional shot at a *Zeke* that got in too close, but I didn't see any of our planes leave the formation to get in an extra shot. I was awfully proud of the type of cover the fighters put on." Despite the pressure to run up their individual scores, the Fighting Corsairs had accomplished their mission in protecting the bombers.

CHAPTER TWELVE

Hammering the Enemy

To most pilots, the aircraft ceased to be just another machine and became almost another person . . . a being to be cherished and looked after, who in turn would respond to one's own demands to an almost superhuman degree.

—GROUP CAPTAIN LEONARD CHESHIRE, V.C.

THE OPERATIONS ORDER ISSUED ON JANUARY 16, 1944, HAD A SHORT BUT interesting and significant comment concerning the battle that had been fought over Rabaul on the 14th:

> To all AirOps, pass to all VF Squadrons.
> From: Strike Command
> To: Fighter Command

Many thanks to the fighters for their magnificent cover today. It was terrific.

Fighter Command takes great pleasure in forwarding this message.

If there was any tangible, objective evidence that the men of VMF-215 had done their job successfully, this message provided it.

There had been no mission for Two Fifteen on the 15th, and the operation for the 16th made it only as far as the rendezvous point before turning back. The cancellation was due to the high cover of P-38s not arriving. Hal Spears was extremely disappointed by the scrubbing of the mission. He was one of the squadron's most aggressive pilots, yet he had not had a chance to mix it up with the enemy since returning from Australia. His division had been scheduled for flights on the 8th, 10th, and 12th, and all had been scrubbed due to weather. He had not been scheduled to fly on January 14, missing a chance at a large number of targets.

Nothing changed on the 17th, with only Don Aldrich and Hap Langstaff flying short test hops over Vella Lavella. The pilots pulled out recreation gear and writing material when not sitting in on lectures about the local area and its diseases. Conditions had improved enough at Barakoma that an outdoor theater had been constructed. Men desperate for entertainment went to the movies night after night, braving rain, insects, and enemy hecklers to view a film that had probably played several nights in a row. Playing cards allowed new pilots to assimilate, whether it was in a high-stakes poker game with the likes of Doc Neber and Don Aldrich or a game of bridge with hard-nosed players such as Bob Hanson and Bob Owens. Contrary to movie and television portrayals in later years, there were no women in the forward areas and no way to reach any. Bull sessions invariably turned to women, home, tactics, or flying. Over rare bottles of alcohol and any spare food that could be found, old-time pilots with a tour under their belt awed the newer men with tales of strafing Kahili or the artillery barrages endured at Munda.

The squadron leaders, Owens, Warner, and Aldrich, spent their time planning the next operation and overseeing maintenance. Different pilots were tasked with teaching classes on climate, geography, survival skills, and aerial tactics. Typical American boys, the pilots were impatient, ready to get on with the necessary missions to get home. Bob Hanson, referred to by correspondents as "Butcher Bob" after the action on January 14, spoke for the impatient pilots when he said, "I came out here to kill Japs." The pilots understood that the best way to get home was through Rabaul and on to Tokyo.

Bob Hanson obviously had postwar dreams like any other young Marine. However, his dreams seemed like something out of a Hollywood movie. He was supremely confident that he could turn his successful record as a fighter pilot into an equally successful and exotic flying career when the war ended. In bull sessions Hanson outlined some of his future goals and most depended upon his aerial accomplishments. He wanted to complete his education at Hamline University and return to India, where he planned to put his flying skills to use. The giant subcontinent had a special hold on him, and his future rested in that great land. Like a character in a novelist's plot or *Terry and the Pirates*, Hanson planned to hire himself as a personal pilot to some wealthy prince or ruler of one of India's many small states. This might lead to a command or generalship in a private air force of some faraway and exotic land. Some pilots, not sure if Hanson could actually attain such lofty goals or even that he was serious, gave him a new sobriquet, "The Maharajah of Rabaul."

Son of Methodist missionaries, Robert Hanson was the highest-scoring Corsair ace with twenty-five victories. USMC Photo

BACK TO RABAUL

The bloodletting above New Britain continued on January 18, a beautiful sunny day with unlimited visibility. Four divisions of Two Fifteen's Corsairs flew up to Torokina at 0610, sitting on the runways after breakfast and refueling until orders were received at 1055 to take off. The Army B-25s passed over at just about the same time heading north without waiting for the fighter escorts. By the time the fighters joined them, they would be completing their bomb runs and heading home.

After rendezvous near Buka, the fighters were in three different layers from two thousand to seven thousand feet. Bob Owens led the Corsairs as high cover, eight Navy Hellcats flew medium cover, and eight New Zealand P-40s were down low. The sixteen Corsairs were from Owens's own division and those of Roger Conant, Dick Braun, and a very enthusiastic Hal Spears. The bombers appeared from the west heading toward New Ireland just as the fighters arrived from the east. The dark green Kittyhawks turned to follow the bombers home. The Hellcats and Corsairs faced fifteen or twenty Japanese pursuing the retreating bombers. The Marines flew straight at the gaggle of Japanese fighters, intending to break them up. Firing as they came in range, the Corsairs forced the Japanese to scatter.

Owens met three of the Japanese aircraft head on, but they broke up as soon as he opened fire. One of the enemy planes made the mistake of trying to escape in front of Roger Conant's division flying to the right and below Owens's Corsairs. Conant, Larry Smith, and Jake Knight all fired at the twisting target. All three of the pilots claimed hits but Conant pulled in behind the *Zeke* to put the finishing touches on its destruction. Conant's last memory of the burning Japanese plane was that of the enemy pilot trying desperately to protect his face from the flames licking at the cockpit.

The three Marines turned hard after the other two *Zekes* and easily caught the slower Japanese plane. Conant had the first shot, hitting the trailing *Zeke*, but the little plane pulled up and away. It flew right into the path of Larry Smith. Smitty turned with the *Zeke* and opened fire, as the other two Corsairs followed just behind hoping to get a shot if the *Zeke* escaped from Smitty. The Japanese pilot tried to turn away, but Smitty's guns tore pieces off the *Zeke* and it banked into the sea.

The last of the three *Zekes* suffered the same fate as the other two, Conant taking the honor of the final shots. Now low on the water, low on fuel and ammunition, Conant decided to return to Torokina. It proved to be a wise decision, as a large formation of Japanese fighters milled around above the three Corsairs.

Nearby, four inline engine fighters, identified as *Tonys*, bore straight in at Spears and his strong supporting cast, cocky little Creighton Chandler, darkly handsome Ed Hernan, and taciturn "Frenchy" Williams. After a head-on pass, the Japanese split up. Two turned away quickly; the others zoomed up. One *Tony* crossed in front of Spears, who felt certain some of his bullets hit home, but Chandler fired the killing shots. Spears confirmed that it went into the water.

Spears and Chandler stalked another *Tony* escaping back to New Britain. Chandler stayed glued to Spears's wing as the Marine followed a very talented Japanese pilot through several abrupt turns just above the waves. It was a long chase, over fifty miles, before Spears put the *Tony* down in the water at a small bay called Put Put. Chandler skillfully stayed with Spears through the entire pursuit.

Turning for home, the pair were startled when a *Zeke* dived in from behind and sprayed them with a long burst. The enemy plane zoomed away before their tardy shots could hit it. Near the tip of New Ireland, the Corsairs encountered a Hellcat pursued by a single *Zeke*. Spears knocked the *Zeke* into the sea before the Japanese pilot even knew the two Corsairs were on his tail.

Leaving Rabaul and New Ireland behind, it appeared as if the day's action was over. The army bombers were long gone and the sky appeared to be clear of planes. Spears and Chandler seemed to be alone in the sky, but a glint of light on metal exposed two Japanese fighters heading south. The Marines knocked down both *Zekes*; Spears's target showered his Corsair with small pieces of debris but caused no damage.

As the last planes left the area, Hernan and Williams engaged two *Hamps* below them. The clipped-wing *Zekes* split up, and each pulled up in a chandelle, one right and one left. Williams took the one to the left and set it afire. Hernan blew the wing off the other.

Not a bad day's work for Two Fifteen: ten claims with no loss. Spears's return to action was successful, claiming three victories. Spears's Corsair had a few nicks and metal creases but was not damaged beyond the level of repair available to them at Vella Lavella.

INTERLUDE AT VELLA LAVELLA

In one of Two Fifteen's tents, the men prepared for sleep. Foot lockers were closed, letter-writing gear carefully put away, and some took a last, lazy look at precious letters that had been read many times. Like many of the others, Al Snyder had an intense aversion to insects and he carefully tucked the corners of the mosquito netting around his cot and himself as he prepared for a good night's sleep. Silence settled over the darkened tent, broken only by occasional snoring or natural tropical sounds.

Less than an hour later, a fearful muttering and thrashing noise was heard from the direction of Snyder's rack. Snyder's flashlight beamed on, followed by more excited thrashing and loud groans. Snyder tumbled from his cot, the rays from the flashlight dancing across the ceiling. Everyone was now awake, and cooler heads attempted to comfort the terrified Marine. All questioned his frantic movements and fear, which had disrupted their much-needed sleep. By way of explanation, Snyder directed the flashlight on his cot and revealed the presence of an enormous spider, the size of a man's fist. He had felt it crawling up his leg. The group made sure of the destruction of the creature and did a quick search of the quarters to ensure that no friends of the gigantic arachnid were in hiding. Never really enamored with the tropics, "Spider" Snyder had found one more reason why few people vacationed in the Solomons.

Nearby stood a hut with a wood floor and wire mesh screening the windows. Above the door was a greeting, in neatly painted letters:

Lavella Vista Lodge
Rates: 2100 per month
American Plan
Laundry: 100

Scrawled in much less neat, though entirely readable, letters below the sign:

Waitress Wanted

BACK TO ACTION
There was no flying scheduled for the 19th, but a mission was laid on for VMF-215 on the 20th to escort thirty-six B-25s to Vunakanau. Thrifty Warner would lead four divisions as part of a large escort of eight

P-38s, eight F6Fs, twenty P-40s, and twenty additional Corsairs from other squadrons. The Marines of Two Fifteen joined up with the other aircraft at about 1215, forty-five minutes from Torokina. Warner and Don Aldrich took their divisions up for high cover, and Hal Spears and Hap Langstaff stayed with the medium cover. True to form, some of the planes couldn't accompany the mission and only thirteen of the Corsairs formed up. Lloyd Cox had been unable to start his F4U after refueling at Torokina. Ed Hernan and Gizmo Gilman had to drop out due to engine failures. John Fitzgerald continued his streak of bad luck. His first mission, on the 8th, had been scrubbed due to weather, which was irrelevant to him because his Corsair had been damaged when he hit a stump while taxiing. On the way to the big fight on January 14, his F4U had been taken out while parked at Torokina. Now, an oil line broke, slinging oil all over the cowling and cockpit, and gradually reducing oil pressure to make further flight unsafe. Fitzgerald would miss another flight. He had yet to see combat.

The Japanese system of coast watchers and radar on New Ireland gave the enemy plenty of time to scramble about forty fighters to meet the first group of nine bombers as they passed the New Britain coastline at the Warangoi River twenty-five miles southwest of Rabaul Town. The Japanese dropped phosphorous bombs on the formation, the explosions sending white streamers throughout the sky in beautiful tendrils but doing no damage. Hal Spears downed a *Hamp* just before the B-25s released their loads over Vunakanau. The bombs burst crisply around the airdrome, and the twin-engine bombers turned for home. It was at this time that the interceptors made concerted efforts to get at the American bombers.

Spears and "Shrimp" Chandler went in low on the airfield to see if there were any Japanese around the strip. Chandler nailed a *Zeke* trying to land, and Spears knocked down a *Zeke* pestering a B-25. Don Aldrich, with John Breneman at his side, downed two *Zekes*. One crashed between Vunakanau and Tobera Airfields and the other near Malakuna Village near the New Britain coast.

Bob Hanson and Lloyd Cox were following the bombers as they exited the area when their attention was drawn to a single B-25 lagging behind the others. A Japanese fighter was pestering the lone Army bomber. Hanson set the *Zeke* afire, and the Marines saw it crash at the junction of the Warangoi River and the New Britain coastline. The B-25 was unable to escape and crashed just off Cape St. George on New Ireland. In a daring rescue under the noses of the Japanese on New Ireland, a "Dumbo" flying boat was able to pluck the entire crew from the sea to safety.

Hanson lined up another Japanese fighter, but "Frenchy" Williams dived in and shot it down before Hanson could close for a good shot. As the *Tony* crashed into the sea, the pilot tried but failed to bail out. The Marines returned to Torokina, fueled, and made it home by 1535 that evening. They had taken off at 0610 that morning.

VIEW FROM THE TOP

The next day, "O" flew down to Munda for a meeting to discuss tactics. He was convinced more than ever that his squadron was demonstrating the best tactics to use when fighting the nimble little *Zekes* and *Hamps* around Rabaul, a view shared by most of the other commanders. Tactics originally developed by Jimmy Thach and Jimmy Flatley in their Wild-cats early in the war, refined by men like John Smith and "Indian Joe" Bauer above Guadalcanal, and finally taught by men like Jim Neefus and Ken Walsh with the more modern Corsairs, were helping to wrest con-trol of the air from the Japanese. The weave was no longer thought of as a purely defensive maneuver to protect your wingman's tail. Now it was used as an offensive maneuver to put the escorts in the best position to get a shot at encroaching interceptors. The meeting touched on a variety of topics. The squadron leaders discussed at length how to organize the different types of fighter cover for the raids on Rabaul.

The types of bomber dictated different tactics. The SBDs were almost impossible to follow once they had committed to their steep dives, but they were also slow going to and from the target. They were nicknamed Slow But Deadly. The Corsairs, Kittyhawks, and Hellcats tended to swing out and away from the Dauntlesses in their dives. The fighters would then pick them up after they had completed their bomb release and pull out. The TBFs were also slow but were easy to follow in their shallow, gliding attacks. The Allied fighters remained with the Avengers throughout their attacks, weaving to match the slower speed of the torpedo planes. The B-24s and B-25s flew in level bomb runs and the fighters had no trouble staying with them. The B-25s were preferred as they were much faster than the other bombers.

Once the bombers had finished their mission and were proceeding safely from the rally point, groups of the fighters, except the close cover, would release and mix it up with the enemy. Freelancing was still frowned on by commanders during the bomb run, but afterward it was free time for the more aggressive souls, like Spears and Chandler did on the January 18 mission, to go after the enemy fighters. Old rules never changed, however, and it was still repeated: "Never dogfight with a *Zero!*" Trying to maneuver with a *Zeke* at a slow speed was usually fatal.

BACK TO BUSINESS

Times had changed. Unlike the pitiful numbers that the Allies had thrown at Kahili three months previously, usually four to six Liberators or Mitchells escorted by less than a dozen fighters, the missions to Rabaul involved more than one hundred planes on every mission. The flight to attack Lakunai Airfield on January 22 involved eighteen Mitchells protected by a massive number of escorts: twelve P-38s of the Army's 339th Fighter Squadron, eight Navy Hellcats from VF-40, twelve P-40s of New Zealand's No. 17 Squadron, and twenty Marine F4Us from VMF-211 and VMF-321. The last two units were operating from the brand new Piva Fighter Strip (also called Piva Two, Piva South, or Piva Yoke). Owens added twenty-seven Corsairs when they joined the formation over Bougainville at 1315. Hap Langstaff remained at Torokina; his prop was damaged when his plane slid off the runway.

The course of the strike took them up past Green Island, cut across New Ireland, and then over the northern tip of Duke of York Island to Rabaul. The Corsairs of Two Fifteen were spread throughout the formation at different altitudes: Owens, Conant, and Braun led their divisions as part of the medium cover, Warner and Langstaff flew low cover with the bombers, and the divisions of Spears and Aldrich were in the "bottom" cover. The P-38s flew top cover, the best position for diving into any opposition.

There was no aerial opposition until the bombers completed their bomb runs on Lakunai Fighter Airdrome. Japanese gunners on the ground responded with gusto, pouring out hundreds of colorful anti-aircraft shells as the planes passed by. Puffs of dark smoke mixed with tracers laced the sky and some found their mark. A B-25 flew right into a large-caliber shell, disintegrating before the eyes of the Allied pilots and crews. Dozens of *Zekes* pounced on the stragglers, and the Corsairs responded by taking quick shots at the fleeting shapes of attacking Japanese. As the bombers withdrew, the Marines held their weaves, refusing to be drawn away from their charges. A P-38 lost power and drifted away from the protection of the Allied fighters. Swarms of *Zekes* pounced, and the Lightning went down in flames.

Weaving with Jake Knight, Roger Conant caught a *Zeke* whose pilot was concentrating on the bombers. Conant remembered this engagement with particular clarity: "That damn thing was no more than . . . 50 to 100 feet . . . 50 yards away. All I had to do was pull the trigger. I could literally see the bullets tearing into his wing. Each made a triangular shaped hole . . . they tore him apart." This *Zeke* had previously dropped a phosphorous bomb on the formation, and Conant noted the irony of the white smoke trailing in long streamers from its wing roots. Knight and Thrifty Warner witnessed the *Zeke* go down, an impressive fire-wrapped kill.

Hal Spears nailed a *Zeke* trying to take off from Lakunai through the dust clouds caused by the explosions of Allied bombs. Two Corsairs from another squadron were mobbed by a swarm of *Zekes* and shot down. Hanson flew into the crowd of enemy planes with a vengeance, flaming two *Zekes* and then scoring an easy kill on an unsuspecting *Tony*.

O. D. Hunter and Frenchy Williams attacked several *Zekes* but separated as they pursued them. Williams destroyed two of the enemy planes before two more latched onto his tail. The Corsair's superior speed paid off, and he escaped undamaged. Hunter claimed his target destroyed by fire. On the trip home, Hunter discovered antiaircraft fire had damaged his right oil cooler, resulting in a mist of oil spraying throughout the cockpit all the way home. He expected the engine to seize up due to oil loss, spending the trip home wiping the windscreen continually. The tough Vought airplane and Pratt and Whitney engine held out. He landed safely.

Down to earth with a dry wit,
O. D. Hunter originally flew with
VMF-214, the "Swashbucklers,"
and finished his South Pacific
service with VMF-215. USMC
Photo

Stragglers reached the rally point after the balance of the formation disappeared to the south. Bob Owens circled to provide cover for any dawdlers. A streak of green flashed by Owens as a *Zeke* flew through the last of the bombers in hot pursuit of a lone blue F4U. Owens lined up the enemy plane but couldn't fire because the other Corsair was in his line of fire. Owens closed to point blank range and fired; the *Zeke* exploded almost immediately and disintegrated. A body floated clear and a parachute appeared, a closer look revealing the figure under the blossoming chute to be the Marine pilot of the Corsair previously under attack. Owens circled the flyer as he lost altitude and hit the water, sending out a contact report to the Rescue Services. Owens also saw pieces of his own victim hit the water nearby.

The last victory of the day went to Don Aldrich. With John Burke on his wing, Aldrich held back to make sure all of the stragglers escaped. Searching the sky, Aldrich spotted a *Zeke* making a firing run on a helpless pilot in a parachute. The *Zeke* tried to escape by pulling up in a loop, normally the best evasive tactic for a Japanese plane, but Aldrich followed his target, picking away with short bursts. The *Zeke* spurted flames, but unfortunately Aldrich could not confirm its demise as two of the *Zeke*'s buddies jumped in. They positioned themselves to make a pass on the Corsair, and Aldrich was forced to break off his pursuit. Before the two Japanese could get within firing range, Johnny Burke turned into them, driving them off.

The Corsairs of Two Fifteen returned to Torokina, pulling up into chandelles and swinging into their final approaches. The Marines eased their F4Us in, let the airspeed tick off, as all the while their eyes were darting back and forth between their instruments and outside the cockpit as the runway enlarged before them. Lifting the nose a bit, the majestic birds settled in one by one. The ground-bound Corsairs made broad S-turns down the airstrip to give their pilots a better view ahead over the long nose. Just off the taxiways, the pilots set the throttle to idle and shut their birds down. Some left their planes for VMF-212 to use the following day. They would fly back to Barakoma via SCAT transport. The others refueled and flew on to Barakoma. Once back at their base, all could relax in their rudimentary camp. It was ever so humble but it was home.

Chapter Thirteen

Rabaul Defiant

Fly with your head not with your muscles!

—Eric Hartmann

THE JAPANESE CONTINUED TO OPPOSE EACH INCOMING ATTACK, SEND-ing thirty to seventy fighters up each time the Allied bombers crossed St. George's Channel. Steady streams of airbursts and colored tracers showed the Japanese gunners were undaunted and unbowed. It appeared as though the Japanese were able to replace any losses they suffered, although their excellent camouflage and cave system made it appear as though the airfields were empty.

If the hardworking flyers in the Allied squadrons could have seen "the other side of the hill," they would have been amazed at how difficult things really were for the Japanese. The garrison of Rabaul had turned completely into moles. Caves, bunkers, and underground galleries were constructed to house nearly the entire army and navy forces in and around the town. Most barracks and living quarters had moved below ground or were dispersed throughout the jungles and plantations that surrounded Rabaul Town. Natural camouflage was used whenever possible. In some cases the Japanese dug through sections of ridgelines to use the natural protection of the hillsides as proof against the blast of Allied bombs. By the end of the war, the Rabaul area would eventually be honeycombed with over 350 miles of tunnels, not including fighting positions and gun emplacements. Coast defense guns were carefully camouflaged and set in well-protected earthen emplacements. Some of the Japanese positions were prefabricated steel bunkers sunk partially into the ground with only firing apertures visible.

Airfields were out of service for short periods of time, whether the result of Allied attacks, rain, or crashes. Repair crews and airmen lost sleep due to the continued air attacks. Nevertheless, the Japanese were never without an airstrip to fly off interceptors. Engineers and construction troops were aided by the labor of prisoners. Hundreds of prisoners died of mistreatment and malnutrition. The work crews continuously improved blast pens, run-up areas, and revetments around the airfields. They constructed dummy aircraft to deceive aerial reconnaissance and strafing planes. Frequent naval incursions by Allied warships around New Britain and New Ireland effectively cut the Japanese supply line and made it difficult for supplies to reach the garrison. Allied submarines destroyed supply ships trying to enter the harbor. Any ship that successfully anchored in Simpson Harbor faced immediate destruction from the air. The first stages of strangulation occurred during late January of 1944, but the Allied pilots had no way of knowing.

The Japanese diet gradually grew poorer in quantity and quality. The Japanese, cut off from supplies from home and unable to trade with locals who they had mistreated, constructed large tracts of vegetable and root gardens. There was, at this time in 1944, no starvation, but sickness due to malnutrition reduced the effectiveness of the tired troops. Mail from Japan was infrequent and undependable. Submarines were the principal source of communication with the outside world. A *Betty* bomber occasionally snuck in from the major fleet base at Truk to deliver dispatches and official correspondence. Medical conditions were medieval, and drugs and antibiotics were limited. Shops located in underground shelters constructed crude artificial limbs for dismembered soldiers and sailors. Many died due to the unclean and bacteria-laced conditions that allowed infection into wounds. Living in the jungle or caves had inherent hygiene and disease problems, and the bombings increased the mortality rate. Allied pilots captured by the Japanese suffered from the same conditions that afflicted the Japanese. Some died quickly, executed by their captors, and others died due to mistreatment, disease, and malnutrition.

The crisis facing the 11th Air Fleet of Adm. Jinichi Kusaka at Rabaul forced the Imperial navy to bring in more aircraft. Adm. Mineichi Koga brought down his carrier air groups from Truk. Koga's groups included carefully hoarded pilots who had fought previously throughout the Pacific, but some were newly trained flyers still without combat experience. It had been hoped that the less experienced airmen and a new collection of airplanes could avoid combat until they were fully trained. Once the veterans and novices had trained together on their new equipment, they would be available for a counterattack against the Allies in the South Pacific.

Circumstances forced Koga, who had become commander of the Combined Fleet on the death of Admiral Yamamoto in November of 1943, to reconsider the priorities of war. Koga made arrangements for the planes of the 2nd Carrier Division to be dispatched from Truk starting on January 20, to be completed by January 25. The last large group of Japan's naval aviators, the men of the 2nd Carrier Division, was expected to breathe life into Admiral Kusaka's garrison and do what the 11th Air Fleet and random army units had been unable to do: stop the Allied aerial offensive.

Aces

By mid-January of 1944, the Torokina Airfield complex comprised Piva Fighter strip, Piva Bomber Strip (also called Piva North or Piva Uncle), and the original fighter field that lay alongside the ocean. VMF-215, stationed at Barakoma on Vella Lavella, still shared its aircraft with VMF-212. Between sorties to Rabaul, the pilots were kept busy with ferrying planes and maintenance flights. John Breneman and Gizmo Gilman ferried a pair of F4Us to Torokina and returned with a pair of F6Fs to Barakoma on the 23rd.

After the first few missions in January, pilots of Two Fifteen and the other fighter squadrons could not help comparing the blossoming scores of Don Aldrich, Bob Hanson, and Hal Spears with the records of great Marine aces like Joe Foss and Pappy Boyington. Both Foss and Boyington were credited with twenty-six victories; Foss scored all of his victories over Guadalcanal, and Boyington's score included six claimed as part of the Flying Tigers. Foss was in the States, and Boyington was a prisoner of war. Another score, closer and more likely to be eclipsed, was that of Ken Walsh. Walsh, who had borrowed a fighter from Jim Neefus the previous August, was credited with twenty enemy planes before he went home in August. Marine commanders frowned on discussions of the great individual score, concentrating on training in teamwork, but such talk was inevitable. Instead of concentrating on a great team like Joe Foss's "Flying Circus," some of the men focused on the individual claims of Jimmy Swett, who shot down seven *Vals* in a single engagement, and Jefferson DeBlanc, who shot down five Japanese in one day. As of January 24, Two Fifteen included several high scorers in its ranks: Aldrich had eleven kills, Hanson had fourteen, and Spears had been credited with ten. Bob Owens disliked the talk of high scores and tried to emphasize the success they had achieved over Rabaul due to section and division tactics. Loner-style fighting did little to encourage team efforts; but on each mission to Rabaul, as soon as the bombers headed for home, some of the pilots turned toward the enemy airfields looking for trouble.

Owens found individuals like Hanson a bad example for inexperienced and impressionable flyers. "You can tell those young men for me to close their ears to any discussion of Hanson's tactics," Owens said in reference to the new and easily influenced pilots. "For every Hanson, there are at least ten dead Marine pilots who tried to do once what Hanson does every day." Proud of the way his men stuck with the bombers and each other, "O" didn't want anyone breaking their weaves to go "chasin' Zeros."

Owens often warned the ever impatient Hanson about going off to fight the Japanese, with or without his wingman. It was not that Hanson was a gifted flyer or better than those he flew with; Two Fifteen contained its share of well-trained or naturally skillful pilots. Some, like gifted Hap Langstaff, flew so brilliantly that others described them as being one with the aircraft. Instead, Hanson flew in a violent and aggressive manner, trying to get the brutish Corsair to follow his wishes through sheer physical force. He was a perfect match for the powerful Vought. Put together they became a flying "demon." Sam Sampler flew on the former wrestler's wing more than anyone else in VMF-215, and he described Hanson's style: "No man on earth can stick with him. He flies at top speed every moment, executing every known maneuver and then some. Sooner or later, Hanson is off by himself tackling huge formations of Zeros." Hanson was not the only target of criticism for being aggressive. Spears and Aldrich were also thought of as being "Zero chasers." Both Aldrich and Spears led their divisions by example, managing to deflect some of the criticism. Other pilots and "O" continued to warn Hanson of the dangers in single combat with the nimble little *Zekes*, but he had a stock reply: "They've had plenty of chances. If they were going to get me, I'd be dead now." Idle bravado? Perhaps, but Hanson was the typical successful fighter pilot: He had complete confidence in himself and his aircraft.

Big Strike / Big Effort

Major Owens was scheduled to lead the largest number of Fighting Corsairs ever assigned a mission, twenty-nine F4Us, on January 24. Seventeen had flown up to Torokina, and the remaining twelve pilots flew up via SCAT to pick up their aircraft. Due to unforeseen magneto problems, unscheduled engine changes, and the usual gremlins, only nineteen faded-blue Corsairs joined up above the field. By the time the squadron reached the coast of New Ireland, there were only thirteen. Assigned to independent high cover, the best spot for attacking the Japanese interceptors, the Corsairs made the rendezvous at twenty-six thousand feet but found there were no bombers.

Ten minutes later, the TBFs arrived and headed to the target area. Once over Simpson Harbor, the Avengers proceeded to circle above the water. Several P-38s cruised back and forth above the torpedo planes as the stubby planes made a second loop over the shipping. Antiaircraft fire blossomed around the bombers until the Avengers found the targets they had been looking for: ten large transport vessels and dozens of smaller craft. Picking out individual victims, the TBFs went into their shallow dives, opened bomb bay doors, and sprinkled the harbor with high explosives.

During the first circuit of the harbor, Dick Braun and Thrifty Warner led their flights toward a gaggle of *Zekes* threatening the bombers. Braun locked on to one, firing as he closed, and it produced puffs of white smoke. The *Zeke* appeared to fall away out of control, but Braun rejoined his flight without confirming its destruction. The Marine assault succeeded in breaking up the intended Japanese attack, sending *Zekes* off in all directions.

Thrifty Warner and Lloyd Cox chased one of the *Zekes* briefly, Warner pounding it with .50-caliber slugs. A thin wisp of brown smoke appeared from the *Zeke*'s cowling and it lost way. The two Corsairs screamed past. Neither Warner nor Cox saw the enemy plane crash. Like Dick Braun, Warner would claim a probable when he returned to Barakoma. The pair of Corsairs returned to their protective position above the Avengers.

Bob Hanson was trailing his division due to a supercharger problem. Sluggishly following the others upward, he was distracted by a distress call that proved to be a wild goose chase. When his division dived on a group of enemy planes, he followed but could not keep up. The Corsairs were unable to close on the *Zekes* as the Japanese spotted the approaching F4Us and pulled up in great, zooming climbs. They pulled up right in front of Hanson, lagging behind, who set two on fire, one after the other.

Heading back over Tobera Field, Hanson wryly noted the takeoffs and landings of the enemy below him. Moving in and out of the clouds, Hanson finally found a new target, an inline-engine Japanese aircraft flying away to the west. From almost dead astern, Hanson opened fire and followed the *Tony* in a slow turn. The Japanese plane lost altitude, smoke trailing in white streamers, and Hanson returned to the clouds.

Hanson flitted between the clouds, unsure of his supercharger, forcing him to remain at lower altitudes. Two *Zekes* presented themselves just below him, and he fired at each in turn. The pair split up, and Hanson followed one to its destruction. Trading fire with another pair of Japanese without results, Hanson made his way to the rally point, noting five aircraft either going down or crashing. He was particularly impressed by the demise of a *Zeke* that went smoking into the drink after a head-on pass with a Corsair.

Slowly he closed on a group of Grumman Avengers leaving the combat area. As the distance diminished, he noted another group of planes joining the Avengers. There were five or six darkly painted *Zekes* moving in for an attack. Hanson attacked, firing at one, then another. He shifted his fire from target to target forcing the Japanese to break up their attack. The Japanese split up and disappeared in the direction of Rabaul. Joining the big Grummans, he tucked his Corsair in close and set course for Torokina.

Japanese fighters continued to pester the bombers leaving the harbor. Dick Braun picked out one and blasted it with a long burst. The *Zeke* took the hits but Braun lost sight of it as his faster Corsair left it far behind. Over the coast, Braun encountered an F4U chasing a single *Zeke* without apparent results. The *Zeke* pulled up in a chandelle that brought him head on at Braun. Braun held the trigger down as the two planes passed each other and the *Zeke* started to emit smoke. Bob Hanson confirmed that the *Zeke* crashed.

Once the bombers were heading home, Owens led his high cover down over Rapopo field in search of enemy planes. A dark-colored *Zeke* detached itself from the general melee over the harbor and wandered toward the airfield. With his division, Owens dived into the attack and caught up with the Japanese fighter at eight thousand feet. It proved to be a difficult opponent, twisting, turning, sliding, and skidding, with "O" firing bursts each time the *Zeke* flew through his sights. The enemy plane showed just a wisp of smoke, and the *Zeke* did an abrupt turn back underneath Owens, apparently successfully evading Owens's attack. But the *Zeke* failed to escape as Owens looked back and saw it plunge into the sea from four thousand feet.

The last Allied planes to leave the target area were the Corsairs of Owens's division. Following a group of Avengers, Owens noted a shape close to the water near the retreating bombers. Motioning to the other planes around him, about twenty Corsairs from different divisions and squadrons, Owens pounced on the enemy plane. Identifying it as an army Ki. 44 fighter, codenamed *Tojo*, Owens opened fire as the stocky Japanese fighter banked right. An explosion at the wing root shattered the Japanese plane's right wing, and the loss of lift hurled the out of control *Tojo* violently to the left, right into Owens's path. Narrowly, "O" avoided colliding with the burning wreck, and his wingman broke left at the same time to evade debris. Pieces of flaming wreckage, and possibly gunfire from an unseen enemy or even another pursuing Corsair, struck the major's plane and started the Corsair on fire.

Flying one of the old birdcage-type Corsairs, Owens was injured. A bit of skin peeled off his face and much of the rest reddened by burns as flames briefly enveloped the cockpit. The Corsair went into a shallow dive, the speed built up until "O" felt like he was making 400 knots. Fighting the air pushing him down, "O" lifted himself up and out of his seat. Resigned to getting out, his body was held only by his radio cord. At that moment, the fire went out and a quick look revealed the aircraft was not as badly damaged as he had assumed. He hoisted himself back over the cockpit rail and resumed flying the damaged Vought. Leveling off, he found himself surrounded by at least a dozen Corsairs weaving protectively around him. The rugged F4U seemed to be functioning smoothly, and the distance back to Rabaul grew with each minute. Reaching Bougainville seemed a possibility, but the protective screen of F4Us stood by in case he had to put down in the Solomon Sea.

Owens's luck ran out just as the planes reached Cape Moltke, some thirty miles north of Torokina. The propeller went faster and faster, shaking the battered Corsair, and Owens was forced to shut down the engine. About twenty miles from salvation, Owens began preparations to ditch. With so little altitude, Owens used what little airspeed he had to maintain control rather than attempting to get closer to Torokina.

The landing went well. Corsair Bureau Number 02285 smoothly came to a stop, floating briefly. Covered with oil, Owens unhooked his straps and stood up. Just as he started to exit the aircraft, a wave swept over him and knocked him forward. His head struck the canopy frame, and he suffered a nasty cut which bled profusely. Shrugging off the blow, Owens inflated his life raft, set it on the wing, and calmly sat down. Slowly the water rose and Owens floated clear. Overhead, the other pilots were circling in the proverbial "protective umbrella." Owens was bombed with spare Mae Wests and life rafts from the covering planes; many pilots had never been this close to a downed flyer and they overdid it a bit.

Within twenty minutes a PBY flying boat appeared on the scene and plucked the soaked but safe major from the water. There was no trouble finding the Marine; the ocean around him was a mass of colors due to the many dye markers and shark kits thrown in by the overzealous pilots covering him. The PBY taxied over a small distance to pick up a downed P-38 pilot who had been in the water for some time and would have been overlooked if not for the attention showered on Owens. The Army pilot was in pretty bad shape, suffering from exhaustion and exposure after days in the ocean. Owens was feeling pretty good despite his injuries. Appearances provided a different picture to the sailors aboard the Catalina, and they treated the two pilots according to the way they looked. Though in bad shape, the Army pilot looked fine, a nice tan and hair bleached nearly white by the sun. Owens, however, looked terrible. His facial injuries made him look as though he had suffered nasty wounds, and the cut on his forehead was still bleeding. Consequently, the crew of the PBY made quite a fuss over Owens. He was soon swathed in bandages, and the sailors ignored the poor Army flyer that could not even raise his arms. In the course of conversation with the soldier, "O" found out the man was from South Carolina less than a hundred miles from Owens's hometown. Once in the hospital in the Treasury Islands, Owens discovered the attending doctor hailed from Greenville! The doctor advised "O" that nature had done a marvelous job of first aid. The slipstream had carried away most of the damaged skin and the saltwater had cleansed the wounds.

With Owens out of action, Thrifty Warner took the reins of command. Warner had given great thought to the Japanese tactic of dropping phosphorous bombs on the Allied formations. He, like many other pilots, believed the bombs were not intended as a weapon but as a method of communications. The plane dropping the bombs was normally a D4Y *Judy* divebomber, a plane often mistaken for the *Tony* fighter due to its inline engine. The bombs marked the sky as a rally point for the assembly of the intercepting Japanese fighters. The bombs also marked the progress of the Allied formations as they neared their target. Japanese radar and vectoring capabilities were not as sophisticated as the Allies, and it appeared to Warner that the phosphorous bombs were a good, though primitive, way of saving assembly time. Thrifty offered a counter-tactic. The effective use of the phosphorous bombs "could be neutralized if we were to duplicate the bombs and sent out small groups to lead the enemy fighters in the wrong course." Salesman though he was, there is no record that the Allied leaders seriously considered implementing Thrifty's suggestion.

Warner Takes the Lead

A P.T. boat returned Bob Owens to the squadron only a day after his water landing, but he was in no shape to fly. His forehead, cheeks, and one burned hand were covered in bandages, and he wore a hospital set of clothes.

VMF-215 pictured after Bob Owens was injured in a crash landing on January 24, 1944. Front row: Conant, Bowman, Evans, Aldrich, Braun, Owens, Warner, Wolff, Burke, Cox, Gilman. Second row: Brewer, Sampler, Tyler (intelligence officer), Hanson, Robinson, Langstaff, Doc Neber with Sydney the dog, Smith, Knight, Chandler, Kross, Hunter. Back row: Sanders, Snyder, Stockwell, Wetzel, Samuelson, Breneman, Spears, Fitzgerald, Leu, Hernan, Williams. Author's Collection

For the next mission on January 26, Warner would lead twenty-four Corsairs in a strike against Lakunai. Typical of the strikes on Rabaul since starting their third tour, there were over a hundred planes. The strike force consisted of sixty-six SBDs and TBFs and sixty-four fighters in addition to Two Fifteen's Corsairs. Larry Snyder and Frenchy Williams were left at Torokina due to engine trouble. The remaining Corsairs of the squadron would fly cover for the TBFs.

It was a beautiful, sunny day with unlimited visibility. The TBFs crossed New Ireland, crossed the coast of New Britain, and laid their loads all over the Lakunai area. The Japanese response was particularly nasty this day, as over fifty *Zekes* responded to the Allied attack. One group of Japanese made head-on passes at the formation in an attempt to draw the fighters out of their protective weaves while other *Zekes* pounced on any fighters that took the bait.

The Japanese put up a terrific fight and the pilots of Two Fifteen claimed fourteen kills and eight probably destroyed. All of Two Fifteen's aircraft returned safely, and the War Diary proudly proclaimed: "All the TBFs we were supporting returned safely. . . ." Only two planes were damaged. Don Aldrich's Corsair was jumped by a pair of *Zekes* that shredded his wings and left elevator, but he managed to lose them by diving away from eight thousand feet. He had trouble pulling out of the dive due to the damage, but his U-bird landed without incident. Thrifty Warner took hits from cannon in the accessory section that sprayed oil all over his plane. He was not sure if the hits came from enemy aircraft or ground fire.

Most of the combat occurred during head-on encounters. Bob Hanson claimed three *Zekes* destroyed, one from head on, and a probable kill. His wingman, Sam Sampler, was credited with a probable kill. Hal Spears put in claims for two destroyed and two probable; one of his encounters was nose to nose. Warner was credited with two for sure, one straight on, and a probable. The probable kill took place when he single-handedly took on ten *Zekes* who were strafing a Corsair pilot in a parachute. The rescue made him a target, and that is when his aircraft was damaged.

Aldrich likewise claimed two and a probable. Dick Braun and his wingman, Gizmo Gilman, each claimed a single score. Dour John Breneman added a victory claim and a probable. Ed Hernan, lost and alone in the sky, received credit for two enemy destroyed. Hap Langstaff attacked a *Zeke*, and his gunfire caused the enemy plane to start smoking. The last he saw of the Japanese plane it was falling away from twenty-five hundred feet. Another flyer also saw it smoking, but neither pilot could confirm that it actually crashed.

All of Two Fifteen's Corsairs returned safely, Hernan behind everyone else. Meeting with intelligence officers for debriefing, scores were tallied and damage logged. After the mission debrief, the number of enemy planes shot down was added to previous totals and accumulated individual scores were examined. Don Aldrich's accumulated score was thirteen Japanese, Hal Spears had twelve, and Bob Hanson led with twenty-one claims.

Such high numbers by the three pilots made it difficult to avoid the topic of competition. Previously, Owens had been able to direct talk to other subjects, but now Hanson had passed the highest-scoring Corsair

Jovial, fun-loving Ed Hernan joined the Fighting Corsairs after a tour with VMF-214. He was killed flying in Korea.

ace, Ken Walsh, who had scored twenty victories. Despite the loss of several pilots and Owens's recent dunking, the enthusiasm of the three top scorers was not lessened. The Japanese were also undaunted; the number of *Zekes* challenging each raid was undiminished. With large numbers of targets, Aldrich, Hanson, and Spears were eagerly looking forward to the next mission and a chance to add to their tallies.

CHAPTER FOURTEEN

Chasing *Zeros*

*Generally he divided courageous aircrew into two categories: (a) men
with acute imagination who realized they would probably die and
who forced themselves to go on, and (b) men, who though intelligent,
could shut their minds off from imagination and carry on without
acute forebodings of the future.*
—GROUP CAPTAIN LEONARD CHESHIRE, V.C.

BOB OWENS WAS GROUNDED DUE TO HIS INJURIES BUT HE CHAFED AT
sitting on the ground and watching others get into action. He felt that
crash landing was something akin to falling off a horse; it was best that
he get back into the air as soon as possible. Unfortunately for the major,
Doc Neber kept him grounded for a full week after his water landing.

Missions to Rabaul were exhausting, leaving Barakoma about six in
the morning and arriving back at after six in the evening, with breaks at
Torokina en route. The flight north was shortened on January 27 when
the men of VMF-215 moved from Barakoma to Piva Yoke airstrip on
Bougainville. T.Sgt. W. L. Minor took care of the administrative work,
ensuring the administrative records made it to their new home. Lieutenant Tyler, the intelligence officer, took command of the few ground
personnel and put them aboard SCAT transports for the journey to Bougainville. Unfortunately, just as Two Fifteen was moving into Piva Yoke,
the squadron's ground crews were moving on to Green Island. Doc Neber
loaded all of the medical supplies, including the special liquid in the little

bottles, into crates and put them on the R4D provided. The dog Sydney, the squadron mascot, made way for himself. Living conditions for the pilots would not be improved with the move as there were no permanent facilities at the primitive airstrip that would be their new home. It seemed to be fate that Two Fifteen would occupy new airstrips that had rudimentary living conditions: Munda, Barakoma, and now Piva were all new with only basic necessities. They would bivouac on a small knoll not far from the flight line, living in tents that had been constructed in a hurry. They would maintain the rotation of aircraft with VMF-212, flying every other day to ensure more pilots would get a chance to fly. Unfortunately, their tents at Piva were also within range of Japanese artillery.

FIRST STRIKE FROM BOUGAINVILLE

The move was completed in time for two divisions to fly a combined TBF/SBD strike aimed at Tobera on January 28. Don Aldrich was the flight leader with his division and that of Hap Langstaff. The strike numbered thirty-six bombers, thirty-six more Corsairs from other squadrons, twelve New Zealand Kittyhawks, eight Navy Hellcats, and sixteen Army Lightnings. VMF-215 provided close cover on the SBDs. It was an impressive display of aerial power, outnumbering anything the Japanese could put into the air. All of the planes except for the Hellcats and Lightnings were flying from Bougainville. The SeaBees and engineers had created a network of three airfields on an island that had been invaded only a couple of months before, and most of the island was still held by the Japanese. The Japanese commander, Vice Admiral Kusaka, had predicted doom for Rabaul if the Allies were able to build airstrips on Bougainville. Missions like that on January 28 would prove his prophecy true.

The flight to Rabaul was much shorter without flying from Barakoma and stopping for fuel at Torokina. The top cover was engaged with enemy planes as soon as they closed on New Britain, but the SBDs were not accosted and were able to drop their loads expertly on the revetments and workshops around Tobera field. Visibility was excellent, the tropical sunlight forming a shining backdrop for the unfolding drama of aerial combat. The Japanese hit the bombers right after they dropped their bombs.

There were about sixty Japanese in the air, and they followed the retreating bombers all the way to the rally point near Duke of York Island. Despite the large number of aggressors, the Japanese were not able to get in close to the bombers due to the swarms of Allied fighters that met every onslaught.

Eagle-eye Don Aldrich and boyish John Burke weaved near the bombers and met each approaching Zeke with six .50-calibers of intimidation. Occasionally a Zeke strayed too close for too long, and the pair of Marines warned them off with a few shots. One Japanese pilot foolishly made a head-on pass against Aldrich and suffered the ultimate regret. His plane was last seen falling to the ocean in flames. A second head-on attack brought the same results. Two Zekes swung in too close and concentrated their attention on the SBDs, unaware that Aldrich and Burke were just above them. Aldrich managed a long burst at one and sent it careening into the sea.

As the pair of Marines rejoined the bombers, cannon and machine-gun fire raked their aircraft. A single Japanese fighter pulled up behind them, spraying bullets in long bursts, but proved unable to get a solid hit as the two Corsairs dived away. Burke's Corsair suffered damage to the right wing and stabilizer, and Aldrich was hit in the left wing and fuel tank. Heading home, Aldrich spotted a lone enemy aircraft at five hundred feet and opened fire. The bullets hit home, and the two Marines watched as the Zeke tried to initiate a split S, a half roll to the inverted and then a half loop to straighten out, at less than four hundred feet with fatal results.

Two Zekes attacked the bombers in a diving attack and then pulled up, one directly in front of Gizmo Gilman. He followed the Zeke and poured bullets into the cockpit and engine. It went down just a mile from Cape Gazelle. A nearly identical scenario played out in front of Gilman just a few minutes later. A Zeke pulled up to escape the fire from the two Corsairs, and Gilman sent it into the sea. A third Zeke took hits from Gilman's guns but he was unable to see the results and claimed only a probable.

Dick Samuelson caught a Zeke just past Cape Gazelle at one hundred feet. Another Corsair joined in, and both hammered the enemy plane until it exploded. What was left of the *Zeke* crashed into the sea. Samuelson shared credit for the kill with Lt. (j.g.) Robert Mims of VF-17, the pilot of the other Corsair.

Aircraft returning to base often discovered damage when they prepared to land. Johnny Burke thought he could land his Corsair instead of bailing out or attempting a water landing. But the Corsair was too badly damaged, and it crashed on the runway at Piva. The aircraft was written off, but Johnny Burke suffered only a bad laceration.

With no flaps and a flat tire, Don Aldrich also had a rough landing. An experienced pilot, he made a better landing than Burke and received a cheer from ground personnel when he brought the battered F4U to a successful stop. His plane was not a total loss and would fly again. Doc Neber received a good deal of satisfaction giving orders to Aldrich as

Doc Neber treats Don Aldrich after he received nine pieces of shrapnel in his thigh during a dogfight over Rabaul during which he downed his fourteenth, fifteenth, sixteenth, and seventeenth enemy plane on January 28, 1944. USMC Photo

he poked at the minor wounds to retrieve shrapnel. The two hammed it up for a camera as Neber bandaged the wounded thigh, the photograph ostensibly to prove that Neber did actually provide some service.

A third troubled landing took place when Dick Samuelson returned. Preparing to touch down, he discovered a cartridge case had jammed his oil cooler shutters. The cartridge case was probably from Lt. (j.g.) Mims's guns. Samuelson's dead stick landing caused no permanent damage, and the aircraft was quickly repaired.

MYSTERY FLIGHT

On the morning of January 30, twenty planes accompanied B-25s on a mission to bomb shipping in Simpson Harbor. Dick Braun commanded the mission, Ray Wolff led Owens's division, and Bob Hanson led Warner's division. Conant and Spears led their own divisions. It was an uneventful trip; there was no fighter opposition and antiaircraft fire was desultory. Yet one pilot did not return, John Fitzgerald. It was a strange disappearance, as his section leader, Lloyd Cox, couldn't remember when he'd last seen the young flyer. Fitzgerald made no distress calls nor was he seen leaving the formation. Roger Conant reported he'd seen a Corsair that might have been Fitzgerald hit by antiaircraft fire. A New Zealand pilot also reported seeing a Corsair falling in the drink and the pilot bailing out. They could not determine what actually happened to poor John Fitzgerald, the unluckiest pilot in Two Fifteen. They could only guess at the cause of his disappearance, as they had with the squadron's first loss, Gerry Pickeral, back in July of 1943. Most believed a large-caliber antiaircraft gun got him.

ROUTINE

The men of Two Fifteen settled quickly into their new home at Piva within earshot of the ground fighting. Food continued to be as bland as it had been on Munda and Vella Lavella. French toast, powdered eggs, and S.O.S. were morning staples and there was always plenty of syrupy coffee. It seemed the entire world, or at least all the men in a world at war, subsisted on dehydrated foods. Thoughts often returned to the plenty of Sydney with its abundance of steaks and fresh milk. Australia was not easily forgotten, as the diet of Spam, Vienna sausage, corned beef hash, and powdered food was often supplemented with mutton. There was little in the way of alcoholic refreshments in these forward areas, but stills were not uncommon. At least one of these "gin factories" at Piva exploded and burned down the tent it was housed in. Pilots often traded for bottles if they made ferry flights to Guadalcanal. Of course there was also a small liquid compensation from Doc Neber after a particularly hard mission.

The morning mission returned by 1240 that afternoon, and many pilots looked forward for the rest of the day to relax. Hap Langstaff and George Kross were sent out later in the morning to escort a PBY in search of a downed flyer. With several New Zealanders in their P-40s, they reached the coast of New Ireland and circled the PBY as it went low to search for the missing pilot. Finding no sign of a man in a life jacket or a life raft, Langstaff and Kross prepared to accompany the flying boat south.

The Kiwi pilots had other ideas. Instead of withdrawing with the patrol plane, they turned and began strafing the lighthouse area on Cape St. George. The Japanese had built small buildings and reportedly had a radar set or a coast watcher position at the site.

The P-40s went back and forth over the cluster of dwellings as the PBY disappeared to the south. Nervously, the pair of Marines remained high, covering the aggressive New Zealanders. They expected a swarm of *Zekes* at any moment but thankfully no Japanese intervened and the Kiwis, out of ammunition, headed for home.

DUBIOUS INTELLIGENCE

The relaxation of the pilots after the morning flight was interrupted by a report there would be another flight that day. It was urgent that they get into the air right away, with as many aircraft as they could fly. An aircraft carrier was reported to have slipped into Simpson Harbor and it was imperative that the Allies attack before dark. At 1600, seventeen Marines of VMF-215 ran to their Corsairs to take off from Piva Yoke.

The seventeen included two spares in addition to Dick Braun, Roger Conant, Ray Wolff, and Bob Hanson's divisions. Conant had a small division with only three planes. The pilots did a quick preflight check, a haphazard walk-around. Some had superstitious routines before each takeoff. They walked around their plane in a certain pattern, a lucky process, before mounting on the right side of the aircraft. Some carried a rabbit's foot or other trinket that was sure to give them luck. Others, like Roger Conant climbing aboard Corsair #259, preferred no lucky charms. Conant preferred nothing personal or individual in his plane for the same reason others carried such talismans. Members of Two Fifteen sadly still remembered the child's booties found in Jack Jordan's crashed plane.

The Bougainville airfields hummed with the deep cacophony of multiple aircraft engines. The runways were lined with idle groups of soldiers, sailors, and Marines as the aircraft of VMF-211, 215, 217, and the Navy's VF-17 waddled out on to the airstrip at Piva Yoke. On nearby Piva Uncle, the TBFs and SBDs lumbered down the Marston matting and lifted off. Closer to the sea, at Torokina Field, the Allison engines of eight New Zealand P-40s rattled the jungle.

The blast of a single Corsair's Pratt and Whitney engine was lost in the sounds of the many. Only a puff of smoke from the exhaust indicated an individual engine starting up. Slowly, mixture controls were pushed to auto-rich and the engines began to run more smoothly. In dozens of F4Us, pilots performed checks: temp, pressures, and magnetos as the engine ran to 1,000 rpm. Flaps, ailerons, and rudders were tested. The supercharger was checked, first switched from neutral to low, and a few seconds later, to high. Prop control fully down, throttle opened, pressure back on the stick to keep the tail wheel down, and the big birds began to move. Noses swung very slowly as the pilots tried to line themselves up on the runway. The field appeared to be a mess, planes moving to and fro, but underneath it all there was an unseen order. Intercooler shutters closed, fuel set on reserve, supercharger in neutral, and the pilots set the manifold to fifty-four inches and 2,700 rpm. The giant machines moved down the runway, lifting off at just about 90 knots and climbing out at 125 knots, the best climbing speed.

The Corsairs were low and medium cover on the Avengers. The fighters scissored with the slower bombers as they passed New Ireland, eagerly hoping for the sight of an aircraft carrier near Rabaul. As usual, some pilots were unable to continue and were forced to turn back for Bougainville.

Abort is the term used when a plane is forced to return before the completion of a mission. The cause of the return was something other than battle damage; an aircraft might lose oil pressure, begin to smoke, or strange noises from the engine or propeller might alert the pilot to a problem. There might be oxygen failure or loss of hydraulic pressure. After a few missions from Bougainville, most pilots were familiar with the planes that were troublesome and those that were relatively trouble free. One particular aircraft was tagged as the comic character "Hogan's Goat," because it was constantly suffering minor mechanical problems. Pilots avoided flying this plane altogether. Eventually that aircraft sported a drawing of the character and nickname painted on the cowling, a warning to inexperienced flyers.

Pilots learned with experience to use visual or auditory clues to help them determine if a problem was serious enough to turn back or only a minor irritant. Some Marines refused to turn back unless there was absolutely no choice. Often they were ordered to turn around by their division leader. Sammy Stidger had died due to a continually malfunctioning airplane that he insisted on flying. Other pilots turned back at the slightest indication of a problem. In many cases it was not possible to tell if something was really wrong or the problem was just a "feeling." This made it suspicious when a pilot turned back and mechanics found nothing wrong. Suspicions were also aroused when a pilot turned back on many flights.

Owens felt lucky he never had a pilot in his squadron who turned back frequently or under mysterious circumstances. The problem was not widespread among the squadrons, as other pilots would soon quickly see who was not pulling his share and the ensuing peer pressure would have been far too much for any Marine. Owens would have disposed of such a flyer, transferring him to a non-flying assignment. The tough Japanese defenses and long flights over the ocean were incentives to avoid any flights to Rabaul.

John Foster of VMF-222 related the story of a pilot in a squadron not his own who would fly to New Ireland with the rest of the formation and then drop out. He would circle alone until the others returned and fall in with the retiring aircraft. It was dangerous to be alone but the pilot could not face the terror of Rabaul. This particular pilot was eventually dismissed from the service, but that was probably a mild punishment compared to the loss of respect among his peers. It would be awkward if they ever met in the States after the war.

John Foster of VMF-215's sister squadron VMF-222 was a close friend of many of the Fighting Corsairs, especially the irascible George Sanders. His book *Hell in the Heavens* details VMF-222's part in the Bougainville Campaign. USMC Photo

In the afternoon of January 30, the Japanese defenders attacked early, just after the formation crossed Duke of York Island. There was no carrier in the harbor but the SBDs and TBFs hit the shipping in the harbor, five-hundred-pound bombs crashing into metal and wood or erupting in giant water geysers from misses and near-misses. They sank or crippled four large cargo vessels and several smaller ships. Antiaircraft fire was extremely vicious, as shells from the big guns reached up to fifteen thousand feet and the lighter guns filled the air with colorful tracers at lower altitudes.

Passing Praed Point on New Britain, Bob Hanson was startled by a Corsair flashing by hotly pursued by a *Zeke*. Hanson turned to intervene. The anonymous Corsair ran away from the *Zeke*, which zoomed up and away. It was a mistake. The climb brought the Japanese plane across the front of Hanson and Sam Sampler. Hanson opened fire and scored flaming hits. The *Zeke* went into the drink about three miles off the coast.

In the clouds above the harbor, Hanson and Sampler continued to look for targets. Climbing out of a layer of white, the Marines found themselves at ten thousand feet behind two *Tojo* fighters. The two Japanese interceptors flew along in a straight line until Hanson opened fire. The enemy split up, one heading for the clouds and the other falling victim to Hanson's guns. Hanson watched the *Tojo* spiral out of control and then led Sampler in search of the other Japanese plane.

The remaining *Tojo* was spotted darting in and out of the clouds below, racing for Rabaul. The Japanese plane was no match for the faster Vought, and Hanson quickly closed the distance. The *Tojo* pilot did not give in easily, flying erratically in an effort to throw off the Marine's aim. Hanson's shots eventually started fires at the wing roots, and the enemy fighter fell off to the right in a fatal dive.

With the redoubtable Sampler still beside him, Hanson arrived at the rally point to find dozens of airplanes engaged in combat or trying to avoid the action. Both Hanson and Sampler fired at various aircraft but couldn't get in a good shot or follow their target. They joined a group of Avengers heading south past the rally point where Hanson shot up another *Zeke* that approached the American planes head on. It crashed just off Cape Gazelle.

Major Owens had warned his pilots several times about strafing the radar site on the tip of New Ireland as the Japanese had hidden antiaircraft guns there. On this day, Bob Hanson had a great deal of nervous energy, as well as a few bullets, left over and led Sampler into a strafing run on the buildings on Cape St. George.

Lloyd Cox and Texan O. D. Hunter were the other section in Hanson's division. They followed the bombers in and strafed a small vessel in Keravia Bay. Rejoining the TBFs, they encountered two *Zekes* trying to slip in for a stern shot on a bomber. Cox fired at one, and Hunter took the other. Cox's target did an abrupt split S and disappeared back to Rabaul. Hunter's enemy was not so fortunate as it tried to make a high-speed turn away from the Corsairs. Notoriously sluggish in such turns, the *Zeke* fell easy prey to Hunter's gunfire. The Japanese plane rolled over and crashed into the water.

Ralph Robinson encountered a *Zeke* at thirteen thousand feet over Simpson Harbor and moved in for a stern attack. His gunfire shredded the *Zeke*, which went into a spin, apparently out of control. Robinson returned to his weave with Dick Evans and lost sight of the *Zeke*.

Evans was lured from his weave by the sight of a P-40 being chased by a Japanese fighter. Evans opened fire and distracted the *Zeke* long enough to allow the Kiwi to escape. Evans watched his bullets enter the darkly painted enemy plane and bore in until the Japanese plane started to smoke, falling away from five thousand feet to splash into the sea.

Traveling at ten thousand feet above the harbor, pugnacious Creighton Chandler also found Americans in distress, two F4Us being pursued by a single, darkly painted *Zeke*. Chandler latched on to the enemy's tail and caught the enemy easily. The .50-caliber bullets set the *Zeke* afire as if lighting a match, and the Japanese fighter fell into the Simpson Harbor wrapped in flames.

Chandler was not finished for the day. He scored an unusual victory. Over Rapopo Airfield he attacked a *Zeke* from astern. As his bullets scored hits on the enemy plane, the pilot bailed out. No smoke or fire, but it crashed into the water.

Twelve *Zekes* pounded after three Corsairs just past the rally point. Dick Braun observed the unequal contest and intervened. Although he only shot down one of the *Zekes*, the others all fled in different directions, allowing the other Corsairs to escape.

Weaving above the harbor, Frenchy Williams was confronted by a *Zeke* chasing a Corsair. Williams swung out and attempted to get a stern shot. He fired several bursts until the Japanese pilot seemed to lose control, and the *Zeke* rolled over slowly, diving in to the drink. It never showed flame or smoke.

The bomber pilots were disappointed not to have located the reported aircraft carrier, but they could be satisfied by the numerous hits they had scored on other shipping. They had several losses that day. John Fitzgerald was missing; no one had seen him after they passed Praed Point. Tom Stockwell's plane was shot up by a brief encounter with a *Zeke*, but the ground crew report laconically stated that his Corsair "can be repaired."

The late takeoff time forced some of the pilots to return as the sky darkened, with the last plane landing at 1930. The long, exhausting flight and poor lighting contributed to another loss. Frenchy Williams overshot the runway due to poor visibility and crashed. Williams was unhurt, but the Corsair was a complete write-off. On the balance sheet, Two Fifteen claimed eleven victims and Bob Hanson's score rose to twenty-five.

Zero-Chasin'

At the end of January 1944, Ray Wolff took a Corsair up for a test flight. Lloyd Cox and Chief Leu took older Corsairs back to Guadalcanal and returned with newer aircraft.

Bob Hanson's score of twenty kills in a little over two weeks had drawn more attention than normal to the squadron. Though the action had yet to be covered by the stateside press, local and military press took notice. A comic strip and several small articles about Hanson appeared in the *Bougainville Bulldozer*, spreading the story around Torokina and the adjoining airstrips. It was probably fortunate that the major news outlets did not get the story of Hanson and provide the publicity they had showered on Boyington during his attempt to pass Joe Foss's record of twenty-six kills. Hanson would have been a disappointment. He had none of the flamboyance or outspokenness of the leader of the Blacksheep. The big Marine was affable enough and enjoyed joking around with others of his squadron, but he was somewhat reserved when dealing with outsiders. New to the squadron after the first tour, he sometimes appeared to be a loner to the older members of the Fighting Corsairs. His life experiences and ability to speak several different languages gave him a more worldly character than some of the more provincial or inexperienced members of Two Fifteen. But he was more than willing to play bridge, wrestle, or participate in silly pranks. Roger Conant was his favorite, though often reluctant, wrestling partner. He recalled that Hanson often performed the vulgar but slightly humorous spectacle of lighting his farts.

Fame had little effect on Hanson. "Hanson is the least changed ace I've ever seen. No matter how many planes he gets, he's the same old Hanson," said the intelligence officer, Lt. Jim Tyler. Hanson was not the only well-known personality in the squadron; both Don Aldrich and

Hal Spears had high scores at the end of January, Aldrich with seventeen claims and Spears with twelve. After many flights to New Britain, pilots of the various squadrons knew each other as many had served or trained together previously. There was a common bond among the fighter pilots who had served several tours that was not confined to the Marines. They wore the same golden wings as the aviators in the Navy squadrons VF-17, 30, and 40 who flew Hellcats and Corsairs from the same airstrips as the Marines.

George Sanders had been part of VMF-222 before joining VMF-215, and his old flying buddy John Foster of Two Twenty Two recorded a conversation about the high scores being racked up over Rabaul. Foster queried Don Aldrich and Hal Spears about their recent success:

"Mainly luck," was Spears's opinion. "But there is also a certain amount of aggressiveness necessary also."

"When you see a plane you can get without exposing yourself unnecessarily to Japs waiting above—okay. Go ahead and get him," chimed in Aldrich.

"Above all, don't get separated from the bomber formation going wide and coming in on the Zeros by surprise. The Zeros are getting smart now. They form two or three different groups along the route they think we'll follow: then they change off with each other in staging their attacks.

"The little yellow bastards have been very unethical. Instead of coming in after the bombers, most of them are content to sit up there above us and try to pick off our fighter planes whenever they get a chance. We've got enough planes now so that we can have a roving high cover and at the same time help out the poor devils protecting the bombers. It's a hell of a feeling to sit there in your cockpit, and watch Zeros flying off to the side, doing slow rolls, loops, and anything else they can think of. Whenever they want to, they form a regular column and play follow the leader. They fly over you and as soon as one of the fighters gets in an exposed position in his weave, one of the Japs is always in the right position to make a run on him." Foster and the other Marines were unaware of a recent order from the Japanese command instructing their flyers to "attack or defend yourself only when battle circumstances particularly favorably to you." Talk drifted to other topics, such as the new radios

Bob Hanson, Don Aldrich, and Hal Spears composed a true Murderer's Row. These three accounted for 51 claims against the Japanese. The shorts were not a regular part of flying gear. USMC Photo

being installed in some of the planes, and the young men broke up their bull session and headed back to their bivouac areas.

Not all the pilots were happy with the talk about the higher-scoring aces like Aldrich, Hanson, and Spears. The aces themselves appeared relaxed and made no big deal of their victory claims, but non-flying and inconsiderate administrative personnel made thoughtless comments when praising the bigger scores. Many pilots felt it was unfair to single out any one member of a unit when the squadrons were supposed to operate as a team. Major Owens overheard one of his pilots, one of the best flyers in VMF-215, comment after hearing a rather tactless remark concerning the prowess of the top scorers. The disgruntled, and rightfully so, pilot said that he would load up the guns of his Corsair right then and face any other pilot in a duel to see who really was the best. While only half-serious, this challenge reflected how unthinking publicists could misread the events taking place. While a few pilots eagerly wanted to add to their scores, most of the experienced flyers knew it was not about high scores, as they had another, more important mission.

"It's not right to go Zero chasing when there's guys who can't defend themselves," sensitive and perceptive Lloyd Cox said, referring to the men in the SBDs, TBFs, and Army bombers that could not match the speed and maneuverability of the Japanese interceptors. His comments reflected the feelings of the squadron as a whole. Even with all the talk, the men of Two Fifteen were proud of their record, and their individual high scorers, but they were also determined to stick together, protecting those guys unable to defend themselves.

Navy and Marine pilots claimed eight victories on a mission to Rabaul on January 31, including kills by aces Philip DeLong and Hugh Elwood. During January, bombers had flown 1,038 sorties against the fortress. They had paid a high cost, losing eight B-24s, fourteen B-25s, eight SBDs, and five TBFs. The fighters contributed 1,850 sorties, losing thirty-seven Corsairs, five Hellcats, nineteen P-38s, and six of the New Zealanders' near obsolete P-40s. During the same month, Allied pilots were credited with 627 Japanese planes in the entire South Pacific area, with 458 downed in the Rabaul area.

The pilots of Two Fifteen received credit for eighty-five enemy aircraft in January. They contributed 209 sorties and suffered the loss of eight Corsairs, operationally or in action. Owens, Kross, and Aldrich had nearly been killed. Fitzgerald, Knight, and Moore were lost. The worst loss was that of Sammy Stidger. An original member of the squadron at Goleta, survivor of two tours, his death hurt the most. The fact that his death was an accident only made it seem more futile and senseless.

CHAPTER FIFTEEN

Final Flights

*Always pray, not that I shall come back, but that I have the courage
to do my duty.*
— Lt. Anthony J. Tutora Jr., killed in action,
October 15, 1942

Originally scheduled to start the month of February escorting a B-25 strike, the Fighting Corsairs stood down when the mission
was canceled due to poor weather. The next day they gave up their planes
to VMF-212 and took another day off. Still, life on Piva Yoke was not
without excitement.

Patrick Gildo Santin, the would-be priest, decided to do his impression of Johnny Weissmuller in the Tarzan movies. One afternoon he was
seen swinging through the upper branches of trees near the runway. It
must be noted that the vines of Bougainville were not nearly as plentiful or as strong as those depicted in Hollywood. His performance did
not match that of the cinematic ape-man, and poor Santin fell, ripping
through the canvas top of a visiting colonel's jeep. The colonel was very
understanding, and Santin, unhurt in the fall, ended up with only a quick
lesson in canvas stitching and repair.

Aerial activity resumed its pace on the third of February. As if to
make up for the last two days of relative inaction, the day saw every pilot
in the air on some type of mission. Starting with a dawn patrol, Two
Fifteen flew two escort missions, two search missions, and ended with

dusk patrol. The two escort missions were part of the strategy to keep pounding the Japanese at different times to keep their interceptors, and their pilots, in the air. It was a war of attrition.

DEADLY MISSION

The first escort took off at 0940 in company with eighteen Avengers, seventy-four Dauntlesses, and the Hellcats of VF-38 to hit Tobera Airdrome. Hal Spears led his division and that of Bob Hanson. There was little organized opposition. Groups of three to six *Zekes* tried to get at the bombers but were for the most part unsuccessful.

Hal Spears dived on a group of three *Zekes*, shooting one down, but its mates were able to escape. Over Blanche Bay, Spears noticed a division of Corsairs closing in on a single enemy fighter. Spears used his diving speed and position to cut in on the attack and shot the *Zeke* down, sending it crashing to the earth. He fired on a third target of the day but it pulled up and away from him, right into the gun sight of "Spud" Chandler on his wing. Chandler fired at the *Zeke* and it began smoking, the smoke growing worse as it dived toward the sea.

Once the bombers turned for the rally point and headed for Torokina, the pilots either looked for aerial targets to engage or went down to strafe. One of these pilots was Bob Hanson and he appeared as a tethered dog, the Japanese managing to stay just out of reach, looping and rolling until confronted by American fighters and then zooming up and away. George Brewer, on loan from Don Aldrich's division, flew as Hanson's wingman and tried to stay with him throughout the twisting and turning pursuits of Japanese interceptors. A *Zeke* and two Corsairs flashed close by, and Brewer ignored the chance to join the engagement to stay on Hanson's wing. Hanson evidently saw none of this, as the action took place a little behind and below him.

A *Zeke* slashed through the formation a few seconds later. The Japanese pilot sprayed bullets and cannon shells as it streaked up and away. Shells smashed into the engine and accessory section in the upper deck of Brewer's F4U, and it began to lose power. Brewer's Corsair lost altitude and airspeed. Smoke pouring from his plane, Brewer decided to abandon his aircraft. He unstrapped his harness, unplugged his cords, and stood up in the slipstream as he prepared to jump from the damaged Corsair.

As he straddled the cockpit sill, the lanky Marine looked below him and noted he was back over Tobera field. Thoughts of being captured by the people who had just been the focus of the morning's bombing made him uncomfortable, and he changed his mind. Perhaps he could ride out the flight a little longer, at least until he was clear of New Britain. Setting course for home, he was joined by a pair of Hellcats and the three managed to clear the harbor without being engaged by Japanese fighters. Brewer nursed the bent-wing bird all the way back to Torokina and landed with little trouble. The aircraft was repaired. His fellow pilots would later kid Brewer about his approach to Bougainville, trailing a long streak of black smoke that must have stretched all the way to Rabaul!

The American formation flew away from Cape Gazelle and Duke of York Island, approaching New Ireland, stragglers joining up with those that had maintained formation. Bob Hanson still had bullets and decided to expend his restless energy, and full load of ammunition, on the suspected enemy radar installation at Cape St. George. After checking with Hal Spears, Hanson pointed the nose down and dived, firing on the group of nondescript buildings and possible antiaircraft gun emplacements. Spears stated what happened next: "He strafed all right. Some ack ack shot at him and tore off part of one wing. He pulled up low over the water and skimmed along to make a water landing. Then one wing hit the water and he cartwheeled over and over in a big splash of water. Nothing but debris and an oilslick remained."

Creighton Chandler also saw the crash but discounted the amount of antiaircraft fire: "I saw the Corsair make a strafing run on Cape St. George, New Ireland. But the Corsair pulled up too late. The plane's right wing struck the water, the gasoline tank burst into flames, and the plane somersaulted into the water. I dropped down low but could see nothing except pieces of debris."

Lloyd Cox, fighting to see ahead through his oil-streaked windshield, knew Hanson was dead. He could tell from the way the plane struck the water that there was no chance that Hanson could have escaped instant death. Hal Spears led them back to Bougainville.

Aftermath

Don Aldrich led two divisions on a B-24 escort mission that left before the planes of the morning mission had returned. The flight to the target was uneventful. The bombers made their runs from north to south on Lakunai from twenty-two thousand feet. According to the Unit Diary, "Bombing of Lakunai was effective." The B-24s suffered no losses, and there was no aerial action. Ten to fifteen Zekes made an appearance but were satisfied to attack from twelve o'clock and then break away. VMF-215 suffered no losses but reported a PV-1 Ventura going down near Buka Passage.

Hope was not lost for Bob Hanson. Many pilots had been shot down and returned. Bob Owens, George Sanders, George Kross, Ken DuVal, and Hanson himself the previous November had been shot down but survived. Despite the negative nature of the eyewitness reports, Hal Spears took Johnny Burke, Lloyd Cox, and Hanson's wingman and diving partner, Sam Sampler, back to New Ireland later that afternoon for signs that the missing pilot could be rescued. After crisscrossing the area in a vain effort, the four Marines returned to Piva at 1730 that evening. Robert Murray Hanson died a day short of his twenty-fourth birthday.

Hanson died with twenty-five Japanese to his credit. His passing was too quick for the journalists, and they were never able to sensationalize his exploits as they had those of Gregory Boyington when he drew close to Joe Foss's magic mark of twenty-six victories. Hanson claimed twenty victories on six flights within the brief span of two weeks. He died before news of his feat could reach the general public, and he missed out on the accolades of his country. Perhaps it was best for the pilot and the writers, as Hanson would have disappointed the media with his reserved ways. For him, the unwanted publicity would have made his life uncomfortable. Death is a high price to pay for such convenience.

Earlier, when Hanson had been listed as missing in action off Bougainville, his parents had written to the commandant of the Marine Corps: "Even as a missionary to nonviolent 'Ghandi-land' I have never been able to accept the Pacifist position; so that none of our four sons have had any encouragement from us to avoid a share of the sacrifice Bob had to face. Mark, the eldest, is in the army; Stanley, the third, is in the Navy V-12 training program and is a sophomore in college; and Earl, not yet seventeen, is a high school senior. Mark, Bob, Earl and their four-year-old sister were born in India; Stanley here. In spite of having lived most of our lives in India, the USA is home—and worthy of the best we may have." They did not reply to the notice of his death.

Bob Owens, not much older than his charges but more mature than his years, talked little of the departed Hanson. Though hardly an intro-vert, Hanson was never as outgoing as someone like Sammy Stidger, and his loss was mourned differently. Owens spoke bitterly of the departed wrestler, as though Owens himself might have been able to stop Hanson from his almost self-destructive urges: "He wasn't afraid of anything. He took unnecessary risks, though. It was his own fault. He was probably trying too hard to pass Foss and Boyington." It is ironic that the final line of that epitaph wasn't entirely correct. The hard-flying, talented, and aggressive Bob Hanson had not died in any attempt to raise his score. He died strafing a group of decrepit and derelict structures on the ground.

On February 4, Robert Hanson's birthday, the commanding officer of Marine Air Group Twenty-Four presented Distinguished Flying Crosses and Air Medals to nine members of Two Fifteen. Like some macabre joke, one of Col. William L. McKittrick's awards included an Air Medal for Grafton S. Stidger, 1st Lt., USMC. That same day, Roger Conant and five others flew to Guadalcanal to pick up new aircraft. The pilots were disappointed with their replacement airplanes, as the Unit Diary acidly noted: "New ships were old rebuilt crates of the '02 series." The older Corsairs were of the birdcage variety with poor visibility.

Old or new aircraft, the pilots of Two Fifteen were in the air the next day. Nineteen planes accompanied B-24 Liberators to raid Lakunai. Gizmo Gilman was unable to make the flight after his Corsair refused to start. Japanese antiaircraft fire was intense but inaccurate, and bombers were able to plaster the northwest end of the runway, already burning in places due to an earlier light bomber attack. After their loads were gone, the bombers turned south, and four Zekes flew over them, dropping phosphorous bombs.

There were few targets, and the only claims were a "probable" by Conant and a "damaged" by Ralph Robinson. The squadron suffered no losses, but close cover was not as active as the outer layers of protection, and it provided few opportunities to shoot at the small number of enemy.

ON THE GROUND

The Japanese in the jungles of Bougainville continued to contest each advance of the Army and Marine units that were hacking their way inland. The sounds of nearby fighting carried easily back to the airstrips, and, like the old days on Munda, the noise made the aviation people uneasy. The Japanese possessed a few large-caliber artillery pieces and occasionally interdicted the airfields.

The biggest nuisance to the flyers and ground crews was the night heckler missions, typically single aircraft that dropped bombs at irregular intervals in the early morning or late evening hours and changed engine sounds and altitudes, all with the goal of interrupting sleep, annoying those on the ground, and performing reconnaissance. They struck in the early morning or late evening hours. The Japanese would often fly planes down to Buka, hide them during daylight hours, attack in the middle of the night, and then fly all the way back to Rabaul. The planes were usually obsolete *Val* divebombers or seaplanes. It was over Bougainville that the first Allied night fighters achieved success, and it was increasingly difficult to disrupt the routine of the Allied defenders. Nevertheless, sleep was a precious commodity.

The Marines of Two Fifteen were grateful for the abundance and proximity of shelters at Piva. They had become nocturnal combat veterans, having learned the value of a good foxhole after service at Guadalcanal, Munda, and Vella Lavella. The Marines dug personal shelters close to their tents, under the tent flaps, if possible, to keep out the rain.

George Sanders was the unintentional source of entertainment during one of the nocturnal raids at Torokina. He already had a reputation for strange incidents during alerts on Vella Lavella, once nearly drowning after diving into his fighting hole after frequent tropical rains. Another, less humorous incident, occurred after the dunking. Japanese aircraft were spotted on radar, and night fighters were dispatched when the first alarm was sounded. Pilots lay awake on their cots, debating whether or not the danger was great enough to warrant another run to the slit trenches.

The decision was made for them by the sound of aircraft engines closely followed by the shrill noise of bombs falling. Figures poured from tents and huts, scampering for their dugouts and bomb shelters. Poor George ran helter-skelter for the nearest trench and met a tree with his face. His countenance was badly lacerated, but the tree was uninjured.

Now, weeks later on Bougainville, Sanders again encountered problems during night alerts. During one of the regular visits by the Japanese, the men of Two Fifteen heard a banging and clanking sound as they dashed for cover. Through the half-light of a jungle night and antiaircraft fire, the figure of George Sanders was seen stumbling toward a shelter, a helmet securely attached to his foot.

MAXIMUM EFFORT

There were two flights to Rabaul on February 7. Four divisions escorted SBDs to Vunakanau at 0800, and two divisions took B-24s to the same target a half-hour later. It was a very busy day for some of the pilots. Dick Braun's division did an hour morning patrol and flew the second mission. Hap Langstaff, Ralph Robinson, and George Brewer missed the morning flight due to mechanical problems, but Langstaff and Brewer joined up with the later B-24 escort.

Sixty Dauntlesses, twelve Corsairs of the "Flying Deuces" from VMF-222, twelve Corsairs from VMF-212, twelve Kiwi P-40s, and VMF-215's thirteen planes made up the early attack. The Japanese fought fiercely both with antiaircraft fire and interceptors. There were at least fifty Japanese in the air, slashing across the formation, spraying bullets both at fighters and bombers.

The men of Two Fifteen scored big. Don Aldrich, Frenchy Williams, and Ed Hernan all claimed double kills. The pilot of a *Zeke* attacked by Hernan tried to exit his aircraft just as Hernan fired; he crumpled and went down with his plane. Johnny Burke and Hal Spears also scored. The squadron was also given credit for three probable kills and one damaged. The only damage to Two Fifteen's planes was a few holes in Ed Hernan's wings, the result of a hit-and-run attack by a *Zeke*.

The Japanese met the afternoon run with heavy antiaircraft fire, but their planes were less aggressive; only about ten *Zekes* appeared. Langstaff made the only claim, driving off four *Zekes* that tried to get in close and getting a "probable."

The planes cleared Cape St. George and were headed home when a streaking shape flashed through the fighters before anyone could react. The courageous, foolish, or lost Japanese pilot did no damage before diving away and disappearing to the north. "Its speed appeared to be in excess of 500 knots, as it quickly ran away from F4Us which nosed over and dove after it," noted the aircraft after-action report apologetically. Interestingly, the diving red line for the latest model of the *Zero* series was 455 knots! A trifle embarrassed, the Corsair and Kittyhawk pilots returned without further incident.

THE LAST BIG FIGHT

VMF-215 escorted a group of B-25s to Vunakanau in company with Corsairs from VF-17 and VMF-217 on February 9. Twenty-three planes from Two Fifteen were scheduled for the flight, but gremlins cut that number down. Tom Stockwell found he had a faulty voltage regulator and returned early. George Sanders and Gizmo Gilman also suffered small mechanical problems and did not complete the mission.

Lloyd Cox was unable to get his Corsair to start. He picked up a spare F4U and attempted to catch up with the already departed formation. Passing Buka Strait, Cox spotted something in the water and went down to have a look. The object in the water appeared to be an American life raft with someone in it. Circling slowly, Cox contacted Air-Sea Rescue and continued lower to buzz the flyer with an eye on Japanese gun positions on the nearby coastline. Cox flew a solo vigil over the gently rolling raft until he was forced to break off due to low fuel. Dumbo had a good fix on the downed airman, and he was rescued later that day. Cox soon after learned the man in the raft was a TBF gunner who had been afloat for twelve days. Unable to beach his raft on the enemy-held island, the man floated offshore the entire time.

The rest of the mission went off as planned. The B-25s approached Vunakanau from the west, dropping dozens of five-hundred-pound bombs on the target. Crews watched the results of their bombing, a giant cloud of smoke and dust that hid the airfield. The Japanese antiaircraft fire poked the sky in an effort to disrupt the bombing, but no interceptors arrived until the successful bombing was completed.

Approaching the target, Ray Wolff found he could not purge his wing tanks and decided to head home. Alone, he used clouds to hide his retrograde from the target area. Exiting from one cloud, two *Zekes* left the cloud at the same time. Unaware of the Marine, they casually flew on. Wolff was able to close on one and ripped it into pieces before its pilot could react. Having lost the second *Zeke*, Wolff went into a dive and sped home, not wanting to get caught with fumes in his tanks.

Don Aldrich, flying close cover on the B-25s, spotted a *Tojo* as it opened fire on another Corsair. Aldrich opened fire from long range, causing the *Tojo* to break away, and the other Corsair escaped toward the water. Aldrich stayed with the *Tojo* through several violent maneuvers but finally sent a telling burst into the enemy plane, which crashed near Rapopo Plantation. It was his twentieth victim.

Ed Hernan had a busy day, shooting down two *Zekes* and a plane he described as a Japanese army *Oscar*. In doing so he was nearly shot down twice. Once he was saved by his wingmen, O. D. Hunter and Frenchy Williams. The second time he dived away in his faster Corsair to leave an attacking *Zeke* lagging far behind. Nearing Bougainville, he found that his Corsair was banged up a bit and he was unable to get his gear down, making a landing in that configuration back at Piva. He was unhurt and the aircraft was repaired. Williams received credit for one of the *Zekes* that tried to nail Hernan.

Cox returned late and all of the others returned undamaged except for Ed Hernan. It was the second straight mission that Hernan returned with a damaged aircraft.

GOING HOME
VMF-215's final combat flight took place on February 12. Bob Owens was still unable to command; he had only flown a test hop to see how he felt and decided to stay on the ground. Thrifty Warner would lead an early mission to Tobera. It was a relatively uneventful flight in, and the bombers exited the Tobera without aerial opposition. The SBDs were a little slow to reach the rally point, and Warner and Larry Snyder turned

Ten days after Robert Hanson's death on February 3, 1944, the remaining nine aces of VMF-215 posed. Front row, L to R: Ed Hernan, eight victories; Don Aldrich, twenty kills; Bob Owens, seven kills; Hal Spears, fifteen kills; G. M. H. Williams, seven kills. Back row, L to R: Arthur "Thrifty" Warner, eight kills; Roger Conant, six kills; Creighton Chandler, six kills; Dick Braun, five victories. Author's Collection

back to protect them. About twenty enemy planes made an appearance during the withdrawal. Warner led Snyder in an attack on the tail end group of four fighters. Snyder attacked a *Tony*, and Warner attacked a *Zeke*; and both targets went down in flames. The enemy attack was broken up. These were the last two aerial victory claims for Two Fifteen. The third tour was over, but the battle to isolate Rabaul would go on.

On February 14, the pilots of Two Fifteen boarded R4D transports and left for Efate via Guadalcanal. Some were so happy to leave that they left everything they owned, except for what they had in their pockets or

Seventeen pilots of VMF-215 returned after completing their three six-week tours. Fourteen posed on return to San Diego in March of 1944. Back row, L to R: George Sanders, O. D. Hunter, Don Aldrich, Lloyd Cox, Thomas Stockwell, and John Breneman. Front row, L to R: Roger Conant, Reinhardt "Chief "Leu, Dick Braun, Arthur Warner, Bob Owens, Hap Langstaff, Lawrence Smith, and George Kross. Author's Collection

on their backs, in the desolate tent camp they had lived in for the last few weeks. Third-trip pilots would go home, while first- and second-tour flyers would go to Sydney and return north for another tour under the command of Maj. James K. Dill, who had served in VMF-212 as executive officer with two aerial victories to his credit.

At Efate, the flying echelon was reunited with the ground echelon for the first time since July 22, 1943. For a few days the men were able to enjoy the relative comforts of Dallas huts and peaceful, uninterrupted nights. The pilots who were remaining for another tour left for Sydney on the 18th. Ten days later, seventeen pilots headed for home, Uncle Sugar in local parlance: Bob Owens, Thrifty Warner, Don Aldrich, Hal Spears, Hap Langstaff, Dick Braun, Chief Leu, Ray Wolff, Roger Conant, Lloyd Cox, John Breneman, Ed Hernan, George Sanders, O. D. Hunter, Larry Smith, Tom Stockwell, and George Kross. Eleven of these tired Marines had formed the squadron back at Santa Barbara.

CHAPTER SIXTEEN

Afterwards

To a far greater degree, they deserve credit for having knocked the enemy out of the sky in the Solomons and over Rabaul. . . . In accomplishing this, Marine fighters were the majority throughout the ascent of the Solomons, and man for man, plane for plane, they were certainly the equal of any American in aerial combat.

—Peter A. Isely and Philip A. Crowl,
The U.S. Marines and Amphibious War:
Its Theory and Its Practice in the Pacific War

Things did not go well for Admiral Kusaka and the Japanese airmen at Rabaul after VMF-215 left. Conditions steadily grew worse, as supplies from the outside were effectively blockaded by the Allies' naval and air power. Submarines and *Betty* bombers brought in supplies at infrequent intervals, but any large merchantman risked destruction attempting to enter Simpson Harbor. Still, the Japanese refused to become disillusioned by the poor situation and continued to challenge each Allied air strike. It was not just the blockade that determined the fate of Rabaul but events elsewhere that contributed to the final fate of the once mighty, now impotent, aerial bastion.

The US Navy in 1944 possessed the most powerful, well-trained, and numerous carrier force in the world. It was decided by the Chiefs of Staff to use this mighty fleet to strike a decisive blow, one that would cripple Japanese air and naval power in the Pacific. On February 17, the fast carriers struck the massive Japanese fleet anchorage and naval air station at Truk Atoll. No major Japanese fleet units were present, but forty ships were sunk in the raid. The air strikes wiped out Japanese naval airpower in the Central Pacific, destroying over 250 enemy planes in two days of raids. A follow-up raid hit the Marianas with similar, though less spectacular, results.

In addition to the severe losses of aircraft, newer Allied planes outclassed their Japanese opponents. The agile, sleek *Zero* series was improved by adding armor and self-sealing fuel tanks like Allied fighters, but this reduced its range and maneuverability. The newer versions of the Hellcats and Corsairs were superior to the *Zeros* in nearly every category, and the newer Army P-38s replacing the older P-40 Warhawks and P-39s were more than a match for the *Zeros* when used properly. The Japanese were building newer types of aircraft, but they did not reach frontline units until later in 1944. Even with airplanes that could match the Hellcats and Corsairs, the quality of Japanese pilots had deteriorated; training was shortened, and many were sent to operational units in the field for final training.

In view of massive attacks on the interior lines of the Japanese Empire, the Imperial High Command decided that Rabaul was too far forward to maintain safely. The remaining Japanese aircraft at Rabaul were ordered to fly to Truk. Kusaka was left with a hollow fortress that could not defend itself or project any power. The aircraft began leaving on February 20, 1944, and the last aircraft left on the 25th. There would still be some occasional aerial opposition to Allied attacks, but the greatest number of interceptors available would be only seven. Intelligence surmised that these were composite planes, constructed by hardworking mechanics from wrecks, not an influx of Japanese air strength.

"We broke the back of the Japanese Air Force, at least the Naval Air Force, at Rabaul," said Bob Owens. Coupled with the losses at Midway, battles in the Solomons, and the Navy raids on Truk, he was correct. The Allies in New Guinea, primarily the Fifth Air Force, must also be credited with the destruction of the Japanese army air forces during the same time period. For the rest of the war, both Japanese army and navy units operated with large numbers of obsolete aircraft, operated by inexperienced pilots and ground crews. The infamous kamikaze attacks were one of the last-resort tactics that Japan used due to the lack of trained personnel and outdated aircraft.

THREE TOURS FINISHED

The excellent ground crews of VMF-215 stayed on until October of 1944 with a succession of air echelons, serving most of that time on Bougainville. They not only serviced the planes they were most familiar with, Corsairs, but any type of single-engine fighters and bombers as well as multi-engine planes such as the Douglas R4Ds (the famous DC-3). During March, the Japanese ground forces on Bougainville made a major effort to drive the Americans out of Torokina. The massive artillery bombardment and ground assault nearly succeeded. The ground crewmen of Two Fifteen were smack in the middle of the action, and some of the men were put into foxholes on the front lines. Nearly every day the Marines went into the shelters due to artillery fire and night hecklers. As the Japanese crept closer, bullets from infantry weapons flew through the service areas, and one man was killed by small-arms fire. Nevertheless, the crews of Two Fifteen kept the availability of aircraft they serviced at 95 percent.

The remaining flight echelon under Maj. James K. Dill began their next tour of duty from the strip at Piva Uncle. They continued to fly to Rabaul but also hit targets on New Ireland as far away as Kavieng on the northern tip of the island. From Bougainville, the planes moved on to the new airstrip at Green Island and continued their attacks on the Rabaul/Kavieng area. They flew escort missions, but with the lack of aerial opposition, they spent most of their time perfecting divebombing tactics from the Corsair. Several pilots, including John Burke, were lost due to antiaircraft fire. Burke, known for his pleasant disposition and eager smile, joined Two Fifteen after the first two tours. Credited with two aerial kills, he died in a poorly planned attack on Buka on April 18, 1944. The remainder of Two Fifteen returned to the United States in October of 1944. The designation VMF-215 finished the war as a training squadron in Hawaii.

Many of the original pilots remained together and were assigned to the same escort carrier group commanded by Bob Owens. Others were sent to new squadrons as cadre personnel; combat experience was valuable to leaven out the hundreds of new pilots joining operational units. The original pilots of Two Fifteen, those who had served the first three tours in the Solomons, set several air combat records, and this was acknowledged by the US Navy in a Unit Commendation for the period of July 24, 1943, to February 15, 1944. They were officially credited with 137 enemy planes (later research revised this total to 135½ kills), with another forty-six probably destroyed in the air and twenty-one destroyed on the ground. This was in addition to numerous barges and small vessels they wrecked. The squadron lost thirteen pilots in various circumstances. Three were killed by fire from Japanese planes. Three were killed by enemy antiaircraft fire. Twenty-seven Corsairs were lost, including the one borrowed by Ken Walsh.

It is important to note that the Navy Commendation contains a line remembering the "resourceful, tireless, and skilled ground personnel who serviced and maintained the planes despite daily hostile shellfire and nightly bombing attacks." The writer of the citation was unaware that the flight and ground echelons had spent most of their time separated, but the description was both accurate and deserved. The men who serviced Two Fifteen's planes, no matter their service or unit affiliation, and Two Fifteen's ground crews that serviced other squadrons' aircraft, were resourceful and tireless.

There were ten aces in the squadron, ace being an overworked but easy measure of a fighter pilot's success. Hanson's twenty-five kills led the pack. Sharp-eyed Don Aldrich ended the war with twenty, and gutsy Hal Spears had fifteen. Ed Hernan and Thrifty Warner each bagged eight Japanese, and Bob Owens and Frenchy Williams finished with seven apiece. Both Roger Conant and Creighton Chandler claimed six, and Dick Braun added five more. Six of these aces had left Midway together, and only one failed to return home.

Counting skill by numbers of victories was not always a fair measure of a pilot's skill as Roger Conant confessed: "Being an ace is not a big deal. It was simply a matter of simply being in the right place at the right time." Most felt their job was to protect their wingman and if that resulted in aerial victories, then so be it. Conant had done his job well, as three of his kills and three of his probable kills were shot off the tail of his section leader, Bob Owens. It was a pity that some very capable flyers received little attention simply because they didn't shoot down five enemy planes. The original members of Two Fifteen remembered Ray Tomes as the best combat pilot, but he had only four credited victims at his death. Pilots acknowledged the skill of Hap Langstaff, Tomes's pupil. Bob Owens later stated that if he had a choice of wingmen, Langstaff would top the list.

The squadron was the highest-scoring Marine fighter unit in the battle for Rabaul, second only to the Navy's VF-17 in total number of enemy downed. VMF 215's total was the fourth-highest Marine squadron of the war, yet it served only in the Solomons Campaign. Other squadrons served early in the war in the Solomons and then flew against kamikazes later to add to their totals. The people at Vought kept a portfolio of press clippings concerning the squadron that carried the name of the firm's most famous aircraft. This was presented to Bob Owens and the first group of returning pilots.

Deactivated on November 13, 1946, VMF-215 was reactivated as a reserve unit in Olathe, Kansas, on June 1, 1951, flying F4U-4 Corsairs. After a short period flying jets, the squadron was decommissioned permanently on January 30, 1970. On March 8, 1970, Maj. Gen. Robert Gordon Owens Jr., who had been awarded the Navy Cross for his service with Two Fifteen, wrote: "It is with deep regret that I see this unit leave the rolls of the Marine Corps. Its name will long be remembered by myself and all others as they recall those units which have given so much in the defense of this country." The unit designation VMF-215 ceased to exist. The story they wrote in the sky above Rabaul was easily eradicated with the simple stroke of a pen.

THE BENT-WING BIRD

The aircraft that lent its name to VMF-215, the F4U Corsair, enjoyed a long career, staying in production until 1952. The pilots of Two Fifteen lauded their mount. O.D. Hunter fondly remembered: "The meekest aviator became a tiger at the controls of a Corsair. It is the greatest fighter plane of all time. We had complete confidence in its capabilities as a stable gun platform, ability to withstand high G loads and continue to fly when damaged by enemy fire." As the war progressed, rocket and bomb racks were added to the Corsair, and it became the premier close support aircraft for the Marine Corps.

As the Corsair improved and newer models were produced, it became a favorite of those who flew it. Tommy Tomlinson praised the Vought Company: "The first Corsairs really were not safe. . . . One of the astounding things that happened during the war was how rapidly they improved the Corsair, how the engineers kept modifying the bird, with incremental changes that improved the plane at every stage." Newer models of the Corsair served as the primary close air support weapon of the Korean War. Capable of carrying a substantial bomb load and staying on station for a long time, Marines, soldiers, and Allied fighting men all were cheered at the sight of the propeller-driven fighters. Over 70 percent of the close air support missions flown by the Navy and Marine Corps, day and night, were flown in Corsairs. They continued in their role as fighter planes, downing North Korean aircraft throughout the war including a Russian-built jet fighter. The only Navy fighter ace, Guy Bordelon, shot down all five of his victims in an F4U-5N night fighter. Corsairs were provided to the French who flew them in Indochina, Algeria, and the Suez. Corsairs also flew in the air forces of Argentina and El Salvador as well as Argentina's navy. One Salvadoran Corsair pilot scored three aerial victories in the so-called Soccer War in 1969 between El Salvador and Honduras. The last Corsair retired from operational service in Honduras during 1979.

WHERE DID THEY GO?
For the leading aces of VMF-215, fame was fleeting. Bob Hanson never got to be a personal flyer for a great maharajah, but he did shoot down more planes than any other Corsair pilot, Navy or Marine. He was the Marine Corps' second-highest ace, behind the great Joe Foss. On August 19, 1944, Maj. Gen. Lewis G. Merritt presented the Medal of Honor to Mrs. Harry Hanson, Hanson's mother. The medal was specifically awarded for his flight in breaking up the torpedo attack on November 1, 1943, and his action on January 24, 1944, when he downed four *Zekes*. A

destroyer, USS *Hanson*, DD-832, was commissioned on May 11, 1945, serving until March of 1973 before being given to the Republic of China where it served another thirty years. The Marine Corps remembers the exploits of Hanson each year through the Robert M. Hanson Award to the "Most Outstanding Fighter Attack Squadron."

There is no grave for Bob Hanson, but there are two cenotaphs in his memory, one in Newton, Massachusetts, and the other in India. His school in India named their athletic field in his memory. His name is also listed at the Manila American Cemetery and Memorial in the Philippines. Ironically, his younger sister Edith became an actress and activist in Japan.

Hal Spears also dreamed of turning his flying career into something special, but was unable to fulfill his dreams. On December 6, 1944, Spears and Thrifty Warner took an SBD on a routine flight out of El Toro, California. Trouble developed during the landing and the old Dauntless crashed in flames. Harold Spears, victor in fifteen combats, was killed in the blaze. Arthur T. Warner, victor in seven combats, spent two years in the hospital before he was medically retired. Warner would live the rest of his life in the shadow of that tragic event.

Don Aldrich was awarded the Navy Cross for his actions over Rabaul and chose to remain in the service after the war. Unfortunately, the postwar world is not always kind to returning servicemen. In May of 1946, Aldrich, gifted leader and ranking ace of those that returned home, experienced some personal problems while stationed at Cherry Point, North Carolina. Given leave, Aldrich decided to fly home to Chicago but encountered bad weather en route. Unable to reach home, Aldrich decided to land at a small airport he had used before the war. Unfortunately the airstrip was in disrepair and his Corsair flipped over on its back upon landing. Donald N. Aldrich, credited with twenty victories, broke his neck and died.

The mystery of John Fitzgerald's disappearance was answered after the war. Years later, members of the squadron found out that the unfortunate pilot, unlucky so many times, had been shot down and taken prisoner by the Japanese. Sent to Rabaul, Fitzgerald met another pilot who had also mysteriously disappeared, Charles Lanphier. It was Lanphier who had been lost in the bad weather the day that Alvin Jensen swept in and destroyed a large number of enemy planes on the ground at Kahili. Lanphier's brother, Thomas, was a member of the attack that killed Admiral Yamamoto on April 18, 1943. Fitzgerald and Lanphier were part of a group of Allied prisoners who were systematically starved, denied medical care, and beaten by the Japanese. The majority of Allied prisoners died of this abuse, including Fitzgerald and Lanphier.

Another missing Two Fifteen flyer was Jack Knight. His aircraft was lost due to oxygen failure or possibly enemy fire on January 14, 1944, and he was taken prisoner at Rabaul. On February 20, 1945, Knight was placed on the Japanese merchant ship *Kokai Maru* and sent to Japan. A day later, the ship was attacked by Allied aircraft and sunk. He was presumed to have died in the sinking.

Curly-haired Ed Hernan stayed in the Marine Corps. While in California, the lanky Marine held court in a place called the White House. He entertained bystanders with tales of his exploits in the war, some true and many not even close. Sitting on a barstool, the affable and irascible flyer would tell the assembled patrons of his aerial escapades like any fighter pilot with a great deal of hand motions. Invariably his hands would go up and over in chandelles and loops, palms going up and over his head. He would end up sprawled on the floor. Invariably he would repeat the performance every few days. Flying as a night fighter pilot in Korea, Edwin J. Hernan, victor in eight aerial battles, was shot down and killed by an anonymous antiaircraft gunner on July 19, 1951.

More than any other member of the squadron, Bob Owens imprinted his personality on the Fighting Corsairs. He was awarded the Navy Cross, the nation's second-highest award, for his service and personal bravery with Two Fifteen. He downplayed his personal bravery, later stating: "When you're the leader, you have to be brave. The choice isn't up to you." During the remainder of the war he served in various assignments, including command of a Marine air group assigned to an escort carrier.

After leaving Two Fifteen, he took part in an interesting flight on May 22, 1944. With two other pilots, he was given an FG-1 Corsair and given the task of flying from San Diego to New York to test the aircraft's limits. The three flew at over thirty thousand feet all the way from San

Diego to a refueling stop at Indianapolis, Indiana. Owens averaged 410 miles per hour during the first leg of their trip. After taking off from Indianapolis, the trio ran into a storm short of their goal. He was tossed about and flung up to thirty-eight thousand feet when he lost consciousness. Awakening at six thousand feet, he got his Corsair under control. "I was plenty scared because my plane was in a steep dive, on its back and going like a streak." He managed to land in Harrisburg, Pennsylvania.

Everyone agreed that Bob Owens was a crackerjack pilot. Here he is pictured with fellow FG-1D pilots who attempted to break the coast-to-coast speed record on May 22, 1944. USMC Photo

Owens stayed in the Marine Corps after World War II. He served in a variety of line and staff posts over the years. Not content with his fighter training, he earned his rotary wings in May of 1955. His career included command of squadrons, groups, and a Marine air wing in Vietnam. As the assistant chief of staff of the Marine Corps, he was part of a special honor guard at President Dwight Eisenhower's funeral in Abilene, Kansas, on April 2, 1969. He retired as a major general in 1972. Afterwards, he spent his time in real estate and raised orchids. He enjoyed playing golf, often with his old wingman Roger Conant. He died in 2007 and is buried in Arlington National Cemetery.

The man who prepared and took the squadron to war, Jim Neefus, continued his career in the Marine Corps after World War II. He served in the Korean War and a variety of other assignments before retiring in 1962. Fellow Marine pilot John L. Smith, an ace over Guadalcanal, helped Neefus get a job in the aerospace industry. Tom Stockwell remembered his old commander: "He deserves a lot of credit for welding us into a team. In light of later experiences I can appreciate his effort to create competent pilots functioning as a unit, and to train young officers to accept the responsibilities inherent to operations in a squadron."

Tom Stockwell remained a Marine, serving in a number of interesting assignments, including a stint in night fighters with Hap Langstaff. Faced with the choice of flying rotary-wing aircraft or becoming an infantryman, Stockwell chose to become a grunt. He ended his military career as a ground pounder. Retired, he moved to Louisiana to enjoy his sailboat.

Roger Conant left the Marine Corps after World War II but was called up again for the Korean War. He flew a variety of missions, including night fighters, close air support, and even transports. After the Korean War, Conant went to work for Douglas Aircraft Company, flying for over thirty years until age grounded him with over fifteen thousand flying hours. During his time with Douglas he became an ace again, shooting down five B-17s in missile tests.

Lloyd Cox finished World War II as the commander of the fighter element in a Marine escort carrier group. He left the Marines after the war and became a successful businessman.

George Brewer retired after twenty years in the Marine Corps. Brewer was admitted to the bar in 1957 and practiced law in California.

Cool, calm O. D. Hunter retired after twenty-six years in the Corps. He worked in a manufacturing company and then formed his own company. A true Texas gentleman, he owned a few oil wells.

Johnny "Loophole" Downs led a notably interesting life after Two Fifteen. He flew with Charles Lindbergh on a strike against New Ireland while serving with VMF-222. After the war, Downs returned to practice law in his home area of St. Joseph, Missouri. He did much better with his new clients than he did defending Doc Neber during the mess hall altercation. He served as a state representative for two years and state senator for ten years. Downs served on President Jimmy Carter's staff and as US minister to the International Aviation Organization in Montreal. His entire career was spent practicing law and consulting on aviation affairs.

Larry Smith stayed in the Marine Corps as a reservist. He went into industrial sales in 1948 and later opened his own business.

Sam Sampler pursued a career as a reserve officer. He flew with New York Airlines, fulfilling the dream of his old wingman Bob Hanson, to use his flying skills to make a civilian career in aviation.

Dick Samuelson worked with the Indiana State Police after World War II and was called up for the Korean War. He returned to the state police in 1955, finally retiring from the Inland Container Corperation after working as a pilot. During a reunion dinner in 1983, his impromptu and stirring rendition of "Paper Doll," a hit from 1943, brought tears to the eyes of the assembled veterans.

Gizmo Gilman, stuck with that improbable nickname by some long forgotten Navy chief, stayed in the Marine Corps until 1961. After working in law enforcement for Orange County, he retired for good in 1978.

Always a gentleman, Dick Braun became a successful academic after commanding a squadron in the Korean War. He was professor of law at Georgetown University, a US assistant attorney general, dean at the University of Detroit School of Law, and the founder of the University of Dayton law school. Finally, he retired from the Campbell University law school in 1989. A scholarship for second- or third-year law students is awarded in his name at Campbell.

Colorful George Sanders was sent overseas again, seeing action on several occasions, including the bloody fighting on Peleliu. After twenty years as a Marine, Sanders worked as a photographer for the US Civil Service. He retired to Oregon, in a beautifully forested area not far from another Marine fighter pilot, Marion Carl.

Jake Knight sold real estate after the war. Talented and creative, Knight was an art director and designer at an advertising agency. Finally, he ended up as a vice president of a small manufacturing firm.

"The Kid," Ray Wolff, was no longer a kid after his combat experiences but the nickname stuck. He flew night fighters later in the war but his most vivid memories were those of visiting Nagasaki and the victims of the atomic bomb. He resigned his commission in 1947. He spent his career mostly in sales. At a reunion, Bob Owens's former shadow found himself being kidded for still being the youngest looking of the assembled fighter pilots.

The leader of "Hap's Junior Birdmen," Hap Langstaff, was another career Marine, including seventy-five missions with VMF-311 in Korea. He became one of the most respected Marine pilots and after military retirement continued in aviation with Aerojet Corporation. Hap's old division mate, Chief Leu, was a Marine's Marine. Leu served through the Vietnam War ducking bullets while flying helicopters. Leu had a deep interest in history, and living in Virginia allowed him to immerse himself in our nation's past.

George Kross, another member of Hap's division, retired from the Marine Corps in 1957. The former enlisted pilot worked in defense-related jobs until 1963 when he joined Bay Area Rapid Transit in the San Francisco Bay area. He finally retired in 1978. He was very active in the Silver Eagles, a group of former Navy enlisted pilots.

The center of Two Fifteen's positive morale during their first three tours, Doc Neber, found himself at odds with the Navy when the war ended and was only too happy to shed his uniform when hostilities ceased. He became medical director at a small college in Hickory, North Carolina, and opened a small family practice there. Years later, Jim Neefus told the good doctor: "I always felt that you had a tremendously good effect on the pilots and men of the squadron, and was in a large way responsible for a good deal of the success the squadron had from the beginning to the return from combat. You were a great help to me in keeping up the morale at all times and I am thankful that I was fortunate enough to have you assigned as squadron flight surgeon." O. D. Hunter added: "Even the powdered eggs tasted better with Doc at the table with you."

Billie K. Shaw became a very successful businessman. He enjoyed flying so much that he underwent heart surgery to remain current. Spider Snyder became an inspector for the Federal Aviation Administration.

Gerry Shuchter retired first from the Marines in 1963 and worked for Douglas until full retirement. Ray Wetzel died in a flying accident.

Red Lammerts, one of the pilots who left Two Fifteen early in an effort to get into the action, became a successful businessman and mayor of his hometown in Oklahoma. He also had the unique opportunity to own and operate his own F4U Corsair.

Some Marines who rubbed shoulders with Two Fifteen deserve further mention. Alvin Jensen, whose daring attack on Kahili destroyed twenty-four planes, finished the war with seven aerial victories. George Kross witnessed Jensen's death at Patuxent River, Maryland, in a flying accident in 1949.

Gregory Boyington, who took over VMF-214 after Bob Hanson and several others left to join Two Fifteen, has told his story in books and on television. He ended the war with twenty-eight victories, if his six claims with the Flying Tigers are counted. He remains one of the Marine Corps' most enigmatic personalities, his civilian life as varied as his military career. He enjoyed the spotlight and spent much of his last years signing autographs at air shows.

Kenneth Walsh retired in 1962, respected as a Marine Corps aviator rivaled only by his contemporaries Joe Foss and Marion Carl. After shooting down twenty planes during the Solomons Campaign, he added another kill to his record flying an F4U-4 off Okinawa late in the war. He flew missions in Korea and retired from the Marine Corps in 1962. At a reunion in 1983, Jim Neefus vividly recalled the steely-eyed young man who borrowed a Corsair at Munda but never returned it.

The men of VMF-215 were successful as a fighter squadron for a variety of reasons. One reason was that the original pilots who arrived in the South Pacific had been together as a unit, for a long period of training, in some cases a year. They got to know each other on liberty in Santa Barbara, and during training in California, Hawaii, and Midway. They were a close-knit group that knew each other intimately. Most of their replacement pilots were experienced with other squadrons and some had already been credited with aerial success.

Their success was also due to the time of their arrival in the war zone. In July of 1943 the Corsair was more than equal to the *Zero* fighter and the Allies were nearly equal in numbers to the Japanese. Slogging through the Solomons, they overcame poor living conditions and inadequate maintenance and logistics to defeat the Japanese over Rabaul. Their aerial success must also be attributed to the number of targets. Flying over Rabaul provided a target-rich environment that allowed Two Fifteen the opportunity to shoot down many Japanese.

The final component was leadership. Starting with Jim Neefus and Bob Owens then trickling down to the division and section leaders, leadership formed a basis for the new pilots, whether they joined at Midway or before one of the combat tours, to be integrated seamlessly. It allowed the novices to learn to stay alive long enough to learn through their own experience the skills to survive. Jim Neefus called them the "greatest group of pilots ever put together." When asked what it was that made them so successful, he said that it was the "things that they brought

Scoreboard drawn by
Hap Langstaff. Author's
Collection

with them," acknowledging the variety of personalities in the squadron. There were personality conflicts and disagreements, but the Marines of Two Fifteen were a tight-knit group. Like many squadrons, they believed they were the best and flew as a team. There were many excellent aircraft beside the F4U Corsair and there were many excellent military units that fought well in World War II, but there was only one outfit that was the "Fighting Corsairs."

Aerial Victories

A few lives would feel empty, as they had while he was away at college and out in the Pacific, fighting. The father and mother and the sisters and the brothers would always remember him and regret that he had to die so young. The sweetheart would be brokenhearted and hysterical.

Time would pass and the family again would laugh at jokes and enjoy the dancing, the theatres and their fellow men; the sweetheart would find that someone else could matter. She would marry, have children, and soon but faint remembrances of the pilot who died so young, so long ago, would remain.

Very quickly in the lives of mankind all is forgotten. All that remains is the record—DIED IN ACTION.

—JOHN FOSTER, VMF-222

THE MISSION OF A MARINE CORPS FIGHTER SQUADRON IN THE PACIFIC was to destroy enemy aircraft, but more than 80 percent of Marine fighter pilots never saw an enemy airplane. Along with their Navy and Army counterparts, they accomplished their mission only too well. As the war progressed, the Japanese turned to kamikazes, and the fighters shot them down by the hundreds. The fighters were increasingly used as attack aircraft due to the introduction of bomb and rocket racks and the lack of enemy air opposition.

"Show me a hero and I'll show you a bum," said Pappy Boyington. Of those who did see and engage enemy aircraft, there has recently been a great deal of controversy as to the credibility of their claims. Two important researchers, Frank Olynyk and Robert Sherrod, combed the records to see how many Marines were officially "aces," credited with more than five aerial victories, and they came up with a total of 125. Ten of these aces flew with VMF-215. Unfortunately, the number of enemy aircraft downed, and thus the number of kills for these pilots, has now been questioned. When consulting Japanese records in an attempt to reconcile the number of enemy aircraft lost, researchers like Henry Sakaida found that the total number of aircraft claimed by American fighter pilots far exceeded the number of aircraft the Japanese recorded as lost.

The controversy arises because the number of victories is based on "claims" made by the individual pilots. Intelligence officers were tasked with sorting through the after-action reports to verify pilots' claims and credit them with victories. After each mission, Robert Clark or James Tyler in Two Fifteen wrote down the detailed information that returning pilots gave them at the debriefing and entered their words verbatim into the aircraft action report. They may have taken the pilots' word for each claim; there is no proof that they used corroborating evidence from other pilots. Rarely was there gun camera film in the Solomons; in some cases it was unavailable, but also the corrosive conditions in the area made it impossible to keep the film for any length of time. Some aircraft were simply not equipped with gun cameras.

The claims of the pilots are open to scrutiny because of the lack of more credible confirmation. The biggest reason for this criticism is the absurdly high number of downed airplanes the pilots claimed. Both Allied and Japanese flyers claimed more enemy aircraft than their opponents actually possessed. An example of over-claiming appears in Barrett Tillman's book *US Marine Corps Fighter Squadrons of World War Two*. During the month of January 1944, Two Fifteen's biggest month with eighty-five claims, Marine and Navy fighter pilot claims for destroyed Japanese *Zero*-type aircraft totaled 393. Japanese figures, which may be incomplete due to paperwork lost in air raids or purposely destroyed after the war, admit to the loss of only seventy-three *Zekes*. Due to these discrepancies, which were not unusual and took place in all theaters of war and involved many nations—with or without gun camera evidence—many people look upon the aces' claims with doubt.

The furious pace of aerial combat made it easy to make mistakes. A pilot fires at an enemy plane, and the victim catches fire and seems to fall from the sky. Is it a kill? Did he see it crash? He is busy going after another target or taking evasive action after being bounced by an unseen enemy. Does he deserve credit? Perhaps one or two other pilots fire at the same aircraft, and it catches fire and begins to dive for the sea. All three pilots claim credit for the same aircraft. In the end, however, the fire goes out and the enemy pilot brings his aircraft in for a successful landing and it is repaired. The enemy does not record it as a loss, but three pilots think they deserve credit for an aerial victory. An example of this was when the flames on George Brewer's plane went out after exiting the combat area. He successfully returned, and the plane was repaired. The *Zeke* pilot who attacked the young Marine probably reported Brewer's Corsair as a sure kill.

Most fighter aircraft spewed smoke at some time or another; coolant leaks on inline engine fighters, oil leaks on any aircraft, changes in throttle or supercharger settings, and firing of fixed guns resulted in puffs of smoke or even tendrils of smoke from undamaged aircraft. This smoke led many pilots to think an enemy diving away from combat was damaged. A large number of the kills reported by Two Fifteen involved some type of smoking enemy aircraft. In the big action on January 14, 1944, eight of the enemy planes were "smoking" when last seen by the claiming pilot. The exact phrase used in three of the actions was " I saw him smoke. . . ." It is not only possible but quite probable that many of Two Fifteen's credited victories survived the combat action in which they were claimed.

The number of kills was difficult to verify, and this leads some to question the honesty of some pilots. Did they intentionally inflate their scores in a quest for fame, status, or reward of some kind? Gregory Boyington is an example of this controversy. He claimed to shoot down six enemy planes as part of the American Volunteer Group (Flying Tigers), but he is variously credited with only two or three and one half victories with the AVG. After he was shot down in January 3, 1944, other pilots reported that Boyington shot down another enemy plane before he was forced to bail out. That would have been his twentieth victory as a Marine. Added to the six that he claimed with the AVG, Boyington would have tied Joe Foss as the highest-scoring Marine pilot. When the war ended and Boyington returned to the United States, he claimed an additional two victories scored on his last mission, but there were no eyewitnesses. These two kills gave him a total of twenty-eight, giving him the title as the highest-scoring Marine fighter pilot.

Noted aviation historian Barrett Tillman is kind when he states that some pilots made "extravagant" claims. With the pressure from peers and journalists, some pilots may have claimed anything that was close to going down without waiting to verify complete destruction. Some intelligence officers or senior officers did little to verify claims due to the competition between units, especially during the big battles above Rabaul.

In Two Fifteen, the scores of three pilots, Don Aldrich, Bob Hanson, and Hal Spears, were closely scrutinized. After missions to Rabaul, these three typically left the bombers at the rally point and returned to Simpson Harbor in search of enemy planes. Occasionally, these pilots returned alone after a big scrape. During the weeks that Bob Hanson ran up his score, he frequently lost his wingman and made claims for enemy aircraft after he was on his own. Occasionally his claims were verified by his wingman, as Sam Sampler did after a mission on January 24, 1944, for which Hanson claimed four enemy planes. But what about the times a pilot returned alone? Many of the entries in the war diaries and action reports include verification of enemy planes seen crashing either by wingmen or flyers from other squadrons, but many lack eyewitness corroboration.

In addition to not being able to reliably confirm enemy losses, Two Fifteens's pilots misidentified aircraft on occasion. These occasions of misidentification created doubts as to the veracity of all their claims. Bob Owens claimed to shoot down a *Tojo*, as did Sammy Stidger and Bob Hanson. This type of aircraft was operated by the Japanese army and was only present for a short time at Rabaul. Both Sammy Stidger and Bob Owens made a point of identifying their target as some type of aircraft they were not familiar with. Intelligence officers used pilot's descriptions to identify the type of victims. Stidger's was called a "Fred" or unknown aircraft. The author has used the detailed description to identify it as a *Tojo*. An *Oscar* and several *Tonys*, both army types of aircraft, were also claimed by pilots of Two Fifteen. Both the *Tojo* and *Oscar* are radial-engine aircraft that resemble the *Zero* series of Navy fighter, and this may account for the mistake. The mistaken identification of the Ki. 61 *Tony* as a victim is a little more difficult to explain as the *Tony* in no way resembles the *Zero* series. The Japanese navy units at Rabaul included D4Y *Judy* divebombers, which had inline engines similar to the *Tony* and may be the source of confusion. Another explanation for these erroneous identifications may be that damaged or mechanical problems had forced the army units to leave damaged *Tojos* and *Tonys* at Rabaul when they withdrew from the area, and they were rebuilt or repaired and used by naval units. Identification of fast-moving aircraft in the swirling mael-strom of battle at speeds is not easily done.

It will never be known how many enemy aircraft the men of Two Fifteen shot down. It is certain that they lost twenty-two Corsairs and thirteen pilots, but only ten of the Corsairs were lost to aerial action. Four, possibly five, of the pilots who died were killed in battles with enemy aircraft. What is sure is that the men of Two Fifteen engaged large numbers of Japanese fighters and bombers, destroying or damaging many of them. To concentrate on scores of enemy planes downed or to focus on their overabundant claims does a disservice to the men of Two Fifteen. They also strafed enemy positions, endured enemy antiaircraft fire, flew in terrible weather conditions while living in primitive jungle conditions, and yet they accomplished every mission asked of them. Victory in the Pacific is their legacy.

VMF-215 Losses on First Three Tours

Hap Langstaff—July 25, 1943—twenty-seven bullet holes

Ray Tomes—July 25, 1943—water landing

Gerry Pickeral—July 26, 1943—killed in crash into ocean, oxygen failure

D. B. Moore—July 26, 1943—shot down and killed by *Zeke*

Jack Nichols—July 30, 1943—shot down and killed by *Zeke*

Sammy Stidger—August 1, 1943—shot down and injured by *Zeke*

Bill Deming—August 12, 1943—hit by artillery fire, injured

Ray Tomes—August 18, 1943—four bullet holes

George Sanders—August 19, 1943—water landing, rescued by natives

Don Aldrich—August 26, 1943—aircraft damaged, wounded

Dave Escher—August 27, 1943—out of fuel, slightly injured

Robert Owens—August 30, 1943—Corsair damaged

Kenneth Walsh—August 30, 1943—Corsair shot down by *Zekes*, pilot survived

Reynold Tomes—September 2, 1943—shot down and killed by antiaircraft fire

Don Aldrich—September 2, 1943—Corsair damaged in dogfights

Harold Spears—September 2, 1943—Corsair damaged in dogfights

Jack W. Petit—October 20, 1943—missing due to weather

Kenneth DuVal—October 22, 1943—downed by weather, rescued

B. P. O'Dell—October 22, 1943—Corsair damaged by weather

Jake Knight—October 29, 1943—water landing, oil leak, rescued

Robert Hanson—November 1, 1943—shot down by *Kate* gunners, rescued

Robert Keister—November 1, 1943—killed in accident on takeoff

George Kross—November 3, 1943—aircraft damaged in ground accident

Jack Jordan—November 3, 1943—killed in crash caused by early morning lack of visibility

George Kross—November 4, 1943—aircraft damaged by antiaircraft fire

Jake Knight—November 7, 1943—minor damage, brake failure, ground crewman killed

Ledyard Hazelwood—November 15, 1943—killed while strafing Kieta

Al Snyder—November 17, 1943—water landing, rescued

Dick Braun—January 7, 1944—gunfire damage to wings

John Fitzgerald—January 8, 1944—damaged by hitting a stump on takeoff

Jack Knight—January 12, 1944—ground accident

John Burke—January 12, 1944—damaged by *Zeke*

John Fitzgerald—January 14, 1944—tail demolished by runway accident

Sammy Stidger—January 14, 1944—killed in crash landing

Jack Knight—January 14, 1944—unknown cause, died as POW on prison ship

Earl Moore—January 14, 1944—killed by *Zeke*

Lloyd Cox—January 14, 1944—damaged by *Zeke*

George Kross—January 14, 1944—damaged by *Zeke*, water landing

Bob Hanson—January 14, 1944—damaged by *Zeke*

Hal Spears—January 18, 1944—damaged by debris from destroyed *Zeke*

Bob Hanson—January 20, 1944—two 20mm hits from *Tony*

O. D. Hunter—January 22, 1944—minor damage from antiaircraft fire

Bob Owens—January 24, 1944—damaged by *Zeke*, water landing, wounded

Don Aldrich—January 26, 1944—damaged by *Zeke*

Thrifty Warner—January 26, 1944—damaged by gunfire, unknown origin

Don Aldrich—January 28, 1944—damaged by *Zeke*, pilot wounded

John Burke—January 28, 1944—damaged by *Zeke*, crashed on landing, wounded

John Fitzgerald—January 30, 1944—downed unknown cause, died in captivity

Tom Stockwell—January 30, 1944—damaged by enemy fire

G. M. H. Williams—January 30, 1944—destroyed in runway crash, pilot uninjured

George Brewer—February 3, 1944—damaged by *Zeke*

Bob Hanson—February 3, 1944—killed when plane was destroyed by antiaircraft fire

Ed Hernan—February 7, 1944—damaged by *Zeke*

Ed Hernan—February 9, 1944—damaged by *Zeke*, wheels up landing

John Burke—April 18, 1944—killed by ground fire

Medal of Honor Citation for Bob Hanson

The President of the United States takes pleasure in presenting the MEDAL OF HONOR to

FIRST LIEUTENANT ROBERT M. HANSON, USMCR.,

For service set forth in the following

Citation:

"For gallantry and intrepidity at the risk of his life above and beyond the call of duty as fighter pilot attached to Marine Fighting Squadron TWO FIFTEEN in action against enemy Japanese forces at Bougainville, November 2, 1943, and New Britain Island, January 24, 1944. Undeterred by fierce opposition and fearless in the face of overwhelming odds, First Lieutenant Hanson fought the Japanese boldly and with daring aggressiveness. On November 1, while flying cover for our landing operations at Empress Augusta Bay, he dauntlessly attacked six enemy torpedo bombers, forcing them to jettison their bombs and destroying one Japanese plane during the action. Cut off from his division while deep in enemy territory during a high cover flight over Simpson Harbor on January 24, First Lieutenant Hanson waged a lone and gallant battle against hostile interceptors as they were orbiting to attack our bombers and, striking with devastating fury, brought down four Zeros and possibly a fifth. Handling his plane superbly in both pursuit and attack measures, he was a total master of aerial combat, accounting for a total of 25 Japanese aircraft in this theater of war. His great personal valor and invincible fighting spirit were in keeping with the highest traditions of the United States Naval Service."

FRANKLIN D. ROOSEVELT

Navy Unit Citation for VMF-215

THE SECRETARY OF THE NAVY,

Washington

The Secretary of the Navy takes great pleasure in commending

MARINE FIGHTING SQUADRON TWO FIFTEEN

For service as follows:

"For outstanding heroism in action against enemy Japanese forces in the Solomon Islands and Bismarck Archipelago Areas from July 24, 1943 to February 15, 1944. Undaunted in the face of hostile fighter opposition and intense antiaircraft fire, Marine Fighter Squadron TWO FIFTEEN carried out numerous patrols and fighter sweeps and escorted many bombing attacks against Japanese shipping, airfields and shore installations. Individually heroic and aggressive, the gallant pilots of this fighting squadron shot down 137 enemy planes, probably destroyed 45 others and accounted for 27 on the ground, an exceptional combat record attesting to the superb teamwork of the daring flight echelon and the resourceful, tireless and skilled ground echelon which serviced and maintained the planes despite daily hostile shellfire and nightly bombing attacks. The destruction and damage inflicted on the enemy by Marine Fighting

Squadron TWO FIFTEEN contributed substantially to the successful completion of the New Georgia, Bougainville and Rabaul Campaigns and reflect the highest credit on the United States Naval Service."

All personnel attached to the flight and ground echelons of Marine Fighting Squadron TWO FIFTEEN are hereby authorized to wear the NAVY UNIT COMMENDATION ribbon.

JAMES FORRESTAL,
SECRETARY OF THE NAVY

BIBLIOGRAPHY

Abrams, Richard. *F4U Corsair at War*. New York: Charles Scribner's Sons, 1981.

Action Reports, VMF-215, January–February 1944, Washington, DC, History and Museums Division, Headquarters Marine Corps.

The Allied Campaign Against Rabaul. Washington, DC: United States Strategic Bombing Survey, 1946.

Bartlett, Tom. "Hanson Remembered," *Leatherneck*, May 1985, 18–21, 57, 62.

Baxter, Gordon. "Corsair," *Flying*, June 1977, 46–52, 102.

Bell, Dana. *F4U-1 Corsair, Vol. 1*. Tucson, AZ: Classic Warships Publishing, 2014.

———. *F4U-1 Corsair, Vol. 2*. Tucson, AZ: Classic Warships Publishing, 2015.

Berniere, Andre. "The Ace Business," *Flying*, August 1944, 26–27.

Blankenship, John. "Goleta Airfield's Advantages Provided Base for Marine Corps Air Station," *NOOZHAWK: The Freshest News in Santa Barbara*, July 22, 2015, https://www.noozhawk.com/article/john_blankenship_marine_corps_air_station_santa_barbara_20150722.

———. "Marines Invade Goleta: World War II Brought Big Changes to Goodland," *NOOZHAWK: The Freshest News in Santa Barbara*, February 25, 2016, https://www.noozhawk.com/article/marines_invade_goleta_world_war_ii_and_training_base_brought_big_changes.

———. "1st Months of Marine Corps Air Station Santa Barbara Often an Adventure," *NOOZHAWK: Freshest News in Santa Barbara*, September 3, 2015, https://www.noozhawk.com/article/john_blankenship_marine_corps_air_station_santa_barbara_20150903.

Braun, Saul. *Seven Heroes*. New York: G.P. Putnam's Sons, 1965.

Christy, Joe, ed. *World War II: U.S. Navy and Japanese Combat Planes*. Blue Ridge Summit, PA: Tab Books, 1981.

"The Corsair Experience," E Fighter Productions, 2005. Video of "The Gathering of Corsairs and Legends," at Mt. Comfort, IN, including interviews with various Corsair pilots and archival footage.

"Corsairs Return: Famed Squadron Arrives in U.S. With New Record," *Marine Corps Chevron*, Vol. 3, no. 11, March 18, 1944, 3.

Craven, Wesley, Frank Craven and James Lee Cate, *U.S. Army Air Forces in World War Two, Volume IV: The Pacific: Guadalcanal to Saipan, August 1942 to July 1944, Office of Air Force History, Air Historical Group, USAF Historical Division*, Chicago, University of Chicago Press, 1948–1958.

D'Angina, James. *Vought F4U Corsair*. New York: Osprey Publishing, 2014.

Dean, Jack. "Vought F4U Corsair Flying Freebooter and Pirate of the Pacific," *Airpower*, Vol. 19, no. 5, September 1989.

DeChant, John A. *Devilbirds*. Washington, DC: Zenger Publishing, 1979.

Dial, Jay Frank. *The Vought F4U-1 Corsair, Profile #147*. Leatherhead, Surrey, England: Profile Publications, 1965.

Dorr, Robert F. "Nocturnal Hunter: Frank Lang and the Rare F4U-2," *Flight Journal: Corsair*, September 2014, 38–43.

Downs, John E. Interviewed by Will Sarvis, May 14, 1996, by the Politics in Missouri Oral History Project, http://digital.shsmo.org/cdm/ref/collection/ohc/id/585.

Feist, Uwe, and Edward T. Maloney. *Chance Vought Corsair*. Fallbrook, CA: Aero Publications, 1967.

Flight Characteristics of the Japanese Zero Fighter, Intelligence Service, US Army Air Forces, Washington. Reprinted by Tucson Books, 1981.

Foster, John. *Hell in the Heavens*. New York: Charter Books, 1961.

Francillion, Rene. *Japanese Aircraft of the Pacific War*. Annapolis, MD: Naval Institute Press, 1979.

"From the Catwalk: What Kind of Day Was It?" *The Hook*, Spring 1983.

Gamble, Bruce. *The Blacksheep; The Definitive Account of Marine Fighting Squadron 214 in World War Two*. Novato, CA: Presidio Press, 1998.

———. *Target: Rabaul*. Minneapolis: Zenith Press, 2013.

———. *Swashbucklers and Black Sheep: A Pictorial History of Marine Fighting Squadron 214 in World War II*. Minneapolis: Zenith Press, 2012.

Graham, Garrett. "You'd Be So Nice To Come Home To," *Marine Corps Gazette*, Vol. 28, Issue 3, March 1944.

Grinsell, Bob, and Hap Langstaff. "Sweathogs of the Solomons: Over 'The Slot' with VMF-215, 'The Fighting Corsairs'," *Airpower*, January 1978.

Harris, Bonnie. "Marine Squadron VMF-215," http://www.bonniesbiz .com/8455/15801.html, several video interviews with VMF-215 veterans.

Hata, Ikuhiko, and Yasuho Izawa. Don Cyril Gorham, trans. *Japanese Naval Aces and Fighter Units in World War II*. Annapolis, MD: Naval Institute Press, 1989.

Honda, Minoru. Series of Interviews with Japanese Aces on Japanese Television, www .youtube.com/watch?v=JitLr5D77LSI.

Japanese Fighter Tactics for Combat Intelligence Officers, Washington, DC, Office of the Assistant Chief of Air Staff, Intelligence, January 1945. Reprinted by Tucson Books, 1981.

Jauregui, Jannette. "Of War and Life: Nagasaki Remains Vivid Memory of Ventura Pilot's World War II Days," *Ventura County Star*, February 15, 2013.

Johnson, Frederic. *F4U Corsair*. New York: Crown Publishers, 1983.

Kinzey, Bert. *F4U Corsair*. Carrollton, TX: Squadron/Signal Publications, 1988.

Langweische, Wolfgang. "Flying the F4U," *Flying*, June 1977, 52, 102–3.

"The Last of the Corsairs," *Naval Aviation News*, March 1953.

Matheson, Bruce J. "The Corsair and Its Contributions," *Marine Corps Gazette*, May 1981.

McAulay, Lex. *Into the Dragon's Jaws: The Fifth Air Force Over Rabaul*. Mesa, AZ: Champlain Fighter Museum Press, 1986.

Melson, Major Charles D. *Condition Red: Marine Defense Battalions in the Pacific*. Washington, DC: History and Museums Division, US Marine Corps, 1996.

Mersky, Commander Peter B. *Time of the Aces: Marine Pilots in the Solomons, 1942–1944*. Washington, DC: History and Museums Divisions, US Marine Corps, 1993.

Mikesh, Robert C. "The Last Corsair," *Airpower*, September 1981.

Modugno, Tom. "The Marines Invade Goleta," February 23, 2016, *Goleta History*, http://goletahistory.com/the-marines-invade-goleta/.

Morrissey, Rafe, and Joe Hegedus. *The Vought F4U Corsair: A Comprehensive Guide*. Bedford, United Kingdom: SAM Publications, 2010.

Musciano, Walter. *Corsair Aces: The Bent-Wing Bird Over the Pacific*. New York: Aero Publishing, 1989.

O'Leary, Michael. *Fighting Corsairs*. Canoga Park, CA: War Eagle Productions, 1984.

Olynyk, Frank. "New Research Could Alter Aces List," *Fortitudine, Newsletter of the Marine Corps Historical Foundation*, Vol. X, Summer 1981, 8–10.

———. *Stars and Bars: A Tribute to the American Fighter Ace 1920–1973*. London: Grub Street, 1995.

———. *USMC Credits for the Destruction of Enemy Aircraft in Air-to-Air Combat, World War 2*, published by the author, 1982.

Owens, Robert G., Jr., Video Interview, *Veterans History Project*, The Library of Congress, October 26, 2011, http://memory.loc.gov/diglib/vhp/story/loc.natlib .afc2001001.12343/mv0001001.stream.

"Pictorial History of Marine Airpower, 1938–1975," *Air Classics Quarterly Review*, 1975.

Pilot's Manual for F4U Corsair. Appleton, WI: Aviation Publications, 1977.

Rentz, John N. *Marines in the Central Solomons*. Washington, DC: Historical Branch, US Marine Corps, 1952.

Sakaida, Henry. *Winged Samurai*. Mesa, AZ: Champlain Fighter Museum Press, 1985.

———. *The Siege of Rabaul*. St. Paul, MN: Phalanx Publishing Co., Ltd., 1996.

Shaw, Henry I., and Douglas T. Kane. *Isolation of Rabaul, History of Marine Corps Operations in World War II*, Vol. II. Washington, DC: Historical Branch, G-3 Division, Headquarters, US Marine Corps, 1963.

Sherrod, Robert. "Fighter Aces List Updated," *Fortitudine, Newsletter of the Marine Corps Historical Foundation*, Vol. X, Spring 1981, 7–12.

———. *History of Marine Corps Aviation in World War Two*. San Rafael, CA: Presidio Press, 1980.

Sims, Edward. *Greatest Fighter Missions of the Top Navy and Marine Aces of World War II*. New York: Harper & Brothers, 1962.

Styling, Mark. *Corsair Aces of World War Two*. London: Osprey, 1995.

Sullivan, Jim. *F4U in Action*. Carrollton, TX: Squadron/Signal Publications, 1977.

———. *F4U-Corsair in Color*. Carrollton, TX: Squadron/Signal Publications, 1981.

Szlagor, Tomasz, and Leszek A. Wieliczko. *Vought F4U Corsair*. Lublin, Poland: Kagero Publishing, 2013.

Technical Air Intelligence Summary #11: Performance of New Japanese Aircraft, Anacostia, DC, Technical Air Intelligence Section. Reprinted by Tucson Books, 1981.

"Thirteenth Air Force Writes Rabaul Epitaph," *Impact*, April 1944.
Tillman, Barrett. *US Marine Corps Fighter Squadrons of World War II*. Oxford: Osprey, 2014.
——. *Corsair*. Annapolis, MD: Naval Institute Press, 1979.
Tolivar, Raymond F., and Trevor J. Constable. *Fighter Aces of the U.S.A.* Fallbrook, CA: Aero Publishers, 1979.
Tomlinson, Thomas. *The Threadbare Buzzard: A Marine Fighter Pilot in World War Two*. St. Paul, MN: Zenith Publishing, 2004.
Veronico, Nicholas A., with John M. and Donna Campbell. *F4U Corsair: Combat, Development, and Racing History of the Corsair*. Osceola, WI: Motorbooks, 1994.
War Diaries, VMF-215, History and Museums Division, Headquarters Marine Corps, March 1943–February 1944.

CORRESPONDENCE

Those listed below are persons who corresponded with the author. Many sent several letters but only those letters used in the text are listed:

Alfonso, Fred (Ground Echelon), letter September 15, 1988.
——, letter February 15, 1989.
Amerman, Annette, Branch Head and Historian, Historical Reference Branch, Marine Corps History Division, email April 10, 2017.
Braun, Dick, undated letter.
Brewer, George, "A Tribute to 'O,'" letter June 18, 1982.
Conant, Roger, audiotape March 29, 1982.
——, audiotape with George Kross, May 2, 1982.
——, letter October 21, 1984.
Cox, Lloyd, letter April 5, 1982.
——, letter December 13, 1988.
——, letter June 8, 1989.
Hewitt, Kimberly, Reference Librarian, Newton Free Library, 330 Homer St., Newton, MA 02459, email April 6, 2017.
Hunter, O. D., letter October 11, 1982.
——, letter November 27, 1982.
Kingsley, Bill (Ground Echelon), letter October 1, 1981.
——, letter, January 20, 1982.
Knight, Jake, letter April 24, 1982.
——, letter May 8, 1982.
Kross, George, letter undated
Musinski, Gene (Ground Echelon), letter August 19, 1987.
Neber, Ernest, letter March 26, 1982.
——, letter April 25, 1982.
——, letter April 30, 1982.
——, letter May 26, 1982.
——, letter June 16, 1982.

————, letter September 3, 1982.
Neefus, Jim, audiotape, April 15, 1982.
————, letter to Neber, June 8, 1982.
————, letter June 12, 1982.
Snyder, Alan, letter January 10, 1983.
Stockwell, Tom, letter February 6, 1982.
————, letter March 4, 1982.
————, letter April 28, 1982.
————, letter May 1, 1982.

INTERVIEWS
Conant, Roger, November 14, 1981.
Cox, Lloyd, telephone conversation, February 28, 1982.
————, telephone conversation, March 3, 1982.
————, interview, March 5 and 6, 1982.
Guilford, Bob, private owner of F4U Corsair, February 3, 1983.
Kross, George, telephone conversation, November 2, 1982.
Owens, Bob, telephone conversation, February 23, 1982.
————, interview, November 13, 1981.

INTERVIEWS WITH VETERANS OF VMF-215 DURING REUNION IN SANTA BARBARA, FEBRUARY 2–6, 1983
Jim Neefus
Bob Owens
Roger Conant
Lloyd Cox
Dick Braun
Sam Sampler
Hap Langstaff
Reinhardt Leu
Ernest Neber
Ray Wolff
Dick Samuelson
Creighton Chandler
George Kross
George Brewer
George Sanders
B. K. Shaw
Al Snyder
Larry Smith
George Gilman

INDEX

leaving, 37, 41–43
Pirates' Den, 33, *33, 34*
training, 29–37, *31*
Minor, W. L., 209
Moak, Dave, 139
Moore, Donald B., 24, 25–26, 53, 181
Moore, Earl, 172
Moore, J. B., 9
Munda Airfield
Barakoma Point comparison, 132
conditions, 71–74, 101–2
first uses after capture, *67,* 67–69, *74,* 85–87
Kahili attack from, 87–90, *88*
Medal of Honor flight, 98–100

N
Neber, Ernest "Doc"
appreciation for, 248
background, 8–9
first tour, 43, *45,* 63
gooneys incident, 34
health conditions of squadron, 73, 101–2
life after VMF-215, 248
mess hall incident, 119–20
at Midway, 26
recreational interests, 66, 146, 147, 184
third tour, 209–10, *212,* 212–13
Neefus, James L.
background, 5–8, 11, 12, 13, 15–16, 18

first tour, 49, 53, 57, 58–59, 63–64, 71, 124
leadership style, 34–36
life after VMF-215, 246
at Midway, 27–29, 29
training pilots, 23, 30–32, 44
views on VMF-215 success, 250
Walsh's friendship with, 98–99
New Georgia area, *58*
Newhall, Richard "Tripod"
at Espiritu Santo, 115
first tour, 50, 64–65, 73, 78–79
in Hawaii, 27
leaving VMF-215, 144
at Midway, 30, 36
second tour, 142–43
Nichols, Jack, 53, 58–59, 60
night heckler missions, 230–31

O
O'Dell, Bennie, 135–36
Olynyk, Frank, 254
Owens, J. J., 11
Owens, Robert G., Jr., *35*
awards, 241, 244
background, 2–4
first tour, 43, 49, 64, 78–81, 86–90, 92–95, 103, 106–7
on Hanson's death, 229
injuries, 201–3, *204*
kills, 240, 256
liberty in Australia, 121
life after VMF-215, 244–46, *245*
at Midway, 29, 31, 34, *35,* 36